WAILING PRAYERS to the DEEP Reloaded

THE SECRETS TO EMBRACING OUR *Eternal Life* NOW!

DR. Y. BUR

Available Titles

ASITPLEASESGOD.COM

Wailing Prayers To The Deep *Reloaded*
The Secrets To Embracing Our *Eternal Life* NOW!

Copyright © 2020 by Dr. Y. Bur. All rights reserved.

Visit www.RoarPublishingGroup.com for more information. No part of this publication may be reproduced, stored in a retrieval system, or transmitted in any way by any means, electronic, mechanical, photocopy, recording, or otherwise, without the prior permission of the author, except as provided by USA copyright law.

Book design copyright ©2020 by R.O.A.R. International Group. All rights reserved.

R.O.A.R. Publishing Group
581 N. Park Ave. Ste. #725
Apopka, FL 32704
www.RoarPublishingGroup.com

Published in the United States of America
ISBN: 978-1-948936-46-0

$22.88

As a FORMAL DISCLAIMER: I am not a medical doctor, nor do I proclaim to be. If one has a health issue, please consult with a LICENSED DOCTOR before embarking upon any sort of food-restricted fast. This book is not designed to diagnose any health condition; it is only used to bring about an awareness of the Power of Fasting from a Spiritual Perspective, along with its benefits.

Dr. Y. Bur

www.DrYBur.com

TABLE OF CONTENTS

INTRODUCTION 9

CHAPTER 1 15
- RELOAD YOUR PURPOSE 15
  - Material or Spiritual Flattery 16
  - Irrevocable Gifts 17
  - Instinctual Nature 19

CHAPTER 2 25
- RELOADED STRATEGY 25
  - Godly Edge 26
  - Approaching Issues 28
  - Spiritual Triggers 29
  - Taming the Beast 31
  - Trip Triggers 34
  - Developing Enthusiasm 37
  - Thinking Cap 39
  - Strategic Love 42

CHAPTER 3 49
- RELOADED PRIDE 49
  - Spiritual Ammunition 51
  - The Helpmeet 52
  - The Bonding Factors 55
  - Mastering the ROAR 58
  - The Big Cats Golden Rule 65

CHAPTER 4 67

THE 24-HOUR ANOINTING 67
    Eye of God 68
    The Change 70
    Where Is My Faith 71
    The Seed 73
    The Anointing 74
    When Praying 77
    Wonderworking Power 79

CHAPTER 5 81

TOXIC INFLUENCES 81
    Spirit of Resilience 84
    Getting Rid of Mental Toxins 87
    Getting Rid of Emotional Toxins 96
    Getting Rid of Physical Toxins 100
    Getting Rid of Spiritual Toxins 103

CHAPTER 6 107

WAILING PRAYERS TO THE DEEP RELOADED 107
    Wooing God 108
    Wail of Dominion 110
    Spiritually Deep 111
    Resisting Spiritual Attacks 114
    Halting Waywardness 117
    Taking Action 120
    Spiritual Negotiation 121
    Divine Favor 123

CHAPTER 7 125

ETERNAL LIFE NOW 125
    The Doorpost 128
    Building Others 129
    The Experience 130
    Spiritual Language 130
    Divine Expectations 133

It Is A Wrap 135
Overcoming Spiritual Lethargy 136
Divine Illumination 138
The Divine Cornerstone 142
Spiritual Integrity 143

CHAPTER 8 147

USEFUL EXPECTATIONS 147
Breaking The Spirit of Coveting 148
Understanding a Wailing Prayer 149
Becoming Spiritually Deep 150
Expectations of the Holy Spirit 151

CHAPTER 9 155

THE FASTING CHAMBERS 155
When Not To Fast 157
When We Fast 158
The Hidden Secrets of Jonah 167
Details of Fasting 171
When to start a fast? 175
Types of Fasting 177
Choices of Fasting 177
The Chamber Of Fasting 179
How To Break A Fast 181

CHAPTER 10 183

THE "SECRET PLACE" 183
Divine Refinement 184
Divine Grace 187
Understanding the Bow 191
Spiritual Armor 193

CHAPTER 11 195

THE REAL PROPHET 195
The Prophet's Glitch 196
Understanding The Inner Child 198

 Overcoming Blasphemy 202
 Testing The Spirit 203
 Character Building 207
 Spiritual Regrafting 220

CHAPTER 12 227

 THE 4-FOLD 227
  My WHY 228
  Testimonial Marriage 230
  The Fold Breakdown 231
  The Real Reality 234
  Understanding Doubt 240
  Developing Our People Skills 240

INTRODUCTION

What do we do when our soul is crying out? Do we keep crying? Do we pick up the pieces and move on? Do we fight for what does or does not belong to us? Do we lie down, allowing life to happen? Do we try to make sense of it, or do we go with the flow? Better yet, in the reloading process of life, do we run and hide? When our soul is wailing or buffering in ways we cannot articulate, who do we run to for help? If one has not asked or answered these types of questions, just live a little longer. The Vicissitudes and Cycles of Life have a way of putting us to the test to determine what we are made of.

So, once again, I pose this question: What do we do? Wait, wait, wait, I have more questions: Why do we need to do it? Where do we need to do it? How do we go about doing so? When do we need to get it done? And, the last question is: With whom do we do it? From my perspective, when dealing with the 'it' factor, it is best to get an understanding of the wailing process to ensure we are not setting our own booby traps, Emotionally, Mentally, Physically, and Spiritually.

What is the 'it' factor? Everyone has an underlying 'it' or a proposed 'type' that will vary based on one's beliefs, thoughts, desires, mindset, traumas, strengths, weaknesses, and conditioning. But do not worry, fret, fuss, or fight about the 'it' factor because the *Wailing Prayers To The Deep Reloaded* is designed to open our Spiritual Eyes to a few fundamental Spiritual Principles from a conventional and Divine Perspective. What does this mean for us? As we look beyond the process of uploading and downloading information, thoughts, and beliefs, we cannot overlook the reloading process, especially in a God-Ruled Nation. Why? If we do not reboot ourselves occasionally, *As It Pleases God*, we will become weak or overloaded, regardless of how well we pretend to be on top of our game.

The simple edifices of our hidden predictability are overlooked time and time again due to our natural human defaults or deflections. When we underestimate the Power of God or our reason for being, we can safely say our belief system is not where it should be. Better yet, we can also say we are in some form of secret or open denial as well.

Why do we battle with secret denial as Believers? Without knowing our Divine Purpose or Predestined Blueprint, it creates an internal longing or wailing within the human psyche. Unfortunately, if we are not Spiritually Trained on this matter, *As It Pleases God*, we can whitewash it or blame it on the Devil to avoid dealing with reality from the inside out. Please make no mistake about it: The wailing of the soul is loud and clear, which can be heard a mile away by those who are NOT Spiritually Blind, Deaf, or Mute.

Of course, most often, we will not openly admit we are in a great battle from within. As a matter of fact, we tend to hide it because it is embarrassing to appear out of control, reckless, or less than. So, we play tough or attempt to appear better, stronger, and wiser to weaken or intimidate our opponents, to avoid properly gearing up Spiritually as we should, or to get a temporary adrenaline fix to feed the ego.

By approaching life lacking humility or respect and not gearing up, *As It Pleases God*, we will tend to create a disservice to ourselves in the Spiritual Realm. How so? It has Mental and Emotional implications that are noticed through our PHYSICAL ACTIONS and the lack of self-control. Therefore, it behooves us to examine ourselves, our motives, as well as our inner self-talk and mental chatter.

Why is governing our self-talk and inner chatter important in the Eye of God? For the most part, regardless of our conditioning or how well we cover the wailing from within, our self-talk and inner chatter are captured in our actions, words, thoughts, excuses, responses, beliefs, biases, or egotistical attitudes, positively or negatively.

As we live life in real-time with or without a Biblical Foundation, there are many things we can do in our own strength, not having to answer to anyone. Yet, there are some things in life that we need Divine Intervention or Accountability for God to intercede. From a Spiritual Perspective, this is where the WAILING process comes into the equation to intervene on our behalf, only if we learn how to use it properly.

When we lack the knowledge, know-how, how-to, or secrets to move God on our behalf, we will find ourselves running to and fro, looking for a solution, comfort, or quick fix. Most of the time, the solution to our dilemmas is in the palm of our hands, or it resides within the depths of the soul. If we can find a way to move from our carnal state of mind to a Spiritual State when it comes down to solving problems, we will find that solutional solving and understanding will become second nature, *As It Pleases God*.

Spiritually Speaking, regardless of where we are in life, we have so much POWER hidden within the core of our being that it is not funny. But, for some odd reason, we overlook it by some sort of misconceived default. When, in fact, our POWER is hidden in plain sight through the ability to know God, pray, repent, forgive, develop an understanding of all things, utilize the Fruits of the Spirit, and behave Christlike.

So, instead of using what is within us, we expect others to do what we are unwilling to do or what we refuse to do for ourselves. Then, we have the nerve to blame someone else for our mishaps, setbacks, selfishness, negligence, and atrocities in life. Or, better yet, we blame it on the Devil, often saying, 'The Devil made me do it!' When in all actuality, the Devil did not lay a finger on us, them, or that! Thus, this sort of hypocritical behavior must stop!

Now, the question is: 'Has anyone ever seen the Devil lay a finger on anyone or anything?' The answer is a big 'NO.' The truth is that He uses people, places, and things to do His bidding. Why is outsourcing necessary? He knows the Spiritual Rules better than we do; therefore, He uses us, them, and that as TOOLS to hurt ourselves or others if we allow it or do not know any better.

Here is the deal: He (meaning the Devil) only plants the seed, and it is our responsibility to water, counteract, accept, reject, or uproot it. Really? Yes, really! We have more of a connection to our issues in life than anyone else, primarily when the Fruits of the Spirit are readily available at the drop of a dime. So, why are we expecting others to fix it, fix us, or fix them? This book, *Wailing Prayers To The Deep Reloaded*, aims to empower individuals to take their lives by the horns and blow their own trumpets.

How is it possible to blow horns and trumpets, especially when we are going through it, or we have real issues? It is through the ability to put our bodies under the subjection of the Holy Spirit with the mindset of 'FIX ME,' 'LEAD ME,' or 'TEACH ME,' O'Lord. Just so we are crystal clear, I am not here to point fingers because we are all a work in progress. However, I am here to share the information needed to ease the RELOADING process, *As It Pleases God*.

In the RELOADING process, on your behalf or mine, I can only bring forth such information through many experiences, trials, and tribulations. All of these empowered me to become the person I am today with such Divine Revelation, Kingdom Secrets, and Heavenly Wisdom for our Spiritual Exposure, unveiling the veiled for a time such as this.

I have been where you are, and I am not ashamed of where I have been, nor am I holding any grudges. Every issue, person, or enemy was designed as a stepping stone and a lesson to develop my Spiritual Ingenuity. Through my Battle Scars, I have earned my STRIPES, allowing me to effectively repent, pray, forgive, and fast, *As It Pleased God*, to bring forth the *Wailing Prayers To The Deep Reloaded* book, with NO SHAME attached.

However, amid all, I had to uncover my true calling for myself, overcome the atrocities of my past for myself, Spiritually Till my own ground for myself, and contend with Spiritual Warfare to protect the GIFT that lies within. All this means is that you have to want it for yourself selflessly and *As It Pleases God* to evolve into the Powerhouse that you already are.

Before we go any further, here is my secret: It is through my *Spirit to Spirit* Relationship, *As It Pleases God*, that I can write with such Anointing, Precision, Relevancy, and Unctionable Wisdom. As a child, I could not understand why I had such a hard life. But now, as a Child of the Most High, I understand it was the GIFT from within that was under attack.

The adversary was trying to get me to doubt, second-guess, back down, or give up on myself, short-circuiting my Divine Destiny. As a result, I had to learn how to protect my Spiritual Gifts without wavering. In addition, I was not just doing this for myself but for saving, preparing, and equipping others to do likewise. For this reason, I had to get into God's face, *Spirit to Spirit*, and *As It Pleased Him*, without pleasing myself with selfish wants, needs, or desires and showboating.

On this Spiritual Journey, I am often asked how I really overcome issues without losing my cool. Well, here is my answer: One step at a time through repenting, prayer, forgiveness, fasting, purging, canceling, utilizing the Fruits of the Spirit, regrafting my character to become Christlike, and using Biblical Principles, Laws, and Covenants. And, when it is all said and done, I firmly believe in getting to the CORE of the matter by thoroughly questioning the what, when, where, how, why, and with whom.

Why is getting to the core essential for Believers? In the Eye of God, corelessness equates to an emptiness in the human psyche. Therefore, we must get to the ROOT of whatever or with whomever through our queries to regraft or reload, *As It Pleases God*.

Listen, when we are deprived of the facts, it is extremely difficult to obtain a sustainable or viable solution. Then again, without pinpointing the wailing of the soul, we only patch, sugarcoat, overlook, or lie about our issues. Unfortunately, this causes our voids to become airborne craters, not knowing where they will land until the damage is done or the generational curses are levied. Can this really happen to us? Absolutely! In my opinion, it happens all too often under our watchful care. Here is what Hosea 4:6 says, "*My people are destroyed for lack of knowledge. Because you have rejected knowledge, I also will reject you from being priest for Me; Because you have forgotten the law of your God, I also will forget your children.*"

With this book, *Wailing Prayers To The Deep Reloaded*, it is my reasonable service to share how to create miracles with what you already have in your hands. In addition, I will also share with you how to take your prayers DEEP into the Spiritual Realm as well!

Why must Believers engage in DEEP prayers? There are times when a surface prayer will not help your situation, especially when dealing with what money cannot buy, cure, fix, or create!

Why do surface prayers not work for some Believers? It is due to the lack of knowledge and understanding, *As It Pleases God*. Approaching prayers to please ourselves can cause more harm than good. Blasphemy, right? Wrong. Proverbs 19:2 says, "*It is not good for a soul to be without knowledge, And he sins who hastens with his feet.*" And, "*The heart of him who has understanding seeks knowledge, But the mouth of fools feeds on foolishness.*" Proverbs 15:14.

When the issues of life come upon you to sift you as wheat, you must go into SPIRITUAL WARFARE, especially if you are sick, a family member is afflicted, your house is on fire, or you are under Spiritual Attack with a yoke, habit, or symbolic stutter. In my opinion, this is not a matter of IF; it is a matter of WHEN. Who knows what may happen if you are not adequately equipped, right?

But with all due respect, it is your free will choice of what you desire to do and what you choose not to do! Nevertheless, I will give you the Spiritual Tools, and it will then be left up to you to use, share, or discard them. So, if you are ready to RELOAD, continue this Spiritual Journey with me; I PROMISE not to disappoint.

How can I make such a PROMISE? Based on Proverbs 2:10-11, I can make this Divine Decree. It says, "*When wisdom enters your heart, And knowledge is pleasant to your soul, discretion will preserve you; Understanding will keep you.*" So, let us go DEEPER!

CHAPTER 1

RELOAD YOUR PURPOSE

In today's day and age, it seems that everyone has their own idea of how we can achieve the things we desire—at a cost. Whether it's through products, services, or promises, there's no shortage of proposed solutions for fulfilling the desires of our hearts without God Almighty. Everywhere we turn, someone is offering something that promises to make our dreams a reality, but at what price? Is it the price of leaving God out of the equation only to please ourselves?

Then, what do we do? We continue to buy this and that, or we give this and that, hoping it will solve our issues, but yet, leaving us soulishly thirsty. Unbeknownst, this form of trial and error process of selling hope or the illusion of it does not provide any form of solidified guarantees, especially when our God-Given Purpose is involved. Why? Simply put, God cannot be bought, nor can our Divine Purpose come forth without training, testing, understanding, and instructions.

In fact, those selling a worldly system, putting God in a box for sale, should have a disclaimer associated. Why should disclaimers be given? We are playing around with the lives of those who are already fragile Mentally, Physically, Emotionally, or Spiritually, without them knowing they are in such a state. Thus making us more paranoid and skeptical than ever, while wondering if any of these solutions are truly genuine or if they are just preying on our vulnerabilities.

As a result of the omission of our Spiritual Truth or Purpose, we are failing inwardly while appearing to thrive outwardly. Sadly, we cannot tell anyone we have been duped by a system we thought would work on our behalf. Why is this happening to us, especially when giving and doing our best? When we take God out of the equation or do not unleash the true Greatness from within, we will feel a VOID. And regardless of what we do or try, the yearning from the depths of the soul will not go away, so we PRETEND. Yes, we pretend to be better or more than we are. While at the same time, we are outright omitting our God-Given Purpose or missing the mark, not knowing how to get back on track.

The outer glitz has somehow become the measurement of our level of worthiness. From a Spiritual Perspective, the mental glamour of putting on a show to appease the eyes of those around us has somehow caused hidden blindness. How is this possible when we are working for what we want? When we become consumed with conditional materialism to feel better about ourselves or cover up hidden insecurities, we become selfish by default, not realizing what is happening until it is too late. However, all hope is not lost; we will expose the root of this issue to ensure healing takes place right in the nick of time. For this reason, 'Reloaded Purpose' will share the information needed to shift our system into a PURPOSEFUL one.

Here is the deal: Our innate ability to impress others is causing us to forget about the real reason why we are here in the first place. So, the question remains: Why are we here? According to the Heavenly of Heavens, the answer is straightforward: We are BLESSED to be a BLESSING!

Our responsibility is to leave a positive impression on the hearts of those we come in contact with through our INNER influences, not with our outer influences, showboating, or material gain. Why? What have we gained if we give a person the world without caring about them? When we humbly give others what money cannot buy, it builds our value by default in the Eye of God, not man.

Material or Spiritual Flattery

Of course, we need money for our daily essentials, and having the finer things in life makes us comfortable. Still, we must step outside materialism to give more of ourselves positively, using the Fruits of the Spirit.

What is the purpose of using the Fruits of the Spirit instead of material flattery? First, it builds our character, *As It Pleases God*. Secondly, it weeds out those who are using us, and it will also show us who will spit in our faces after they get what they want.

Why does weeding happen when using the Fruits of the Spirit? First, most often, it is because they secretly feel superior in some way. Then again, envy, jealousy, pride, coveting, greed, or competitiveness may be involved. Secondly, apostle Paul tells us in Galatians 5:22 that there is NO LAW against the use of the Fruits of the Spirit. *"But the fruit of the Spirit is love, joy, peace, patience, kindness, goodness, faithfulness, gentleness, self-control. Against such there is no law."* Anything else, there may be a Spiritual Law governing it; thus, it behooves us to know how God views our behaviors, thoughts, beliefs, or words, especially when they are debauched, evil, harmful, or cruel.

Irrevocable Gifts

Our Heaven on Earth Experience requires us to pay attention with all of our instincts intact; if not, we will miss our cues, become sifted, soul-tied, or have our Spiritual Gifts or Purpose snatched away. How is it possible to have things snatched away from us when Romans 11:29 says, *"For the gifts and the calling of God are irrevocable."* Is this not blasphemy? Absolutely not! Here is what we often miss: The Calling of God. We take this scripture and run with the GIFTS to please ourselves without understanding that there is a Spiritual Contingency.

What is a Spiritual Contingency as it relates to Believers? A Spiritual Contingency refers to a plan or course of action that is based on Spiritual Beliefs, Principles, or Divine Missions. Now, if we use our Spiritual Gifts, *As It Pleases God*, they become Divinely Protected by the Heavenly of Heavens.

Whereas, if we use our Spiritual Gifts to please ourselves or we consume our own Spiritual Fruits, we will become VEILED due to a broken Spiritual Agreement regarding our reason for being. For the record, in this state, we can gain worldly or systemic power from men but not Spiritual Power from the Heavenly of Heavens, *As It Pleases God.*

Is power, not power? Man's power is not the same as God's Power from the Heavenly of Heavens. The moment we think that our power can override the Supernatural Power of God, the Vicissitudes and Cycles of Life will begin to read us as a canker sore to take us out of this system or to teach us a lesson. Relatably, we would often recognize this as a VOID from within or a VEIL. Spiritually, John 15:2 says, *"Every branch in Me that does not bear fruit He takes away; and every branch that bears fruit He prunes, that it may bear more fruit."*

Is being a canker Biblical? It is often referred to as being a cancer or plague and having to be pruned. For example, *"But shun profane and idle babblings, for they will increase to more ungodliness. And their message will spread like cancer. Hymenaeus and Philetus are of this sort, who have strayed concerning the truth, saying that the resurrection is already past; and they overthrow the faith of some."* 2 Timothy 2:16-18.

Respectfully Speaking, we as Believers often proclaim to live by the Word of God, but often do not recognize negative words or behavioral cancers thwarting our *Spirit to Spirit* Relations with Him, *As It Pleases Him.* How is this possible when we pray every day and attend Church on Sunday? God is monitoring for the Fruits of the Spirit and Christlike Character Traits. Here is what we must know before moving on: *"But you have not so learned Christ, if indeed you have heard Him and have been taught by Him, as the truth is in Jesus: that you put off, concerning your former conduct, the old man which grows corrupt according to the deceitful lusts, and be renewed in the spirit of your mind, and that you put on the new man which was created according to God, in true righteousness and holiness."* Ephesians 4:20-24.

Now, getting back to losing our Spiritual Gifts. If we do not know what they are, if we neglect them, if we misuse them, or if we become Spiritually Blind, Deaf, Mute, Dull, Lukewarm, or Stiff-necked, we will not recognize their loss or their value. Why will we not recognize our Spiritual Gifts, especially when we are operating in them? Once again, we are VEILED; thus, they must lie dormant, and we will not operate at our Divinely Maximum or

Spiritual Potential. Frankly, there is always MORE to operating *As It Pleases God* as opposed to pleasing ourselves.

It is often said, *'We cannot miss what we cannot measure.'* If we allow people, places, and things to cloud our sense of judgment or instincts, we will fall short inwardly. Let us momentarily look at the Animal Kingdom to convey a proper understanding, *As It Pleases God*. Animals live by their instincts regardless of size, origin, or conditioning. More importantly, they do not deviate from what they are designed to do unless some form of human derailment, domination, or disruptive control is involved. Remember, they will NOT lose their animal instincts; they simply become suppressed.

Nonetheless, the natural instincts of animals will reemerge once placed in survival mode, doing what they were created to do. However, they will exhibit a weakness that can be sniffed out, causing them to become prey to the more experienced. And we are no different!

Instinctual Nature

Human intervention or not, here is the question we need to ask ourselves: 'Why do animals pride themselves on using their instincts?' Whether they are the prey or the predator, they will react when their life is on the line. Why? They instinctively know that life is designed to take them out when they become weak, careless, sickly, disrespectful, etc., and they will react accordingly.

On the other hand, we as human beings overlook this innate characteristic that is designed to save our lives. How is this possible? For example, most animals instinctively know how to swim, and humans must be taught this skill to prevent drowning.

Why is there a double standard between men and animals? If we talk about a double standard of having the upper hand on animals, I would not consider it to be at all. We possess more than they do and use less than they do for our survival. How do we make this make sense as Believers? In all simplicity, we use less of our potentiality due to our inability to become ONE with our instincts. As a result, it causes INNER DIVISION while we think we have it going on.

The division that takes place inwardly is often overlooked because we are not taught to recognize its causes. Why are we not taught about using our instincts if it is so important for our survival? We often do not know or understand this word from a Spiritual Perspective.

According to the Heavenly of Heavens, our instincts are wrapped into our nature, character, fruits, thoughts, desires, behaviors, and mindsets. For example, we want our instincts to work at their full capacity, but we could not give a rat's tail about our Spiritual Fruits or how we treat others. As a result, we get a Side Eye from our Heavenly Father with an internal divide from within the human psyche.

The SECRET to overcoming our internal division is hidden in plain sight. So, if we break down the word DI-Vision—the word Vision is prefaced by the word DIE. Now, before I go any further, let us take it to scripture, *"Where there is NO vision, the people perish; but he that keepeth the law, happy is he."* Proverbs 29:18. Without a Vision or Purpose, we will begin to die a slow death with rotten fruits from the inside out in various ways, such as:

- ☐ Emotional Imbalances.
- ☐ Negative Mental Chatter.
- ☐ Superfluous Ego.
- ☐ Inner Chaos.
- ☐ Envy.
- ☐ Jealousy.
- ☐ Coveting.
- ☐ Competitiveness.
- ☐ Disobedience.
- ☐ Unruliness.
- ☐ Ungodly Character.
- ☐ Bad Attitude.

How can we get back on track with our wailing process to overcome division? The best way I have found is to understand that we are under a Spiritual Covenant and we should operate *As It Pleases God*, getting rid of the pleasing ourselves mindset.

According to the Heavenly of Heavens, God is obligated to us, and we are obligated to Him. He created us in His image with an obligatory choice to remain inside the Covenantal Legalities.

In layman's terms, our Spiritual Covenant is similar to Adam's from the Garden of Eden Experience. In the Book of Genesis, we can pinpoint an Instructional Covenant when God instructed Adam not to partake of the Forbidden Fruit. Spiritually, this was the determining factor governing his stay in the Garden and his expulsion from it. As it relates to his disobedience, he was given instructions to convey to his wife, but we all know how this story ended. Nevertheless, we are not here to dwell on the past or shift blame; we are here to take possession of what rightly belongs to us while using the Fruits of the Spirit instead of the Forbidden Fruits.

As it relates to our '*Reloaded Purpose*,' we are the NEW beginning. How is this possible? Regardless of whether we align our lives with scripture or not, the Garden of Eden is hidden WITHIN. If we understand the Purposeful Covenant, we can restore our Birthrights. But if we become hardheaded or knuckleheads and do not listen to instructions well, we will feel the sting of Spiritual Expulsion within the depths of our souls.

To clarify, I am not pointing the finger or calling people names. I am only referring to specific, relatable, and detrimental characteristics that will strip us bare Spiritually, regardless of who we are, what we have, or how we obtained it. Then again, these characteristics can cause us to pick up negative habits, blinding our Spiritual Eyes, causing deafness to our Spiritual Ears, and contributing to an uncontrollable tongue, making us Spiritually Mute.

Above all, God did not create us as robots. So, if we choose to do our own thing, we can. We have free will to be, do, and create anything, but our Blueprinted Fulfillment is not guaranteed. For this reason, when we are misaligned or out of Purpose, we will feel an inner void. Regardless of who we are, our reasoning, or justifications of why we do what we do, we are not immune to our Divine Design.

Why do we feel as if we are missing something? Once again, we are obligated to God, similar to a parent-child relationship. For example, it does not matter how old a child becomes; as long as the parent is alive, they will have some form of obligation to their child, and likewise for the child to the parent.

How does the parent-child relationship relate to God's obligation to us? Listen, God clothed Adam and Eve in their wrongdoing in Genesis 3:21, and He has also clothed us with everything we need. How does this correlate to us? In or out of our *'Reloaded Purpose,'* He has clothed us with:

- ☐ The ability to REPENT of our flaws.
- ☐ A DIRECT CONNECTION to Him through prayer, *Spirit to Spirit*.
- ☐ The Holy Spirit as our Spiritual Helpmeet and Guide.
- ☐ Forgiveness as an Emotional Bridge.
- ☐ Grace to break Mental and Emotional Strongholds.
- ☐ Mercy and Forgiveness to sever soul ties and yokes.
- ☐ Gifts, Talents, and Callings for Spiritual Provision.
- ☐ The Fruits of the Spirit as a form of instant Self-Correction or Self-Help.
- ☐ Biblical Guidance as a Living Testament.
- ☐ Divine Authority to call things that are not as they are, to open our Spiritual Negev.
- ☐ Spiritual Favor to possess what rightly belongs to us with The-Lord-Will-Provide Mentality.
- ☐ Redemption through the Blood of Jesus as our Spiritual Atonement and Divine Covering.

Once we understand the parent-child obligations from a Spiritual Perspective, we will begin to understand how powerful our prayers are and how well they work when applied correctly! To open up the floodgates of our blessings, we must learn how to pray effectively without doing so amissly. How is this possible? The secrets of how to pray and heal ourselves are hidden in plain sight; therefore, it is my reasonable service to point them out.

Wailing Prayers To The Deep Reloaded wants us to understand that we cannot become clueless or careless about what we want, what we do, what we say, or what we become. We are held accountable for our actions, reactions, thoughts, words, beliefs, biases, or the lack thereof when it comes to our Spiritual Walk with God. Also, we must account for the prayers keeping us on track or on a straight and narrow path.

Before I end this chapter, let us return to instincts for a moment. Regarding prayer, our instincts are indeed a Spiritual Navigational Tool used to determine what to pray for, when to pray, how to pray, where to pray, and why we need to pray. But more importantly, here are a few things we need to know:

- ☐ Our instincts wake us up in the middle of the night to pray.
- ☐ Our instincts let us know when something is right or wrong.
- ☐ Our instincts allow us to embrace the Ancient Wisdom of God.
- ☐ Our instincts awaken the Spirit from within.
- ☐ Our instincts enable us to connect with the Holy Spirit at the drop of a dime.
- ☐ Our instincts alert us to the presence of God.
- ☐ Our instincts bring us into a peaceful state of Holiness.
- ☐ Our instincts allow us to heed the Spiritual Warnings of impending danger.
- ☐ Our instincts allow us to move in the Spirit.
- ☐ Our instincts illuminate our Spiritual Eyes, Ears, and Tongues.
- ☐ Our instincts help us to move in Faith.
- ☐ Our instincts reload our Purpose.

Our instinctual nature has a powerful influence on our tenacity to Wail or Reload on a level that will put our enemies to boot. How is this possible? It is often referred to as Unwavering Faith. Also, when we follow Spiritual Protocol, use the Fruits of the Spirit, and exhibit Christlike Character, there are certain things the enemy cannot do to us unless we are clueless about our Spiritual Rights or do not know how to Spiritually Enforce them.

When dealing with our *Reloaded Purpose,* it behooves us to avoid leaving an open door to be sifted by those who already did their homework on us or know more about Spirituality than we do. More importantly, we must ensure we do not violate our conscience when settling for negativity, waywardness, or wrongdoing. We must pride ourselves on positivity, goodness, and Christlike Spiritual Etiquette to develop a *Reloaded Strategy* that is designed, *As It Pleases God.*

CHAPTER 2

RELOADED STRATEGY

We all have been preloaded with the bare essentials needed in developing, resurrecting, or reerecting our Spirituality. Regardless of how we feel, think, or categorize ourselves, we all need a Spiritual Refresher occasionally. Why do we need a Spiritual Refresher as Believers? We are human and will tend to adapt or become complacent in areas where we are not corrected, challenged, or tested.

What is the big deal, especially if we are satisfied? Most often, our satisfaction is at the level of the settling involved. From a Spiritual Perspective, it is considered settling if we are not growing, becoming better, stronger, useful, wiser, helpful, or proactive. Why are we predesigned in this manner? We are designed to bear good fruit and multiply. Listen, if we are bearing bad fruit, destroying, or condemning, we have work to do!

The Spiritual Framework of God is very strategic. The moment we come to ourselves as it relates to who we are from God's Divine Perspective, we will begin to understand the value of having a Plan of Action and a Plan of Strategy.

Why do we need some form of strategy when dealing with God Almighty? We cannot go wrong with developing strategies, *As It Pleases Him*. But what if we get it wrong? It is okay to get it wrong in the Eye of God because it gives us a chance to hear the correction, Spirit to Spirit, developing our Spiritual Muscles. For this reason, I advise everyone to document, document, document because this is where the Spiritual Corrections most often will occur. Then again, God may give us half of the information while Spiritually Preparing us for more.

Why does God not give us all the information or corrections at once? Most often, He is TESTING our obedience or downloading capabilities. For example, Divine Wisdom is more often given to those who responsibly document and share it for the Greater Good. Conversely, Divine Wisdom is withheld from those who do not document, share, or misuse it for selfish gain.

Is the dispersal of Divine Wisdom fair? I cannot judge fairness in this matter because God will temporarily grant a fool Divine Wisdom to save the fallen, weak, sick, wounded, or helpless. Thus, I can only convey Spiritual Protocol when developing strategies, be it Divine or not. However, I will say this: God's Divine Perspective MATTERS in the Kingdom and when dealing with His precious sheep, especially when it comes to pleasing ourselves or PLEASING God.

Godly Edge

When we see people, places, and things from God's point of view without complaining, blaming, or degrading, we naturally become grateful for the simple things in life. As a bonus for doing so, by Divine Default, we open ourselves up to Divine Wisdom and Spiritual Know-How. By far, with the silent dysfunctions among us today, operating *As It Pleases Him* gives us a Godly Edge we would not obtain otherwise.

What is the Godly Edge for Believers? It is the state of having a Spiritual Advantage, often attributed to individuals who actively seek a deeper connection with the Holy Trinity, *Spirit to Spirit*. Plus, they strive to embody God's Divine Principles in their daily lives, use the Fruits of the Spirit, and behave Christlike, *As It Pleases Him*. What will God give us in exchange for our obedience to this?

- ☐ He gives us Spiritual Insight and Wisdom.
- ☐ He gives us Spiritual Utterances and a Profound Voice.
- ☐ He gives us Spiritual Understanding and Relevance.
- ☐ He gives us Spiritual Instincts and a Divine Compass.
- ☐ He gives us Spiritual Discretion and Discernment.

- ☐ He gives us Spiritual Influence and Leverage.
- ☐ He gives us Spiritual Prudence and Stance.
- ☐ He gives us Spiritual Savvy and Pristineness.
- ☐ He gives us Spiritual Maneuverability and Conveyance.
- ☐ He gives us Spiritual Fruits and Oil.
- ☐ He gives us Spiritual Gifts, Creativity, and Talents.
- ☐ He gives us Spiritual Coverings and Provisions.

Who does not want Spiritual Benefits, right? We all have a longing to possess some form of Supernatural Power, especially if we have underlying pain, trauma, or guilt. How is it possible to possess Supernatural Power without becoming perceived as an unstable or crazy lunatic? We were created in the Image of God; therefore, if we are bound by emotional or mental torment, we can do something about it. However, we were not designed to run around bragging, boasting, or putting our Spiritual Power on display. Unfortunately, this is how we 'get got' by the enemy's antics designed to discredit the Spiritual Power that we all possess.

For the most part, if we desire to activate our hidden powers, we must up the ante on our problem-solving skills from a Spiritual Perspective. How do we up the ante in the Realm of the Spirit? We must 'Reload' our strategies with Spiritual Principles by putting on the Whole Armor of God as referenced in Ephesians 6:11-18. The moment we learn the value of suiting up Spiritually in Holy Armor, we put ourselves into a position to learn the 'How-To' of using it effectively and succinctly.

If we pursue the issues of life in our own strength, we will find ourselves becoming exhausted, dealing with the wiles of the enemy. Why do we become exhausted with the Vicissitudes, Issues, and Cycles of Life? According to scripture, *"For we do not wrestle against flesh and blood, but against principalities, against powers, against the rulers of the darkness of this age, against spiritual host of wickedness in the heavenly places. Therefore take up the whole armor of God, that you may be able to withstand in the evil day, and having done all, to stand."* Ephesians 6:12-13.

Approaching Issues

According to the Heavenly of Heavens, we must approach our lives with a *Reloaded Strategy* and *As It Pleases God*. By far, if we do not understand who or what we are dealing with from a Spiritual Perspective, we or the ones we love can be hung out to dry due to our lack of understanding or outright negligence. Sadly, there are times we may NOT survive our battle scars of trauma, mainly if we do not position ourselves to get the Spiritual Nourishment needed to survive.

Listen, we are not designed to approach life independently without the Spiritual Edifices designed to protect us. If we do, we may succumb to the intricacies associated with the elements of surprise. What do the elements of surprise have to do with Believers? We will become Spiritually Blind, Deaf, or Mute. The issues we should have seen coming, we will not see. The red flags we should have noticed will go unrecognized. The cues we should have heard, we will not hear. The Spiritual Utterances to cast down ill will, negativity, deceit, or destruction cannot be said due to the loss of words or willpower. But more importantly, we will respond to people, places, and things that DO NOT deserve our time or attention.

How can we approach our '*Reloaded Strategy*' in a way that keeps us Spiritually Protected? First, we must understand WHO we are. Secondly, we must understand WHY we are. Thirdly, we must understand our Spiritual Armor. Now, I cannot determine the WHO and WHY for anyone; we have to determine this for ourselves. However, I can give a point of direction of where we need to begin searching and how to Spiritually Gear Up, *As It Pleases God*.

Why can I not determine the Divine Blueprint or Instructions for anyone? First, we have free will. Secondly, we are all unique, with different Missions, Gifts, Talents, or Callings. Thirdly, we must take it to God in prayer, *Spirit to Spirit*, to MASTER our Spiritual Hunt from within. Fourthly, it is Spiritually Guarded, with everyone possessing their own unique KEY. Nevertheless, if we do not become a MASTER over our very own soul, *As It Pleases God*, we will become easily manipulated, bullied, or sifted, falling for anything or anyone.

Spiritual Triggers

Spiritually Speaking, our naivety should never make us Spiritually Reckless. If it does, it could become detrimental to our soulish being. However, PRAYER is our 'EXODUS.' What does this mean? Prayer is 'The Way Out.' But more importantly, it is also the meaning of Exodus as well.

The wailing from our soul can indeed move mountains, and it can move God if we have it adequately triggered, *As It Pleases Him.* Triggered? What does God or our prayers have to do with triggers? If we desire to move God, we must give Him what He likes or requires, *As It Pleases Him.*

Listen, before I get into the nitty-gritty of Spiritual Triggers, let me reel this in for a moment. For example, we as humans are triggered by:

- ☐ Good Charity.
- ☐ Positive Benefits of Security.
- ☐ Love and Hope.
- ☐ Compassion.
- ☐ Our Unique, Personable Language.
- ☐ A Listening Ear of Understanding.
- ☐ Getting what we want.
- ☐ Stability and Loyalty.
- ☐ Encouragement and Motivation.
- ☐ A Caring Heart.
- ☐ Gifts.
- ☐ Smiles and Laughter.

As we can now relate to triggers that benefit us, we can better understand how God is triggered positively or negatively. But for this book's sake, we will stay on the positive side of the spectrum. Should we not know both? Absolutely. I stand corrected; therefore, I will share both to ensure we are in the Spiritual Know.

Proverbs 6:16-19 says, *"These six things the Lord hates, Yes, seven are an abomination to Him."*

- ☐ A proud look.
- ☐ A lying tongue.
- ☐ Hands that shed innocent blood.
- ☐ A heart that devises wicked plans.
- ☐ Feet that are swift in running to evil.
- ☐ A false witness who speaks lies.
- ☐ One who sows discord among brethren.

When we behave in such a manner, it can block our prayers or reap coals upon us in ways that may create generational curses, yokes, retaliation, and recompensable atrocities. But more importantly, we must also become very cautious about a few character traits contributing to these behaviors. Listed below are a few things we need to take note of:

- ☐ Pridefulness.
- ☐ Selfishness.
- ☐ Envy.
- ☐ Jealousy.
- ☐ Greed.
- ☐ Coveting.
- ☐ Competitiveness.
- ☐ Lusts of the Eye.
- ☐ Lusts of the Flesh.
- ☐ Slothfulness.
- ☐ Disrespectfulness.
- ☐ Revengeful Anger.
- ☐ Disobedience.
- ☐ Cruelty.
- ☐ Hatefulness.
- ☐ Willful Debauchery.
- ☐ Rebellion.
- ☐ Bullying.

Remember, we all appear right in our own eyes, so we must do a check-up from the neck up often. Why do we need to do a check-up on ourselves, especially when we have it going on, and everyone loves us? It is challenging to see ourselves without looking through an outside source. For example, the only way to see our outside appearance is to use a mirror, right? The same applies to our inside appearance as well; we must use a Spiritual Mirror.

What is a Spiritual Mirror? It is the reflection and correction of our Christlike Character and the echoes of our Fruits of the Spirit. Above and beyond the call of duty, it also consists of our ONENESS with the Holy Spirit. Really? Yes, really! This ONENESS helps us heed the Spirit's leading or correction. What makes this so important? Without chastisement, we become selfish, disobedient, disrespectful, dull, or unruly by default, creating a sense of normality, which contradicts Christlike Character to the 10th degree.

Why the 10th degree? Is it that serious? Yes, this is serious when it comes down to our Spirituality, *As It Pleases God*. Why is this so sensitive in the Eye of God? It is His sore spot from the Garden of Eden; therefore, we should tread very carefully in this area while exhibiting the utmost RESPECT.

Having a high level of shady characteristics or a corrupt character is a hidden weapon of mass destruction to the psyche without us realizing its impact. From my perspective, having too many negative triggers will keep our personalities split, making us oblivious to the great divide.

How is it possible to have a split personality as a Believer? We are often conditioned to DENY our slated emotions, attitudes, behaviors, conversations, or masks. The contradiction becomes quite apparent when we switch from person to person from within, in a single encounter.

Taming the Beast

However, we are quick to point the finger at those with the obvious condition of having a split personality. But the truth is that we all have one in the Eye of God. Blasphemy, right? Wrong. Here is the deal, and with all due respect: We all have this little nudging beast from within that we do not often talk about. Yet, it is the one thing that brings the Book of Revelation to life.

Am I going too far with this beast thing? Absolutely Not! The lies we tell ourselves speak louder than the beast itself. I am not here to sugarcoat or feed this lie; I am ripping this VEIL from top to bottom and from left to right with the Holy Fire of the Most High God from the Heavenly of Heavens.

So, my question is, 'Who is the Beast of the Earth?' Wait, wait, wait, I have another question. 'Who opens the Gateway to the other Beast?' 'Do we know why we need the Fruits of the Spirit to combat what is already within us?' The last question, 'What is the number of men?' Now, let us take this thing to scripture: *"Then I saw another beast coming up out of the earth, and he had two horns like a lamb and spoke like a dragon. And he exercises all the authority of the first beast in his presence, and causes the earth and those who dwell in it to worship the first beast, whose deadly wound was healed. He performs great signs, so that he even makes fire come down from heaven on the earth in the sight of men. And he deceives those who dwell on the earth by those signs which he was granted to do in the sight of the beast, telling those who dwell on the earth to make an image to the beast who was wounded by the sword and lived. He was granted power to give breath to the image of the beast, that the image of the beast should both speak and cause as many as would not worship the image of the beast to be killed. He causes all, both small and great, rich and poor, free and slave, to receive a mark on their right hand or on their foreheads, and that no one may buy or sell except one who has the mark or the name of the beast, or the number of his name. Here is wisdom. Let him who has understanding calculate the number of the beast, for it is the number of a man: His number is 666."*

As a result of our lack of understanding, the transitioning characters of the beast play their role without us questioning it at all. As a matter of fact, we often think of a beast as a gory monster, but the human mind can really play tricks on us. The term 'beast' can refer to an animal, especially a large or dangerous one. Often, it is also referred to as an animal's nature, which we all have within our DNA. To be clear, I am not calling anyone an animal or beast; I am referring to the characteristics of a beast.

On the flip side of the coin, to be glorified as a beast is used informally to describe a person who is exceptionally skilled or successful at something, often in the context of sports or other competitive activities. So, regardless of how we deem the projection of the beast, we all have it and will use it at the drop of a dime to survive or save the lives of our loved ones. The bottom line is that it only takes the right trigger to evoke the beast that we tend to downplay or lie about.

How is it possible to become triggered, especially when we have excellent self-control? Self-control has nothing to do with how God has designed our bodies to release hormones to protect us. Thus, it behooves us to understand it, *As It Pleases God*, in order to tame it for Kingdom Usage. Why is this so important in the Eye of God? Our Spiritual Being must supersede the physical being. If not, our physical being and the psyche will dominate the underlying beast.

What are the signs that are designed to help us calculate the effects of the beast properly?

- ☐ When we are on an emotional rollercoaster, not knowing whether we are coming or going.
- ☐ When reacting or lashing out at others without realizing it.
- ☐ When we battle with untrue or delusional thoughts or emotions to get attention.
- ☐ When we have constant thoughts of negativity, evil, ill will, or harming others.
- ☐ When we have an uncontrollable tongue.
- ☐ When exhibiting negative behaviors without realizing it.
- ☐ When mimicking or taking on a sickness without being sick to get attention.
- ☐ When we are driven by bullying others or have an intense desire for control.
- ☐ When we are constantly jealous, envious, or coveting others.
- ☐ When we inflict pain upon others without any form of remorse.
- ☐ When we react with unkindness or take our problems out on those who have nothing to do with our issues.
- ☐ When we are Spiritually Blind, Deaf, or Mute.
- ☐ When we are rude, rebellious, stiffnecked, lukewarm, or dull.
- ☐ When we leave rotten fruits and victims all over the place.

Suppose we are in any of these states too long without interjecting Godly Character, repenting, casting it down, or pleading the Blood of Jesus. In this case, with compounded negative characteristics, rotten fruits, unresolved trauma, debilitating thoughts, or erratic behaviors, we may not be able to transition out of it without the help of God, period.

By not adding God into the equation, *As It Pleases Him*, we will continue having a cycle of relapse. Am I pulling for straws here? Absolutely not! We need to recognize and deal with the behaviors keeping us yoked or soul-tied instead of burying them, pretending they do not exist, or lying about our condition and why we are there.

Trip Triggers

In the same way, we have positive, emotional, or thought triggers, we have negative ones as well. But more importantly, God allows us to change for the better regardless of the type of trigger, who triggers us, and why. If we choose to remain the same, unchanged, or unrepentant, life can turn us upside down, provoking the desire to change without our permission! How would this happen to us, especially if God did not create us as robots? It is usually manifested through self-causation revealed through the issues of life, a constant bout with emotional or mental trauma, a continuous cycle of déjà vu, a trail of failure or defeat, and the list goes on.

Personally, I call negative triggers TRIP TRIGGERS. What is the purpose of this name? For example, when predators seek out, pursue, or ambush their prey, they will trigger them to run. Then, tripping them to bring them down, especially if they have a noticeable weakness or unfair disadvantage. Why is this a Trip Trigger? If they lose their balance or catch them off guard, it provokes fear and panic, interpreted as a preyable (vulnerable) weakness.

Once a viable weakness is triggered, it creates a disadvantage for the prey, Mentally, Emotionally, and Physically, making them vulnerable. On the other hand, if they are well-trained to AVOID panicking, they can think on their feet to avoid becoming tripped up, captured, or preyed upon. More importantly, we are no different!

What are the Spiritual Triggers that move God on our behalf? Listed below are a few triggers to build Spiritual Maturity:

- ☐ Our Spiritual Awakening to Christlike Character.
- ☐ Becoming ONE with the Holy Spirit.
- ☐ The Fruits of the Spirit. (Love, Joy, Peace, Patience, Kindness, Goodness, Faithfulness, Gentleness, and Self-Control).
- ☐ Spiritual Humility.
- ☐ Spiritual Diligence.
- ☐ Spiritual Meditation.
- ☐ Spiritual Trainability.
- ☐ Spiritual Nudgeability.
- ☐ Spiritual Listenability.
- ☐ Spiritual Pliability.
- ☐ Spiritual Righteousness.
- ☐ Spiritual Respectability.

God does not expect us to be perfect; He expects willingness, shareability, trainability, and responsibility with a work-in-progress mentality while Spiritually Tilling our own ground.

If God cannot get anything through us, it is a possibility that He will not use us for specific Spiritual Tasks. Plus, He may develop a deaf ear to us as well. Why would God ignore us or become silent? Do we think for a minute, God is going to answer prayers so we can traumatize the weak, vulnerable, and naive? The answer is no! We must remember the few things God hates, and this happens to be one of them. Moreover, if we are having prayers answered with such negativity, hatefulness, or ruthlessness, it is a possibility that it is not God. So, beware!

The superficial smokescreen prayers for public consumption do not necessarily make us effective in the Eye of God. Our character traits move or detour the implementation of our 'Reloaded Strategy.' What does this mean in layman's terms? Our behaviors or character traits are vital in moving God on our behalf or when contending with the enemy.

If the enemy knows we are torn up from the floor up, he will have a field day tossing us to and fro. Why would he bounce us around like a yo-yo? If we are clueless about Spiritual Protocol, Christlike Character, or Spiritual Ammunition, he will hang us out to dry, Mentally, Physically, Emotionally, and Spiritually. How is this possible when we are a born-again Christian? If we are not behaving Christlike, he knows that pleading the Blood of Jesus over things is of little effect, primarily if we are not pleading it over ourselves first.

Why is pleading the Blood of Jesus of no effect? The Blood of Jesus begins with us, and for us and others! This is blasphemy, right? Wrong! Romans 5:11 says, "*And not only that, but we also rejoice in God through our Lord Jesus Christ, through whom we have now received the atonement.*" If I take this a little further, "*My little children, these things I write to you, so that you may not sin. And if anyone sins, we have an Advocate with the Father, Jesus Christ the righteous. And He Himself is the propitiation for our sins, and not for ours only but also for the whole world.*" 1 John 2:1-2.

What does all of this mean for us? We must use the Blood of Jesus to cleanse ourselves and our houses first. And then, live by example to impact others, *As It Pleases God*. Here is the Spiritual Seal: "*But if we walk in the light as He is in the light, we have fellowship with one another, and the blood of Jesus Christ His Son cleanses us from all sin.*" 1 John 1:7.

If we do not develop our strength, pleading the Blood of Jesus over our lives as Spiritual Atonement, we will lose ground Spiritually by default. For example, during Passover in the Book of Exodus, the Children of Israel were ordered to place the Blood of the Lamb over the doorpost of their houses...not their neighbor's house, not their enemy's house. If they had not followed instructions, the final plague would have affected their household regardless of their loyalty to God.

The bottom line is that we must MASTER our houses first! If we do not, the enemy will place a bullseye target on our houses, shaking it to the core to ruin our credibility, sustainability, and authority from a Spiritual Perspective. Therefore, it is imperative to work on our thoughts, words, behaviors, and reactions to ensure they align with the expectations of God, *As It Pleases Him*.

If we want the *'Reloaded Strategies,'* we must give God what He wants. What does He want from us? It will vary from person to person, but He wants your heart, a personal *Spirit to Spirit* Relationship, to unveil your Divine Blueprint, and an unwavering commitment to lead His sheep into or out of the Fold (The Divine Covering) while always being on your best behavior, *As It Pleases Him.*

Developing Enthusiasm

As life would have it, when thinking about enthusiasm, we think it is this happy, go-lucky demeanor. In all actuality, enthusiasm is our hidden interests stimulating our PASSION or stirring up our Gifts.

In today's time, we have so much jealousy, envy, greed, and coveting, blocking our ability to recognize what or who enthralls our soulish passions. As a result, we tend to settle for worldly acceptance of what should appease us, not realizing we must incorporate what or who ignites our soul as opposed to what or who in-lusts it. Okay, I am creating words here, but it is our overinflated or overstimulated lusts that are drawing us away from our Divine Purpose, throwing our self-control out the window.

Once the newness of superficial excitement wears off, reality sets in, causing the battle of the souls to collide. What does this mean? It means digression is taking place, Mentally, Physically, Emotionally, and Spiritually, luring us away from our Passion, Purpose, or Predestined Blueprint instead of ushering us into it. As a result of our Spiritual negligence, we will lash out at God, ourselves, and others, hoping it will ease the pain. Does it work? It works as a temporary fix while digging us deeper into a pit of seemingly lost hope, misdirected energy, or open and hidden negative habits.

The *Wailing Prayers To The Deep Reloaded* advises that when we are enthused by something or someone, it should make us better, not bitter. It should cause us to grow positively without invoking an inner or outer downfall. It should give us an undeniable glow in our eyes, not tears of regret.

For example, a passionate golfer lights up when talking about golf. A writer writes better when telling their story. A painter illuminates when speaking of their painting. A parent glows when sharing their family. A singer performs better when people enjoy their songs. A person with their SOUL MATE or HELPMEET grows in life, making the corrections necessary to build a WE mentality, instead of going through life embracing the ME mentality or rolling with the punches without self-correction. I can go on for days with examples; however, I have set the tone of understanding how developing enthusiasm works.

If we are not feeling or experiencing any form of enthusiasm, we may be barking up the wrong tree related to our Passion, Purpose, or Blueprint. Really? Yes, really! If you do not feel it in the core of your being, it is often not for you.

How can we pinpoint enthusiasm? It is a matter of finding out a few things, but not limited to such:

- ☐ What brings enthusiasm to our Spirit?
- ☐ What ignites an inner joy?
- ☐ What takes us into a zone of peace?
- ☐ What are we so patient regarding?
- ☐ What do we love with no strings attached?
- ☐ What type of picture can we mentally paint with little or no effort?
- ☐ What makes our Creative Baby Leap?
- ☐ What catches our eyes?
- ☐ What piques our interests?
- ☐ What can we offer to the world, solving a problem, answering questions, or bringing enthusiasm to others?
- ☐ What type of information flows to or through us without any form of training or background?
- ☐ What invokes a level of discipline, taking precedence over what is going on in our lives?

The moment we peel back the layers of trauma, lies, or lost hope, we can better pinpoint the hidden joys of the heart.

According to the Heavenly of Heavens, our Passion, Purpose, or Blueprint is most often hidden in our weaknesses, our kryptonite, or what helps us temporarily zone out. Why? Those are the areas we tend to overlook or avoid at all costs. Suppose we can get past the hurt Mentally, Physically, Emotionally, or Spiritually. In this case, we may find the enthusiasm to unveil our Gifts, Talents, Creativity, or Spiritual Tools to fulfill our God-Given Purpose.

How can we extract our Predestined Blueprint from our issues and weaknesses? It contains the training, information, and experiences we need to make us better, stronger, and wiser, similar to on-the-job training. With experience in Spiritually Tilling our own ground, we can create a win-win situation out of everything through our MINDSET and PERCEPTION, *As It Pleases God*. How? It contains the know-how and how-to wrapped in what is already with the Mindset of God attached. And all we need to do is put our thinking caps on, *As It Pleases Him*.

Thinking Cap

The hidden treasures of life are secretly intertwined in our perceptions. If we are not thinking the right thoughts, it sways our sense of judgment, regardless of how holy we proclaim. How is this possible? The Mind of God thinks totally different from the mind of man, even on our best day. How do I know? Let us take it to scripture, *"For My thoughts are not your thoughts, Nor are your ways My ways," says the Lord. "For as the heavens are higher than the earth, So are My ways, and My thoughts than your thoughts."* Isaiah 55:8-9.

According to the *Wailing Prayers To The Deep Reloaded*, we must begin to think about what we are doing, the reasons why, how we are doing it, where we do it, when we do what we do, and with whom, from a Spiritual Perspective with God in mind. It helps us safeguard or regulate our thoughts more positively, creating a win-win, even when appearing as a lose-lose.

According to the Heavenly of Heavens, we must think inside, outside, around, through, over, and under the box, aligning ourselves with the Fruits of the Spirit, Christlike Character, Spiritual Protocol, or Biblical Scriptures. Why? The best answer I can give is in Romans 12:2, *"And do not be conformed to this world, but be transformed by the renewing of your mind, that you may prove what is that good and acceptable and perfect will of God."*

In our wailing process, going with the flow will not get it. God requires us to renew our minds continually. How can we develop a positive mindset if our thoughts are all over the place? We must develop self-discipline in our actions, thoughts, words, and character. What is the purpose of doing so? *"Whoever heeds discipline shows the way to life, but whoever ignores correction leads others astray."* Proverbs 10:17.

As we grow in our walk with God, *As It Pleases Him*, self-control and discipline work hand in hand. If we cannot perfect the two, obedience cannot reside, causing us to violate our conscience, miss red flags, and thwart our discernment faculties, as we call evil good or good evil. For this reason, the Spirit of Obedience lays dormant in those who do not like being told what to do. Then again, it will do the same for those who intentionally disregard basic instructions, exhibiting dullness, stiff-neckedness, or rebellion.

Why would the Holy Spirit or the Spirit of Obedience go dormant? If we cannot listen to people, we will not listen to the instructions from God in or out of our wailing process. How is this possible? First, God uses people as a TOOL to speak on His behalf, especially when we are Spiritually Blind, Deaf, or Mute. Secondly, *"One who turns away his ear from hearing the law, even his prayer is an abomination."* Proverbs 28:9.

The individuals who are secretly or openly unteachable, rebellious, reckless, unruly, or wayward are usually Spiritually Blind, Deaf, or Mute without realizing their condition, with rotten fruit surrounding them. In addition, we will also find they are gung-ho in asking for advice or opinions from others, resulting in doing what they want to do anyway. Then again, they may pride themselves on capitalizing on others or pilfering to add to their repertoire of pretense.

Spiritually, we must exercise extreme caution with a lukewarm mindset prone to defiance, debauchery, and rebellion. Why should we exercise such caution? Those who possess a DISOBEDIENT MINDSET are usually the ones who abuse others, Mentally, Physically, Emotionally, Spiritually, or Financially. How do we know the difference? *"We will know them by their fruits."* Matthew 7:16. For example, if we would like to determine an individual's obedience, simply pay attention to their level of control, Mentally,

Physically, Emotionally, and Spiritually. If one cannot control these four areas, their display of self-control or discipline is a cover-up or mask.

If we pay close attention, they are usually the bully or control freak who pride themselves on bossing people around instead of serving them. Why do we need to serve? The best way to articulate the answer to this question is to take a look at Matthew 23:11-12: *"But he who is greatest among you shall be your servant. And whoever exalts himself will be humbled, and he who humbles himself will be exalted."*

In the thinking process, we are headed for destruction if we cannot rule over our souls or if our psyche is running the show. Therefore, it is best to repent, pray, and fast over the undisciplined areas to ensure we do not set a booby trap for ourselves. Doing so allows the Holy Spirit to enlighten us in the areas where darkness may be lurking as a snare.

Why do we fall out of Spiritual Alignment, *As It Pleases God?* First, it is due to self-alignment, when we make everything about us, leading to misalignment from within. Secondly, we consume our own fruits without using the Fruits of the Spirit as a replenishing edifice. Thirdly, it is caused by our hidden lusts of the flesh, the lust of the eye, and the pride of life with power, money, and sex.

Our lusts incorporate a lot of characteristics by default. What are they? Let us take it to scripture: *"For the flesh lusteth against the Spirit, and the Spirit against the flesh: and these are contrary the one to the other: so that ye cannot do the things that ye would. But if ye be led of the Spirit, ye are not under the law. Now the works of the flesh are manifest, which are these; adultery, fornication, uncleanness, lasciviousness, idolatry, witchcraft, hatred, variance, competitiveness, wrath, strife, agitation, profanity, envy, murder, drunkenness, revel, and such like: of the which I tell you before, as I have also told you in time past, that they which do such things shall not inherit the kingdom of God."* Galatians 5:17-21.

From my experience, the worst thing we can do to ourselves is to get caught up with those who are determined to get into our heads, brainwashing us away from Purpose or detouring us from our Predestined Blueprint. For this reason, if one needs to draw a line in the sand on something or someone, it is best to align ourselves Spiritually, repent, fast, and pray before we cut it off.

Why can we not just dismiss anyone or anything we do not like? Everything comes into our lives for a reason, a season, a lesson, or a lifetime to avoid inner flatlining; therefore, we must know the difference. Why? We do not know what God is using to teach, train, perfect, mold, or test us without involving Spiritual Discernment, *As It Pleases Him*.

If we are not living up to Christlike standards, cutting people off can cause the joke to fall on us. For example, if we want to cut someone off for having a bad attitude, and our attitude sucks...where is God in this? Just because we feel right in our own eyes, it does not always make us correct. We cannot keep running from our issues; we must deal with them. We must master converting negatives into positives, create a win-win situation out of a negative one, and exhibit the Fruits of the Spirit first.

However, if we take on the Eye of God via the Holy Spirit, *As It Pleases Him*, we can determine our direction without eliminating our Blessings in disguise. How is this possible? With God, our Blessings will always be hidden in plain sight, wrapped in a problem, trauma, adversity, or fear.

Simply because someone is unequally yoked with us does not mean we should be unkind, unruly, nasty, unloving, or negative. So, what do we do? We should exhibit the Fruits of the Spirit and keep it moving without trying to change them. According to the Heavenly of Heavens, it is not our job to change someone! Our job is to change ourselves to become Representatives of the Kingdom *As It Pleases God*, while staying in Purpose on purpose, Spiritually Tilling our own ground, and exhibiting the Love of God with no strings attached.

Strategic Love

Love is often perceived as a spontaneous and uncontrollable emotion driven solely by passion, lust, and chemistry. However, upon closer examination, it becomes evident that successful and enduring relationships are not just the result of chance or luck. Instead, they require a strategic approach that involves careful thought, intention, and planning.

Contrary to what most would think, nothing is totally complete without love. Why are we incomplete without love? We were created to love and be loved. Most of all, we were created to love God, our Heavenly Father.

Love is dedicating time and effort to nurturing the connection through shared experiences, spending quality time, conveying acts of affection, exhibiting unselfish intentions, nurturing bonds, and extending kindness. Although these are only a few examples, they illustrate a deliberate and strategic approach to fostering a healthy and enduring relationship.

Nevertheless, love becomes Divinely Strategic when we add God into the equation with a purposeful and intentional approach to building lasting and fulfilling relationships, *As It Pleases Him*. What is the purpose of adding God into our love life or love endeavors? According to scripture, "*And we have known and believed the love that God has for us. God is love, and he who abides in love abides in God, and God in him.*" 1 John 4:16.

Why is love so important in Strategic Love? First and foremost, we were created in God's Divine Image. Secondly, love gives us hope. Thirdly, love or the lack of it, determines the heart posture of mankind.

What can love really do for us? Then my question would be, 'What can love not do for us?' Yes, you see, as Spiritual Beings, we are drawn by lovingkindness. Here is the scripture: "*The Remnant of Israel Saved, "At the same time," says the Lord, "I will be the God of all the families of Israel, and they shall be My people." Thus says the Lord: "The people who survived the sword Found grace in the wilderness—Israel, when I went to give him rest." The Lord has appeared of old to me, saying: "Yes, I have loved you with an everlasting love; therefore with lovingkindness I have drawn you. Again I will build you, and you shall be rebuilt, O virgin of Israel. You shall again be adorned with your tambourines, And shall go forth in the dances of those who rejoice.*" Jeremiah 31:1-4

The sooner we get it, the sooner we can tap into the Hidden Secrets of God. How is this possible when we have been faithfully serving Him? Anyone can serve God, but when it comes down to the Spiritual Anointing or Gifts, there are Spiritual Prerequisites and Contingencies. Why are there Spiritual Restrictions? To keep us from abusing our power, hurting the innocent, abusing others, using love as a weapon, or bringing shame to His Divine Name. Really? Yes, really.

God gives a Spiritual Side-Eye to bullies who abuse others, especially when it comes to the love factors. Why do they get a side-eye? *"Whoever hates his brother is a murderer, and you know that no murderer has eternal life abiding in him."* 1 John 3:15. What implications are associated with having a bully mentality? They will herd His sheep into the wrong pastures, causing Spiritual Deprivation, Abuse, and Misuse, or a love deficit.

For me, I do not want to hear about the material hype of what a person can do for me; I want to know where they are leading me! Wait, wait, wait...I stand corrected. I want to know where they are leading us. Are they leading us into the Arms of God or into the Pits of Hell? What is the purpose of knowing this as Believers? In all simplicity, with God, all things are possible. Conversely, the Pits of Hell have a one-way ticket; thus, I am not interested, period!

Spiritually Speaking, this is why God has mercy on the Spiritually Naive; however, once we know better, we must do better. Why must we do better, especially when we are all subjected to error? In my experience, the penalty or chastisement for misbehaving is much higher for those who know better and choose not to do better.

In all actuality, what is happening is selfishness, waywardness, coveting, jealousy, envy, pride, competitiveness, and greed have placed conditions on the ability to love God, ourselves, and others the way He designed it. As a result, it has caused us to reject the real Gifts from within and our Predestined Blueprint, which breaks the cardinal rule set forth to become usable, *As It Pleases Him*.

Here is what we must know: *"You shall love the LORD your God with all your heart, with all your soul, and with all your mind. This is the first and great commandment. And the second is like it: You shall love your neighbor as yourself. On these two commandments hang all the Law and the Prophets."* Matthew 22:37-40.

Why is God so adamant about us loving each other? Love contains fruits, be it good or bad. Nevertheless, we have options; we can give our fruits to the Holy Trinity (The Father, Son, and Holy Spirit), or we can keep them for ourselves. If we do not exhibit love to God, ourselves, and others, we create a disservice in the Kingdom of God. How so? It creates spoiled rotten, or damaged fruits. Whereas, if we follow the path set forth by God using the Fruits of the Spirit, we can regraft ourselves from bad into good, fruitful, and productive, *As It Pleases Him*.

Why do we not love as we should? Most often, it is due to a broken heart, some form of trauma, conditioning, or neglect. *Wailing Prayers To The Deep Reloaded* wants us to know, "He heals the brokenhearted and binds up their wounds." Psalms 109:16. Regardless of where we are in our relationship with God, repenting, praying, forgiving, and fasting heal the heart faster than anything else under the sun.

When we are hurting and the pain will not go away, if we repent, confess all known and unknown sins, push the plate away, and take our brokenness to God in prayer, He will heal us. Does it really work? Absolutely. I am living proof. On the contrary, if we think we can do it on our own without God, we only suppress our issues, prolonging the healing process.

Before I move on, let me make a definite distinction about love. Fasting or praying for love or for someone to love us may not be the appropriate prayer or fast. Do we not have free will to pray and fast for whatever or whomever? In the same way that we have free will, so does another. Thus, we must not cross this line. What is the big deal? As a word of caution, forcing love on someone or forcing someone to love us is nothing more than witchcraft, creating a Spiritual Violation. Plus, this is the biggest reason for our emotional hurt and trauma today.

How can we avoid this from happening? It is best to allow people to love us naturally. From a Spiritual Perspective, there is plenty of love to go around, so there is no need to violate anyone's free will. If people cannot love us or appreciate the great person we are, then it is their problem, not ours.

Here is what God expects from us: "*For all the law is fulfilled in one word, even in this; thou shalt love thy neighbor as thyself.*" Galatians 5:14. If someone chooses not to love us, there is nothing we can do about it other than love them with a pure and clean heart with no strings attached, like Christ loves the church. Why must we become the bigger person in this matter? It is our responsibility as children of God to love each other.

Now, on the other side of the spectrum, if for some reason one is having an identity crisis or having a hard time loving oneself, it is best to fast and pray about it. If not, we will set ourselves up for the vultures to prey on our weaknesses and vulnerabilities.

When doing a love fast, do it to become lovable, to show love, to represent the love of Christ, to become a better lover, etc. As long as the love we are fasting and praying about is the love that is within oneself and the love of God, we are safe.

Now, if we are having a hard time in our relationships, or we allow finger-pointing and selfishness to ruin our love lives, it will tend to have a domino effect. Here is why: *"Men ought to love their wives as their own bodies. He that loves his wife loves himself."* Ephesians 5:28. Unbeknown to most, selfishness and ungratefulness are two of the most destructive forces that can poison and eventually destroy any relationship. Whether it is a romantic relationship, friendship, work relationship, or familial bond, the presence of selfishness and ungratefulness can erode even the strongest connections.

In the Eye of God, we must exhaust our resources using the Fruits of the Spirit and behaving Christlike before bailing out of a relationship! What is the purpose of doing so? To ensure the chips fall in our favor. Plus, we cannot expect God to bless our mess, especially when we DO NOT make a conscious effort to fix it, *As It Pleases Him*. If not, the consequences and repercussions could become detrimental to our well-being.

Whether we are falling in love or out of it, or when simply loving our neighbor, open and honest communication is essential. Discussing concerns related to selfishness and ungratefulness while working together to address issues or hopes can help foster understanding and cooperation. Then again, setting respectful boundaries, defining expectations, and actively listening to each other's feelings, needs, wants, and desires are key components of Strategic Love on any level and with whomever.

According to the Heavenly of Heavens, we are the Divine Vessels in which God has chosen to accomplish His love experiment; oops, I mean love experience. Listen, He is not asking for perfection from us. He is requesting genuine willingness, discipline, respectfulness, and obedience to the instructions He has set forth without becoming consumed with the lust of the eyes, the lust of the flesh, and the pride of life.

Our Spiritual Awakening requires a commitment of rational trust between ourselves and God. Without trust, we become indecisive or never satisfied by default. Plus, are these not the factors associated with dissatisfaction that are breaking up our homes and relationships today? Of course, they are. Even if we do not admit it or attempt to whitewash it, it is still a present danger for Strategic Love.

According to the Heavenly of Heavens, we cannot become wishy-washy with the Plan of God and Strategic Love. If we do, we will become misaligned with the expectations God has set forth, becoming easily swayed or exhausted by the expectations of others, causing us to line out (flatline) from within.

In most cases, inner flatlining is often kept a secret among those who pride themselves on doing things their way, pleasing themselves. However, all is not lost; there is hope if we dare to get an understanding of the purpose of adequately aligning ourselves Spiritually.

Why do we fall out of Spiritual Alignment in the Strategic Love Department? First, it is due to selfish misalignment. In all simplicity, this is when we make everything about us with God nowhere in the equation, or we are pimping Him for the benefits and not for solutions. Secondly, we consume our own fruits without using the Fruits of the Spirit as a replenishing edifice while allowing the rotten ones to remain. Thirdly, once again, it is caused by our hidden lusts and pride dealing with power, money, status, and sex.

What is the big deal about lust and pride, primarily when we like what we like? Our lusts incorporate a lot of characteristics by default. Let us take it to scripture: *"For the flesh lusts against the Spirit, and the Spirit against the flesh; and these are contrary to one another, so that you do not do the things that you wish. But if you are led by the Spirit, you are not under the law. Now the works of the flesh are evident, which are: adultery, fornication, uncleanness, lewdness, idolatry, sorcery, hatred, contentions, jealousies, outbursts of wrath, selfish ambitions, dissensions, heresies, envy, murders, drunkenness, revelries, and the like; of which I tell you beforehand, just as I also told you in time past, that those who practice such things will not inherit the kingdom of God."* Galatians 5:17-21. Now, if this is how you roll, then so be it. I have no qualms with allowing your free will to be free. I am just the Messenger!

Nonetheless, when developing Strategic Love, *As It Pleases God*, everything comes into our lives for a reason, a season, a lesson, or a lifetime to avoid inner flatlining; therefore, we must know the difference. Simply because someone is unequally yoked with us does not mean we should be unkind, unruly, nasty, unloving, or negative.

From me to you, please love the skin you are in because God did not make a mistake about you. Once you can do this, *As It Pleases Him*, it will radiate outwardly, making you lovable. Moreover, if someone blocks your genuine love, just keep it moving in the Spirit of Excellence. Your Divine Pride or Tribe is waiting for your love, so do not waste it on those who do not want it or respect it!

Dr. Y. Bur

www.DrYBur.com

CHAPTER 3

RELOADED PRIDE

When we speak of pride, we often think of the arrogant side of our prideful behavior; however, for the sake of *Reloaded Pride*, I am referring to pride as a team effort or a unified group. For the sake of *Wailing Prayers To The Deep Reloaded*, we are not speaking of a Tribe here; we are focusing on a Pride. What is the difference? A Tribe is a conditional grouping of those who will stand with us when it is beneficial. Or, it can be a superficial bond of those who have like interests but will run for cover when it is not in their best interest. On the other hand, our Pride is with us through thick or thin, right or wrong, good or bad, as well as our just or unjust moments. More importantly, they respect our differences, helping us to capitalize on our strengths to build stronger bonds to mentor the up-and-coming.

Just so we are crystal clear, regardless of whether we partake in a Tribe or Pride, God hates selfishness. Why is selfishness a problem for God? Figuratively, it is not a problem for Him per se; it is a big problem for His innocent sheep. The wailing of His children radiates a loud, thunderous noise in His Ear, getting His attention.

For example, even if we do not see the first strike of lightning, once we hear the roaring thunder, we intuitively know another strike will soon follow, right? Absolutely. If one has not noticed by now, this is how God operates as well to get our attention. What does this mean? If we miss the light or if our light is dim, we will eventually hear His sounding trumpet in some area of our lives or from within, causing us to seek cover or initiate the wailing process on our own. Just remember that He will protect those who have mastered the wailing process that gets His attention, and He condemns those who abuse it or cry wolf too much.

According to our Divine Design, it does not matter if we choose a Tribe or Pride; God is not biased regarding who can master the wailing process. However, He is biased on how we go about doing so and who it affects without their permission. How do we make this make sense? In all simplicity, we cannot violate the free will of another, especially if they are not our children, whom we are ordained to raise properly, and *As It Pleases God*. If we violate the free will of others, bully them, or do not raise our children properly, then it can become a Spiritual Violation for us in the Realm of the Spirit.

Now, to 'Reload' this chapter effectively about how He feels about His sheep, let us take it to scripture, *"There is the sound of wailing shepherds! For their glory is in ruins. There is the sound of roaring lions! For the pride of the Jordan is ruined. Thus saith the LORD my God; Feed my flock for slaughter, whose owners slaughter them and feel no guilt; those who sell them say, 'Blessed be the Lord, for I am rich'; and their shepherds do not pity."* Zechariah 11:3-5. For the sake of *Reloaded Pride*, we must crush the selfish pride and replace it with a Spiritual Teamified Pride, giving us a wail that will get God's attention immediately.

In this unification process of our *Reloaded Pride*, God wants us to *"Be sober, be vigilant; because your adversary the devil walks about like a roaring lion, seeking whom he may devour."* 1 Peter 5:8. What does this mean for us? The Devil also has a roar, so we must learn the difference. To get the upper hand on a roaring lion or the wailing process, we must become wise about doing so. In my opinion, we cannot roar back at a lion with a cat's meow! Why can we not behave like a cat? Beyond a shadow of a doubt, they will have us for lunch, just because!

The predatorial Big Cats have little respect for the small ones who are not of their own and those who are weak, untrained, and vulnerable. In the Eye of God, the developmental process counts in the roaring or wailing process. Simply put, we must learn, practice, and become trained by the Big Cats or Mentors to avoid unnecessary trial and error. Therefore, if we put a little strategy behind our roar, we will enable ourselves to go toe-to-toe with the devourer. How can we contend with a devourer as Believers? There is POWER in numbers!

We cannot roll solo when it comes down to building a Roaring Kingdom. Why not? It is dangerous; predators will target those alone, going about as easy prey. Listen to me, and listen well; the devourer will pounce on those who do not have the backing of those who should have their backs. Before I go any further, let me say this: It is the fittest and the strongest that survive. If we do not have someone to watch our backs, the enemy can sideswipe us, knocking the breath out of us. Then again, it can result in some form of Mental, Physical, Emotional, or Spiritual Imbalance or Trauma.

Wailing Prayers To The Deep Reloaded wants us to know that a King cannot be a King alone. Is a King, not a King? We can be a King in the making, but to assume the THRONE, we must have our PRIDE backing us. What do we do if we are approaching our Kingdom alone? We must build in hiding! Spiritually, we must keep our mouths closed by saying less while doing more.

Why is it important to say less and do more in the Eye of God? Let us take it to scripture, *'But when you do a charitable deed, do not let your left hand know what your right hand is doing, that your charitable deed may be in secret; and your Father who sees in secret will Himself reward you openly.'* Matthew 6:3-4. What if our Kingdom is not charity? Building according to our Spiritual Gifts or Purpose, *As It Pleases God*, is considered a Charitable Deed based upon the FREE WILL to do what needs to be done for the Kingdom!

Spiritual Ammunition

As human beings, we will face various challenges and adversities in our lives due to the Cycles, Seasons, and Vicissitudes of Life. These challenges may come in different forms, such as emotional struggles, difficult relationships, financial setbacks, or health issues, to facilitate and equip us for our Heaven on Earth Experiences, *As It Pleases God*. Then again, they may be used to empower us with Spiritual Ammunition to contend with the enemy's wiles.

Who knows what the enemy is going to throw at us, right? But one thing is for sure: We need all the Spiritual Ammunition to ensure the Whole Armor of God works on our behalf. What is the purpose of Spiritual Ammunition and Armor? It keeps us from wallowing or being unequipped. Then again, it can empower us with a yelping wail to our Heavenly Father, putting our enemies to boot.

How is it possible to yelp for a Legion of Angels at the drop of a dime? When we are in Purpose on purpose, God will cover us. And, whatever He allows to happen, it is designed to make us stronger, wiser, diligent, and strategically savvy, *As It Pleases Him*.

The Helpmeet

Merely possessing Spiritual Armor may not always be enough for us. We may need to complement it with Spiritual Ammunition and a Helpmeet. However, Spiritual Ammunition can be understood as the resources, practices, and attitudes that fortify and complement the Whole Armor of God. Without a Helpmeet to pass us the Spiritual Ammunition or help us put on our Spiritual Armor, it may render us dormant and ineffective in the face of Spiritual Battles, especially if we are sick, tired, worn out, or exhausted.

For example, during the battle between the Israelites and the Amalekites, in Exodus 17:8-16, Moses went up to the hilltop with Aaron and Hur. As the battle raged on, Moses raised his hands, and as long as his hands were raised, the Israelites were winning. However, when his hands grew tired and fell, the Amalekites started to prevail. So, Aaron and Hur found a stone for Moses to sit on, and they each held up one of his arms, so that his hands remained steady till sunset. With the support of Aaron and Hur, the Israelites ultimately emerged victorious in the battle.

The truth is that when individuals come together, *As It Pleases God*, they are better equipped to overcome challenges and face the adversities of life by invoking the power of collaboration and support. Is this Biblical? I would have it no other way: *"Though one may be overpowered by another, two can withstand him. And a threefold cord is not quickly broken."* Ecclesiastes 4:12. God knows that when people join forces and work together, *As It Pleases Him*, their combined efforts create a formidable alliance that is difficult to break. For this reason, in due time, if we are in Divine Purpose alone, God will send us a *Reloaded Pride* of our own, especially when UNITY and COMPANIONSHIP are needed for the next level.

On the other hand, if we try to force the Hand of God due to impatience, lack of self-control, or selfishness, we can choose wrong or overlook the Diamond in the Rough. As a result, we may forfeit our Helpmeet to the next in line. How is the forfeiture possible when we are patiently waiting on God? We can wait until we are blue in the face; if we reject, overlook, or lack Spiritual Discernment due to disobedience, a public or private distraction, or acceptance of a counterfeit, God is not obligated to extend a do-over.

Why do we not get a second chance, especially if they were really our Helpmeet in the first place? Because we made a free will CHOICE in the Eye of God without adding Him into the equation, *As It Pleased Him*. Nor did we heed the warnings sent. What if we were not sent a warning? Then my question is, 'What if we missed it?'

When it comes to a Helpmeet, *As It Pleases God*, He will send signs and messages when erring. If we ignore them or lack Spiritual Discernment like those who ignored Noah's warning of an impending flood, then we cannot get mad or poke our lips out for our own folly. What if we are not Noah, and we are not dealing with a flood? The Spiritual Principle of Divine Warnings and Obedience is still relevant from back then to now. Keep in mind that whatever is God-Sent is also Heavenly Protected.

Nevertheless, we may get a second chance at something else after repentance occurs, but it may not be that particular DIAMOND. Why not that same one? Disobedience, arrogance, unforgiveness, complaining, ungratefulness, and rebellion are sore spots for God. Therefore, it is imperative to make sure that we do not exhibit these characteristics when seeking a Helpmeet. Remember, when it comes down to the Divine Treasures of God, obedience is always better than sacrifice.

To add insult to injury, the recipient of our forfeiture will have most often LEARNED from our mistakes to Spiritually Glean what we rejected. Is this fair? Absolutely! Where I am from, it is said, 'One man's trash is another man's treasure.' Plus, they will recognize the Diamond in the Rough right out the gate and be willing to stand in Divine Unity, *As It Pleases God*. Meanwhile, heeding Divine Instructions and keeping people out of their business with a mindset of a Triple Braided Cord.

What is the purpose of keeping people out of their business? First, it allows God to place a Spiritual Seal on the Divine Union. Secondly, to withstand the tests of time, avoid negative influences, maximize the potency of their interconnection, and overcome adversity in the Spirit of Oneness, *As It Pleases God*. Thirdly, to PREPARE while actively seeking wisdom, guidance, and understanding of what is required from the Heavenly of Heavens.

What guarantee do we have regarding a Diamond? A real Diamond knows that it is a Diamond without unveiling its value until it is FOUND or CHOSEN. Better yet, here is another example: The first guarantee is similar to when God created Eve for Adam as a Helpmeet in the Book of Genesis after he completed specific tasks. Do we think for a minute that Adam did not recognize his Helpmeet? He knew who she was instantly, without a doubt.

How did Adam know Eve was his Helpmeet? He was Spiritually Connected to God, *Spirit to Spirit*. Always remember, Spirit knows Spirit. Then, why would God introduce a Helpmeet after the fact? As difficult as it may seem, having a Helpmeet will sometimes distract us from the Spiritual Mission. As a result, God will withhold certain people, places, and things to get us adequately aligned for our benefit, not to our detriment.

Before moving on to the second guarantee, if a person does not make our baby leap from within or cannot positively speak to our inner child, we may need to go back to the drawing board for updates. For the record, there is nothing worse than having someone insult our inner child, degrading our hopes, dreams, and desires, or traumatizing us further. Unfortunately, once the inner child checks out, it becomes harder to reel them back in.

Why must we return to the drawing board? They may not be connected to the Spiritual Mission or our Divine Blueprint. So, we must ask ourselves, 'What are they helping us meet?' Now, if the answer is for lustful pleasures, then we are barking up the wrong tree from the start. Plus, God does not operate like this; He operates for Purpose and Mission for the Greater Good over lustful pleasures.

The second guarantee says, *"And let us consider one another in order to stir up love and good works, not forsaking the assembling of ourselves together, as is the manner of some, but exhorting one another, and so much the more as you see the Day approaching."* Hebrews 10:24-25. We often apply this to a church setting; however, we must think outside the box. Spiritually, this also refers to teamwork, mentoring, or working together to improve for the Greater Good.

Furthermore, it builds our Spiritual Proactiveness in ways that can put our enemies to boot if we dare to learn how to communicate effectively. How do I know? Here is the scripture, *"As iron sharpens iron, So a man sharpens the countenance of his friend."* Proverbs 27:17. Now, if we become a little worried about cutting our Helpmeet with the sharpness of iron because they are not in the friend zone, all we need to do is put a little Holy Anointing Oil on the blade, As It Pleases God.

Please allow me to Spiritually Align this SYMBOLIC reminder about the Holy Anointing Oil that still creates Spiritual Seals to this very day with the Power of the Holy Spirit. *"And you shall speak to the children of Israel, saying: 'This shall be a holy anointing oil to Me throughout your generations. It shall not be poured on man's flesh; nor shall you make any other like it, according to its composition. It is holy, and it shall be holy to you.'"* What if we are not the Tabernacle of Meetings to anoint as such? Now, this is where we are deceived! The Holy Spirit changed the rules of the game...everything we need is WITHIN us! So, ANOINT and SPEAK to yourself, your Helpmeet, your home, your children, or whatever, and be about your Father's Business. The Spiritual Veil has been lifted...the BRIDEGROOM is now seating the TABLE. Please, do not miss it! Sharp rebuke will heal us and save our souls, but the lack of it can cost us everything!

The Bonding Factors

What good is a 'Wailing Prayer to the Deep,' when we are NOT able to break bread with our neighbors? What good is a 'Wailing Prayer to the Deep,' when we are looming curses over the lives of others? What good is a 'Wailing Prayer to the Deep,' when we are full of doubt? What good is a 'Wailing Prayer to the Deep,' when we feel as if we are the only righteous person? I could go on for days; however, the 'Wailing Process' has prerequisites we should not overlook.

To break this down effectively and do this chapter justice, I am going to reflect on the Pride of Lions for a moment. Why? *"Two are better than one, because they have a good reward for their labor. For if they fall, one will lift up his companion. But woe to him who is alone when he falls, For he has no one to help him up."* Ecclesiastes 4:9-10.

The King of the Jungle is perceived to be the most vicious animal, but from my point of view, they have the most developed system of gleanable bonding. How is this possible when a lion is a lion? Their lion-like character has a treasure chest of wisdom, Divinely Designed above man's repertoire. Really? Yes, really! Let us take it to scripture: *"There are three things which are majestic in pace, Yes, four which are stately in walk: A lion, which is mighty among beasts and does not turn away; a greyhound, a male goat also, and a king whose troops are with him."* Proverbs 30:29-30. What can we possibly learn from a Pride of Lions? There are several folds of wisdom or bonding factors that we can glean from this predator:

- ☐ They pride themselves on NOT contaminating their bloodline, period.
- ☐ They pride themselves on protecting their territory, even if it means developing a coalition.
- ☐ They pride themselves on defending their offspring.
- ☐ They pride themselves on taking caution when treading on the occupied, unfamiliar, unchartered, or unwarranted territory.
- ☐ They pride themselves on paying attention to their surroundings and keeping tabs on each other through their unique roaring language.
- ☐ They pride themselves on taking caution and exhibiting respect, especially to the hierarchy.
- ☐ They pride themselves on tolerating, socializing, grooming, communal nursing, and training their own.

- ☐ They pride themselves on mentoring the young as a group effort, catering to the individualized personality of each member of the pride.
- ☐ They pride themselves on exhibiting love, compassion, and nurturing to their offspring or other members through the power of touch.
- ☐ They pride themselves on exuding strength, courage, leadership, determination, and diligence.
- ☐ They pride themselves on watching and guarding their own without blindly slumbering while resting.
- ☐ They pride themselves on being themselves without deviation, balancing work, play, rest, and family time.

The strength of a Pride of Lions is no joke! They are natural-born killers who can rip their prey apart at the drop of a dime to stave off starvation, preserving their bloodline. Conversely, their predatorial skills or survival tactics can build a weakling into a KING through mentorship, knowledge, courage, and practice. What am I saying? A King is comprised of being a lover and fighter, taking care of their own while ruling over their soul or killer instincts. Now, in the language of mankind, this is called Self-Control!

How do predatorial skills benefit us when we are called to exhibit Christlike Character? In all due respect, if we are not exhibiting Christlike Character in our present state of being, we are already exhibiting predatory behavior. How is this possible? We are knowingly or unknowingly killing or tripping up the weak, Mentally, Physically, Emotionally, or Spiritually, especially among our own. Nevertheless, there is hopeful wisdom among the Pride.

So, stay with me; the bonding factors of the *Reloaded Pride* will empower us with strategic ways to rebuild ourselves from the inside out. Thus, giving us the drive to step outside of our comfort zones to polish up our People Skills while *Mastering the ROAR* of the Kingdom.

Mastering the ROAR

The gleanable hunting tactics from a Pride of Lions can be applied to our life's journey or when possessing the Promises of God. How is this possible when they are a predator? Once again, let us take it to scripture: *"The wicked flee when no one pursues, but the righteous are bold as a lion."* Proverbs 28:1. For the sake of this book, I will share information on how to capitalize on the courage and skills of a lion; however, there are contingencies. They are, but not limited to such:

- ☐ We must become hungry enough to pursue.
- ☐ We must use Christlike Character to create the maximization of their method of operation.
- ☐ We must stay alert.
- ☐ We must speak up for ourselves when necessary and back down if needed.
- ☐ We must communicate effectively and speak the communicable language of another, if necessary.
- ☐ We must become transparent, owning our truth.
- ☐ We must exude confidence without being egocentric or wishy-washy.
- ☐ We must become empathetic without looking down on another man's journey.
- ☐ We must become accountable for ourselves while squashing excuses.
- ☐ We must allow others to exercise their free will to avoid creating bondage for another.
- ☐ We must expect people to be who they are while setting a Christlike example to mimic.
- ☐ We must positively renew our minds consistently and succinctly.

Why is this important for us? To maximize *Reloaded Pride*, we must add God into the equation, *As It Pleases Him*. What is the purpose of doing so? Let us take it to scripture: *"The young lions roar after their prey, and seek their food from God."* Psalm 104:21. Always remember, God is our Source, and He takes care of what or who belongs to

Him. Listed below are a few tips on how lions MASTER themselves within a pride:

- ☐ They MASTER the techniques of their clawed hunting tactic through trial and error. This process allows them to know when to extend or retract their powerful claws and with whom.

- ☐ They MASTER the death grip of their prey (goal) by studying their strengths and weaknesses without deviating. They start small, increasing their capacity as they become more experienced.

- ☐ They MASTER their time alone. For the female: to give birth or the bonding process of her new cubs. For the male: to build a coalition, territories, and offspring while serving each other.

- ☐ They MASTER facing their fears and the art of risk-taking to build a Legacy with a long-term objective of Kingship, knowing their purpose, principles, and protocols.

- ☐ They MASTER the strengths and weaknesses of their prey in silence while patiently thinking strategically about their approach without rushing. They also perfect the art of knowing when to lead, follow, and stand down.

- ☐ They MASTER the timing process of when to move and why, when to fight or retreat, as well as when to share their kill and when to stash it.

- ☐ They MASTER the art of willpower, loyalty, unified togetherness, and sociability skills.

- ☐ They MASTER their instincts to know when they are over their head in danger or how to overcome adversity.

- ☐ They MASTER the ability to get close to their prey in silence to hone in on a plan to exemplify their preciseness.

- ☐ They MASTER their losses or defeats like a champ, only to create a win-win with another, and know their target.

- ☐ They MASTER being proactive with the unpredictable, constantly perfecting their tactic and unique savvy.

- ☐ They MASTER their ability to call their prey's bluff, choosing their moment of attack while not risking themselves to severe injury.

Why do we need to become a MASTER? Mediocrity is not going to get it in the Eye of God! We must become strategic in all things to reach the masses we are called to reach. In addition, we also need to become strong enough to cut off the oxygen to debilitating people, places, things, and negativity.

Why does God require us to cut off certain people, places, and things? First, the pruning process must occur with all things concerning God Almighty. Secondly, to transform our lives positively, we must starve it without feeding into foolery! Thirdly, by cutting off negative influences, toxic relationships, or harmful environmental elements from our lives, we create space for positivity and growth, *As It Pleases God*. Lastly, it is often a test of our dedication and obedience to the Will or Blueprint of our Heavenly Father and being about His Business.

We, as human beings, may not consider ourselves animals, but we can certainly learn valuable lessons from observing animal behavior. For example, lions use strategic tactics to catch their prey. This method of operation involves creating panic and anxiety in the prey to make it easier to capture. Once the prey is tripped up, the lion goes for the neck to cut off the oxygen flow. While this process may take longer, it is effective. From my perspective, this strategic tactic demonstrates how male lions have been provided with a mane by nature to protect their neck during this process. The key takeaway is that the same tactics used by lions to maintain their status as the King of the Jungle can also be used against them. For me, this illustrates that we already have the necessary tools to overcome negativity in our own lives.

On the other hand, if a lion is with their pride, they joins forces to take down larger prey. Why would they join forces, especially when they would be required to share their meal? They understand, beyond a shadow of a doubt, that there is POWER in UNITY. With this knowledge, some will fan out, encircle, or herd their prey into a trap by leg grabbing, biting, scratching, or tripping to bring the animal down. Then, one goes for the neck while the other one goes for the mouth and nose, smothering the animal's wailing cry to make the takedown quick.

But more importantly, the bigger the animal, the more of the pride is needed for the chokehold or death bite to occur. How does this vicious act relate to us? The Cycle of Life is designed to work for us and through us, but it has no mercy if we are careless, unrepenting, or unrelenting. How do we make this make sense? Our actions or reactions have life-or-death consequences regardless of who, what, or why we are. So, the bigger the issues are, the bigger the Spiritual Team needed to suit up with the Whole Armor of God for combat.

Here is the deal: We become invincible when we are in Purpose with a UNIFIED Spiritual Grouping backing us. Now, with our *Reloaded Pride*, there can only be ONE leader in the bunch. Why is one leader necessary? A hierarchy is a must to avoid breaking down our system or method of operation. There will be chaos if there are too many leaders, causing a simple ambush to become detrimental.

As a part of the Cycle of Life, we all have strengths and weaknesses, but cooperation is necessary. For example, if a lion lowers its guard in a power struggle, the hunter can become hunted by the onslaught of its rivals or scavengers. With this in mind, let me interject: Is this not happening in our homes or society today?

As life would have it, the scavengers or opportunists are designed to keep us on our toes. If we do all the work, and someone comes in to steal it, getting all the credit or claiming it as their own, it causes us to polish up our skills, right? Of course! In my opinion, it makes us much better and vigorously savvy, only if we dare to fight off the sting of bitterness, anger, or revenge.

Nevertheless, if it is our God-Given right to be who we are, or if we are in Purpose on purpose, we should not deviate regardless of the scavengers, rivals, or opportunists we face. Why should we not deviate or change our strategies? It is all a part of the plan of perfection. Know this: If we do not possess value, they will go elsewhere! For example, the vultures, hyenas, jackals, wild dogs, etc., do not follow elephants around to scavenge. Why? They do not have any value in doing so; they go where they can capitalize.

Besides, we would never go to the beach looking for a jungle experience, and vice versa; therefore, making our environment vital to the appropriate building of our *Reloaded Pride*. In all simplicity, if we desire to be a success, we must avail ourselves to a thriving environment. We must get into a creative environment if we desire to become creative. We must expose ourselves to a conducive writing environment if we desire to write. Although we can go on for days with this list, we do not have to develop a scavenger mentality.

According to the Heavenly of Heavens, scavenging is NOT necessary when we walk in Purpose using our Spiritual Gifts. Why? According to our Predestined Blueprint and *As It Pleases God*, He makes Divine Provisions for us when we align ourselves with His Divine Will and Ways. All we need to do is avail ourselves to the information and follow instructions. As a word of warning, if we become a scavenger, it creates a natural bed of insecurity by default, creating all types of unconducive blockages. So, be careful when doing so, especially when the goal of this book is to become courageously confident.

Now, the question is, does a Pride of Lions scavenge? Absolutely. They will take the meal of another, especially if they are the Leader, if it is in their territory, or if they are in survival mode. But more importantly, according to their Divine Purpose, they will also take the fresh meal of an arch-enemy or weakling as well, as a part of the training process of life. But, they are not too keen on stealing a mouthful of maggots unless they are desperate, in survival mode, or a nomad!

Possessing meals out of rulership and scavenging out of desperation are two different entities. Just keep in mind that predatorial and scavenging behavior resides within everyone and everything as an interbred survival mechanism. So, we must learn the difference to ensure we do not step outside of our Divine Purpose. Does this really make a difference? Absolutely.

We must exercise extreme caution when stepping into another man's territory, especially if we are not equipped or authorized to call for Spiritual Backup. Do we not have equal rights to call upon God? Yes, we do. However, if our call is placed on a phone without service, do we think we would get an answer? Or, if the roar of a lion is replaced with the meow of a cat, do we think the Pride will recognize the call for backup?

Here is a little secret when it comes down to the Cycle of Life. Suppose we are in Purpose on purpose, wailing under God's Authority with a repenting heart. In this case, we have more authority than one who is clueless, rebellious, out of Purpose, or wayward under their own authority. Why is there a difference, especially when God loves us all? Once again, God takes care of what belongs to Him. And if we belong to ourselves, then why are we calling on Him to help us out of a mess that we have yet to repent of or self-correct?

On the other hand, if self-control or discipline is not established accordingly, the scavenging nature becomes habitual. Listen, negative bad habits will hinder a lion's hunting skills, which may result in starvation, disrespectfulness, or engaging in unnecessary battles. For this reason, they must keep their hunting skills top-notch and anointed, fulfilling their Purpose for being here in the first place. If not, life is designed to knock a few notches off their belt or send them back into the Spiritual Classroom to learn that RESPECT and discipline go hand-in-hand.

Why is a Spiritual Classroom necessary, especially when we have free will? God created them to do a specific task, and if they cannot live up to the Spiritual Label God has placed on them, He will DETHRONE them by any means necessary. How is this possible when they are predators? God provides for the predators, scavengers, or whatever is in their rightful place according to their Divine Design.

To make this correlation applicable to us, let me break this down a little more. For some odd reason, when it comes down to the Animal Kingdom, we want everything to be perfect. At least I do; however, I have to respect the Laws of Nature while bringing about a gleanable awareness applicable to our humanistic character, as well as how it affects or propels us.

The bottom line is that, regardless of how we view a Pride of Lions or their method of operation, they were Divinely Created as dangerous predators who take out the weak. The scavengers were Divinely Designed to keep them on their toes, preventing them from becoming lazy and complacent, making the cycle work.

Now, if we begin to pride ourselves on the unusual patterns of scavenging out of laziness, here are a few things that could happen:

- ☐ We can become led astray, threatened by territorial intruders, or encounter perpetual banishment.
- ☐ We can quickly become ambushed or tripped up.
- ☐ We will lose our sense of pride among our own, as well as with the least of animals.
- ☐ We will begin to lose our ability to take ownership.
- ☐ Our milk teeth will keep us suckling, stealing, or using people, places, and things.
- ☐ We will not develop or strengthen our adult teeth to eat real Spiritual Meat.
- ☐ We will play childish games or exhibit childlike behaviors, thoughts, and ways of communication.
- ☐ We will zap our creative or strategic abilities.
- ☐ We will lack the confidence to take ownership.
- ☐ We will exhibit insecurities in our People Skills.
- ☐ We will become deceived by our thwarted perceptions.
- ☐ We cannot live up to the expectations God has set forth.

Before I move to the next chapter, we cannot fall short of the reputation God has in mind for us.

The Balance of Power continually shifts on a sliding scale, favoring the positive and purposeful! We simply need to know this while remaining confident without deceiving others or running our mouths too much with *Prideful Vanity*.

While taking pride in one's accomplishments and maintaining healthy self-esteem are important, the line between confidence and egotistical vanity can easily become blurred, leading to negative consequences. Therefore, it is imperative to focus on getting and staying in Divine Purpose, *As It Pleases God*, without deviating to an unfamiliar roar.

What is an unfamiliar roar? It is a distraction or temptation to lure us away from our Divine Purpose. Or, then again, the unfamiliar roar is usually hidden in our vanity (selfish pride).

Contrary to what most would think, vanity is designed to expose our weaknesses or insecurities, not to make us superior. But more importantly, it is designed to paint a picture of what our heart sees, feels, or covers up. What if we miss what it is saying? Then my question would be, 'What if we do not miss what it is saying?' Plus, if for some reason we get it wrong, we have more of a reason to self-correct to get it right. However, if we keep getting it wrong, it means that we are not paying attention, we do not want to see, or we are not asking the right questions, *As It Pleases God*.

Why should we stay in an unfulfilling Purpose when we are desperate? Desperation is a mindset; if we underestimate our Kingship due to how it appears, doubt will claim the mind, scattering it to and fro.

Remember, Kingdom transfers occur right under our noses without us realizing it. So, suppose we want to become the recipient of Kingdom Transfers, *As It Pleases God*. In this case, we need to target the negative, while repentingly shifting it to the positive, while applying Biblical Scriptures to back it up.

The Big Cats' Golden Rule

Keep in mind that the real Spiritual Big Cats follow the Golden Rule. What is the Golden Rule amongst the Spiritual Cats? We do not sell out our own! We bring about awareness, help them nurse their wounds, correct them, and set them in the right direction. But we do not set our mouths against or slander what God has Anointed.

In the Eye of God, it does not matter if we have made a mistake or made several; the unfailing roar of a Big Cat can be heard in the Heavens. Really? Yes, really! Here is the deal: When one is a Spiritual Big Cat with a Divine ROAR, do not, and I mean do not, deviate from Divine Purpose or engage in uncommon behaviors like wallowing in the mud. Why is so much caution voiced on this matter? God has ordained us to pull prey out of the mud, placing them in a fold of recovery, not to get down with them to play dirty.

When we are a Spiritual Big Cat, it is okay to turn on our Spiritual Nocturnal Vision in our darkest moments to see our way through. Without a doubt, the morning will come on time, every time, without fail; therefore, by Divine Design, we must USE what our Father gave us to heighten our abilities to see what most cannot.

Of course, we all have made mistakes and been shady about something to get attention. Still, we should never lose our voice to public humiliation or defeat. We must lick the wounds of the past, deal with the inner longing for a specific type of love language, wholeheartedly repent, forgive whom we need to forgive, do what God has told us to do, and keep it moving with our heads held high. Here are a few reasons we need to worry, but not limited to such:

- ☐ When we are out of Divine Purpose or the Will of God.
- ☐ When we avoid using the Holy Trinity.
- ☐ When we avoid using the Word of God.
- ☐ When we are not using our Spiritual Gifts.
- ☐ When we are not using the Fruits of the Spirit.
- ☐ When we are not behaving Christlike.
- ☐ When we are pointing the finger and being negative.
- ☐ When we are wallowing in our hypocritical behaviors.
- ☐ When we are operating in outright hatefulness.
- ☐ When we are dull, stiff-necked, or lukewarm.
- ☐ When we lack humility and are selfish, rude, and prideful.

If we are in Purpose, God will bring the correction needed to realign us, guaranteed. Whereas if we are out of Purpose, we dig our own holes, having to transfer our Legacy to the next in line.

Why do we need to self-correct, *As It Pleases God*? According to scripture, "*A good man leaves an inheritance to his children's children, but the wealth of the sinner is stored up for the righteous.*" Proverbs 13:22. Now, if we do not want this to happen, we need to get it RIGHT!

CHAPTER 4
THE 24-HOUR ANOINTING

As we live in a right now world full of distractions and temptations, doing whatever we desire and with whomever, we tend to forget about the Spiritual Tools we have access to. Whether it is through prayer, meditation, fasting, repenting, forgiving, or introspection, reconnecting with God, *Spirit to Spirit*, can provide a sense of grounding and inner peace that is often elusive to those who are just trying to get by without Him.

Nevertheless, in our Spirituality and for our Heaven on Earth Experience, regardless of how low we have fallen, hope and faith can be the calling card needed to reel ourselves in. From my perspective, we have two options when it comes down to *The 24-Hour Anointing Reloaded*:

- ☐ We can take ownership of the calling card we have.
- ☐ We can allow the issues of life to give us a calling card.

Why do we need a calling card? With or without our permission, life happens. If we do not make the right call at the right time to the right Person (God in Three Persons), we can create a disservice to ourselves, others, and our Bloodline. Who are the Three Persons? The Father, Son, and Holy Spirit. What is the purpose of all three?

- ☐ We must know and understand our Headship. Yes, the One who is in charge of us. Who is this? Our God who art in Heaven, the Creator of all things…Who is within us all.

- ☐ We must know and understand the Spiritual Sacrifice of redemption. If not, another sacrifice will be made on our behalf, or we will leave ourselves open to anything or anyone. How can I say such a thing, right? Here is the deal: Spiritually Speaking, we may not like life's choices due to our naivety. Therefore, it is best to cover ourselves, our families, our lives, our Purpose, the doorposts of our houses, etc., with the Blood of Jesus.

- ☐ We must know and understand that we have Spiritual Access to the Holy Spirit for guidance, utterance, or correction.

Let us take this a little further, as it relates to scripture, "*Go therefore and make disciples of all the nations, baptizing them in the name of the Father and of the Son and of the Holy Spirit, teaching them to observe all things that I have commanded you; and lo, I am with you always, even to the end of the age. Amen.*" Matthew 28:19-20. Does this not give us the direct calling card to Heavenly Treasures? Absolutely!

Eye of God

We can tiptoe around our conditioning or what we are being taught, but if we do not understand Spiritual Protocol or how to use it, we cannot get mad at God, period. Why can we not get mad if we are doing the right thing? In addition to doing right, we must also understand Spiritual Astuteness by cultivating a heightened awareness of who we are from the inside out, our reason for being, and connecting to the world around us, *As It Pleases God*.

Although we all appear right in our own eyes, we must learn how to align ourselves with the Fruits of the Spirit and Christlike Character with an openness to Divine Wisdom from the Heavenly of Heavens. Why is this so important in the Eye of God? We are Spiritual Beings having a human experience. If we get stuck on the human aspects of living out of selfishness, we can become an eyesore to ourselves, others, and the Kingdom of God.

What is the Eye of God? Or, better yet, why not the Eyes of God? With this two-fold question, I must speak from a Spiritual Perspective, not from human reasoning, to do this chapter justice. The Eye of God represents ONENESS. If we desire to become used to our maximum capacity, we must MASTER this process to tap in. Tap into what? Tap into our Divine Design, *As It Pleases God*.

Regarding our Spiritual Language, the Eye of God is singular to amplify our Divine Alignment in becoming ONE in Christ Jesus with the help of the Holy Spirit. If not, we will secretly or openly divide ourselves based on our thoughts, words, actions, reactions, traumas, conditioning, or environment.

According to the Heavenly of Heavens, worldly pluralism will not work in the Kingdom. What about the Three Persons (Father, Son, and Holy Spirit)? They are ONE! How do we get ONENESS out of the Three Persons? It is a package deal when seeking wholeness, *As It Pleases God*. But more importantly, embracing this understanding without wavering will exemplify the ability to LOVE and HEAL effectively.

Listen, if we can love unconditionally, we can heal. If we can heal within the depths of the soul, we can love unconditionally. As we are Spiritual Beings, without human emotions or the display of love, we will turn on ourselves in due time. How is it possible to turn on ourselves? Based on the human experiment of emotions, selfishness splits love, traumatizing the human psyche. Whereas selflessness in the Eye of God mends, heals, or seals the psyche in the Spirit of Oneness, *As It Pleases Him*. How do we make this make sense? In the DNA of Love, we are ONE with:

- ☐ Our God.
- ☐ Our Savior.
- ☐ The Holy Spirit.
- ☐ Our Mind.
- ☐ Our Body.
- ☐ Our Soul.
- ☐ Our Spirit.

With this sort of ONENESS, we can pinpoint the moment we jump the track, Mentally, Physically, Emotionally, and Spiritually.

What is the purpose of knowing when the psyche jumps the track? If we desire to become balanced in any area of our lives, we must become ONE from within to become ONE with others. If not, conditional relationships are inevitable, as the cycle of déjà vu takes its rightful place to do what it does, affecting *The 24-Hour Anointing*. As a result, we will begin to pray amiss to control or bully others, regardless of whether we realize it or not.

In the State of ONENESS, we do not have to agree with everyone or everything in the wailing process. Furthermore, because we disagree does not mean we are divided automatically. Why? First, we have free will. Secondly, we can differentiate between being Godly or ungodly, right or wrong, just or unjust, obedient or disobedient, etc. Thirdly, we must also know that right is right and wrong is wrong without becoming Mentally, Physically, or Emotionally tied, bent, keeled, or distracted.

When we do not understand our Spiritual Rights, how to use them, or what type of leverage we have related to our Spiritual Oneness, we will feel divided from the inside out, exacerbating our state of division. The moment we refuse the leading of the Three Persons (Father, Son, and Holy Spirit), rest assured, we will feel the repercussions from within. Why would this happen to us, especially being Believers? Once again, we are Spiritual Beings having a human experience, even if we do not believe in the Holy Trinity.

Why would we not believe in the Holy Trinity? We have free will to believe what we so desire, but it does not change the fact that what is Holy is Holy in the Eye of God. Plus, our perspectives do not change what PLEASES God in the same way that we know what does or does not please us.

The Change

For the sake of *The 24-Hour Anointing Reloaded*, regardless of how life seems, what we are going through, or how wayward we have become, our Spiritual Anointing is already. We do not have to find, create, or manifest it; it is at our beck and call. However, we must master the techniques of gaining Spiritual Access at the drop of a dime.

How do we gain Divine Access to and maintain our Spiritual Anointing? First, we must know we are renewed daily. Secondly, we must OWN it. Thirdly, we must master the art of repenting, fasting, forgiveness, and prayer.

Owning our truth, praying over it, and sacrificing ourselves to the Will of God according to our Predestined Blueprint can rout any stronghold, demon, or bondage faster than anything known to man. Better yet, it can reload anything under the sun, especially if we maximize the power hidden in the *Wailing Prayers To The Deep*.

Instead of running to alcohol, cigarettes, pills, food, or sex for comfort, why not run to repenting, fasting, forgiveness, and prayer for solutions, or *The 24-Hour Anointing?* What can 24 hours do for us? The Bible says clearly, *"God called the light Day, and the darkness he called Night. And there was evening and there was morning, the first day."* In today's language, this is our 24 hours for change.

In the Spirit of Oneness, if the days can change in 24 hours, so can we, right? Absolutely! If one agrees, then here is the Spiritual Seal to enforce it: *"For His anger is but for a moment, His favor is for life; Weeping may endure for a night, But joy comes in the morning."* Psalm 30:5.

The people, places, and things we take for granted are usually the most profound. It is our mindset that governs our prayers, as well as our perception of who is in our lives or our issues. How is this possible? Our faith is directly linked to the MIND in a way that it could BLESS us or bring about a curse, mainly if it is not appropriately governed.

Where Is My Faith

As we all know, our minds will create anything we want, real or unreal. Why? Faith is faith, period. We can positively or negatively create anything we desire with our imagination through our mental portal, based on what the psyche feeds us.

Here is the deal: Faith is for the just and unjust alike; it is no respecter of persons. For the record, it is the same FAITH that fuels the DUALITY of our blessings or curses, successes or defeats, positive or negative outcomes, wisdom or foolery, procrastination or proactiveness, etc.

The Bible says, *"Because of your unbelief; for assuredly, I say to you, if you have faith as a mustard seed, you will say to this mountain, 'Move from here to there,' and it will move; and nothing will be impossible for you."* Matthew 17:20. We often apply this scripture with faith in our Blessings while overlooking the negative mustard seeds, unfruitful seeds, or the hidden lies we feed ourselves. In my opinion, we cannot continue in such a manner when we are secretly hurting those we claim to love.

In the *Wailing Process*, it does not matter how we have been conditioned to think about faith or our seeds; if we take a more in-depth look into our lives, negativity is the culprit of our instability, Mentally, Physically, Emotionally, or Spiritually. How? Our unrestrained thoughts, words, actions, biases, and behaviors create the mountainous volcanoes of selfishness, erupting everywhere. Simultaneously, we are getting the lava and ashes on the innocent while we think we are doing the right thing, with God nowhere in sight. How do we make this make sense? It only takes a little faith to create, tear down, move, beset, or annihilate our Bloodline.

Unbeknown to most, positive or negative faith or the duality of it all carries the same amount of weight Spiritually. Really? Yes, really! According to scripture, *"Death and life are in the power of the tongue, and those who love it will eat its fruit."* Proverbs 18:21. Now, do you think for a minute that our tongues do not contribute to our good, bad, or rotten fruits? Then, think again! Because Luke 6:44 says, *"For every tree is known by its own fruit."*

We must become cautious about what proceeds out of the gateway of our mouths. Do we not have the freedom to say whatever we want? Yes, we have free will. Nevertheless, through this freedom, we have the power to BLESS or curse our *24-Hour Anointing*.

The Seed

The Bible speaks about Seedtime and Harvest a lot, emphasizing the fundamental principle of SOWING and REAPING. Although some may think they are exempt from this Spiritual Principle, but the Spiritual Tilling Process must occur with all mankind. Why? We were created from the dust of the EARTH and the fullness therein, so this applies to our DNA as well. For this reason, our SEEDS are more powerful than we care to imagine, requiring intentionality, nurturing, patience, understanding, and growth.

What is considered to be our seeds? Beyond the agricultural metaphor, our seeds are hidden within our actions, reactions, behaviors, attitudes, words, thoughts, beliefs, non-verbal body language, and character. They are all nurtured by the contents of the heart, environmental conditioning, traumas, and the mindset of the individual.

Based upon the Law of Reciprocity, we must hone in on the seeds we are sowing and the ones we are not. Of course, we will all think differently; however, we must categorize them accordingly, making our best attempts to use the Fruit of the Spirit, *As It Pleases God*.

Our Power of Choice can cast down or build our lives in ways beyond human reasoning. Unfortunately, it is through our choices that we tend to err a little, creating embarrassment for ourselves, and then we try to secretly or openly blame God without assuming responsibility. When we do not follow Godly Principles, we end up hurting ourselves in the long run, losing what or whom we take for granted.

As it relates to *The 24-Hour Anointing Reloaded*, here is an example of the best way to categorize our seeds, but not limited to such:

- ☐ Good or bad.
- ☐ Positive or negative.
- ☐ Fruitful or unfruitful.
- ☐ Blessed or cursed.
- ☐ Just or unjust.
- ☐ Right or wrong.
- ☐ Favorable or unfavorable.

- ☐ Christlike or ungodly.
- ☐ Biblical or unbiblical.
- ☐ Prosperous or unprosperous.
- ☐ Profitable or unprofitable.
- ☐ Faithful or unfaithful.

Is it this simple? Absolutely. It is simple if we practice aligning ourselves with the Fruits of the Spirit. If not, we can make it challenging for ourselves due to the rationalization or justification to support what we are thinking, saying, becoming, doing, or our hidden biases. For this reason, we must become Spiritually Alert and Intuitive, *As It Pleases God*. Doing so will help us balance ourselves on a moment-by-moment basis to ensure we stay on a straight and narrow path with the 3-Fold Anointing, eliminating the ungodly toxins and selfishness.

The Anointing

In the Spiritual Journey of Divine Growth, *As It Pleases God*, we must seek to deepen our connection with Him, our Heavenly Father, *Spirit to Spirit*. If one does not know what a *Spirit to Spirit* Connection is...It is simply connecting the Mind, Body, Soul, and Spirit to our Creator through relating, repenting, praying, forgiving, and fasting while incorporating the 3-Fold Anointing (The Father, Son, and Holy Spirit) into the equation.

Communicating with God, *Spirit to Spirit*, and availing ourselves of the Hidden Treasures of the Spirit fosters a sense of inner purification and renewal. By doing so, we can uproot, regraft, bless, reroute, and anoint our seeds through transparency, confessing, forgiveness, mercy, and gratefulness.

When we repent, fast, forgive, and pray for the right reasons without murmuring, fussing, fighting, or complaining while counting them all as joy with Christlike Respectfulness and Discipline, here are a few things that will take place:

- ☐ Our Spiritual WISDOM will bow down.

- ☐ Our Spiritual Instincts will bow down.
- ☐ Our Spiritual Anointing will bow down.
- ☐ Our Divine Assignment will bow down.
- ☐ Our Spiritual Enlightenment will bow down.
- ☐ Our Spiritual Favor will bow down.
- ☐ Our Spiritual Veil will bow down to cover us.
- ☐ Our Spiritual Blinders will be removed.
- ☐ Our Spiritual Ears will be opened.
- ☐ Our Spiritual Tongue will await its cue to speak.
- ☐ Our Spiritual Eye will be able to see what is hidden in plain sight.
- ☐ The Holy Spirit will bow down to guide us in the right direction.

How can the Holy Spirit bow down to us? This is blasphemy, right? Absolutely not! Let us take it to scripture, *"But you shall receive power when the Holy Spirit has come upon you; and you shall be witnesses to Me in Jerusalem, and in all Judea and Samaria, and to the end of the earth."* Acts 1:8. *"But the Helper, the Holy Spirit, whom the Father will send in My name, He will teach you all things, and bring to your remembrance all things that I said to you."* John 14:26.

When the Holy Spirit comes down to our level to lift us to His level in Christ Jesus, it comes with some real POWER that will shake up the human psyche. How so? In essence, if we encounter someone with a Divine Anointing of the Holy Spirit, *As It Pleases God*, they can speak to the depths of the soul of man, they can cause the soul of man to leap, or they can cause a rebellious minion to stand down without saying one audible word.

For this reason, when someone says the Holy Spirit is speaking, and they are talking crazy, negatively, nasty, and rudely...I do not believe them. Why? Do you think God uses the Holy Spirit or His Ordained Vessels to destroy His sheep or Kingdom? Absolutely not!

Yes, God and the Holy Spirit are humorous at times to break the monotony or initiate a cheerful countenance because He knows,

"*A merry heart does good, like medicine, But a broken spirit dries the bones.*" Proverbs 17:22. And He also knows that "*With joy, you will draw water From the wells of salvation.*" Isaiah 12:3.

On the other hand, He also knows that cringeworthy communication is not ideal in the 3-Fold Anointing. Proverbs 21:23 says, "*Whoever guards his mouth and tongue keeps his soul from troubles.*" Moreover, here is the Spiritual Golden Rule: "*Let no corrupt word proceed out of your mouth, but what is good for necessary edification, that it may impart grace to the hearers.*" Ephesians 4:29.

In all simplicity, and with all due respect, if we do not have the power to choose our words carefully, then it indicates that we must expand our vocabulary to more positive words, use the Fruits of the Spirit, or tame the ego. Is this not a bit rude to tell someone to expand their vocabulary? Unfortunately, it is not!

In Spirituality and *As It Pleases God*, it is imperative to understand the DUALISM connected to each word we use. I, myself, also use Google to choose my words carefully and respectfully. Nevertheless, here is the kicker: Most Believers do not know the difference between positive and negative words, thoughts, beliefs, desires, traumas, experiences, and so on. Nor do they know how to reverse a negative into a positive to create a WIN-WIN, *As It Pleases God*.

Why am I targeting Believers? Then my question would be, 'Is the enemy targeting their own, or are they targeting Believers? Wait, wait, wait...do not answer that question yet. If one is reading this book, it warrants that they are a Believer. Thus, it is my responsibility from the Most High God to PREPARE the Willing, Able, and Ready!

What if we are already prepared? Then, congratulations! But for those who are not 100% prepared and are still a little sensitive or rough around the edges in their Divine Walk with God, then let us do this: "*Let your speech always be with grace, seasoned with salt, that you may know how you ought to answer each one.*" Colossians 4:6.

What if we need to defend ourselves from the naysayers? Please allow me to answer this question with another: 'Do we think the Holy Spirit is helpless?' When someone is truly operating with the Holy Spirit, they do not worry about the naysayers because they know their Spiritual Impact was noticed, but rejected. How do we make this make sense, especially when Believers are advised not to seek attention? The Spirit of God has a Divine Presence that cannot be denied or go unnoticed, nor does it seek attention or glamorization to be seen...it just is. For this reason, we may say to ourselves, 'It is just something about that person, but I cannot put my finger on it!' Due to the mindset of the individual partaking in the Divine Encounter, they can opt for the negative or positive.

Either way, due to the LACK of Spiritual Discernment, the Divine Encounter can be rejected! For this reason, God's Spiritual Elites are well-trained in the area of rejection. Why? If one cannot handle rejection, they are not ready for the Divine Commission. So, it is back to the Spiritual Classroom!

Why do we need the Holy Spirit, especially when God created us a little lower than Angels? Let me counteract this question with another one, *"For what man knows the things of a man except the spirit of the man which is in him? Even so no one knows the things of God except the Spirit of God."* 1 Corinthians 2:11.

The Holy Spirit is not for Himself but for us, period. He is our lifetime GUARANTEE from God, the Manufacturer. Is He really with us for a lifetime? I will let the scriptures answer this question. *"And I will pray the Father, and He will give you another Helper, that He may abide with you forever."* John 14:16. If we do not KNOW this, we cannot redeem ourselves appropriately.

How do we redeem ourselves? By REPENTING! Really? Yes, really. Being that this is a very sensitive area of Spirituality, once again, let us take it to scripture, *"Then Peter said to them, "Repent, and let every one of you be baptized in the name of Jesus Christ for the remission of sins; and you shall receive the gift of the Holy Spirit."* Acts 2:38.

When Praying

When praying, we must ensure we are not violating the will of another and we are not fasting out of selfishness or materialism. It must come from a place of love and not evil. If we violate the will of another person through fasting and praying, it is nothing more than witchcraft! Most people will not inform us about this sort of behavior, but it leads to blocked prayers or prayers that backfire.

Here is a secret...we must continually direct our prayers back to ourselves to avoid violating anyone's free will. When we bring our positive prayers back home to ourselves, we are free from ill-willed intents. Hint, hint...I do not know anyone who would intentionally curse themselves while praying. Therefore, keep it directed toward self positively; it helps to keep our channels of communication open with our Heavenly Father, even when dealing with difficult people.

According to the Heavenly of Heavens, there is a thin line between interceding on behalf of someone and outright violating their free will. For example, if someone is acting like a stone fool, driving you crazy, instead of fasting and praying for God to change the person, simply ask God to help you deal with the behavior and glean the lessons hidden within it.

Here is a sample prayer: *Father, my God, in the name of Jesus, I have a situation at hand, where I feel as if I am going crazy when dealing with _____. I do not choose to be in this frame of mind; therefore, I rebuke this emotion, as I replace it with the Spirit of Peace. I pray that You grant me the wisdom on how to deal with this sort of individual, as I allow the words of my mouth and the meditations of my heart to become holy and acceptable unto You. Lord, calm every raging emotion that is provoked inside of me when this person comes into my presence. I pray that Thy will be done regarding this situation, because I am freely handing it over to You right now. I plead the Blood of Jesus over me, my life, and my situation, and I assume total responsibility for my role in this. Let the light of Your grace, mercy, and forgiveness illuminate my life as I walk by faith and not by sight. Grant me the instinctual wisdom and lessons beyond human understanding, enabling me to deal with any situation or circumstance that comes my way. Let Your love permeate every vein in my body to ensure I say the right words at the right time, As It Pleases You. Father, let it be in me that is also in Christ Jesus as I forgive them for they know not what they are doing. Amen.*

Here is another little secret: Always make the petition, "*If thy will be done regarding _____*," then unselfishly make the request known to God. This secret is KEY, especially when avoiding the violation of the free will of another. On the other hand, it also helps to avoid missing out on what He is using to develop and train us! We must also state the feelings we want God to help us with. A statement such as *"I feel as if _____." "This is how I feel regarding _____." "I assume total responsibility for my role in _____."*

When in the wailing process, we must OWN our prayers without pointing the finger. Statements such as *"They did this," "They did that," "They made me feel,"* etc., are out of the question. Remember, when we begin to point the finger at someone, there will always be three fingers pointing back at us. Put differently, all the roads in our lives will always lead back to us.

Once we have mastered this aspect of the FREE WILL non-violation zone, we are empowered to rout demons in Spiritual Warfare. We can speak to the Mental, Physical, Emotional, and Spiritual MOUNTAINS in our lives, commanding them to obey us. Also, we can call on God, invoking His Divine Presence, or provoke Him to send a Legion of Angels on our behalf, especially when we are forgiving.

Wonderworking Power

According to the Ancient of Days, the Wonderworking Power is wrapped in the Power of Forgiveness. Then again, if we do not desire the Wonderworking Power, we do not have to use it. Still, we must know that we cannot live a truly fulfilled life while walking around full of hatefulness, grudges, or unforgiveness; it contaminates the psyche, affecting the lives of others. Most often, we treat people based on how we feel about ourselves.

In the Eye of God, it is unfair for the innocent to deal with our unresolved issues, especially when it is within our power to become better, stronger, and wiser, or work toward overcoming whatever with whomever. I know it is easier said than done, but it is doable, *As It Pleases God.*

Why is forgiveness so important? We forgive to be forgiven. But let us take it to scripture, *"And when you stand praying, if you hold anything against anyone, forgive them, so that your Father in heaven may forgive your sins."* Mark 11:25. Even if we think we are perfect, we will fall short because we are human. Yet, we should not use it as an excuse but as motivation instead. Before we move on...we do not forgive others for their sake; we forgive them for our own. But more importantly, we must learn how to forgive others quickly to free ourselves from the emotional or mental bondage attached to unforgiveness.

Respectively speaking, I am not saying we will forget about some atrocities that occurred in our lives. But if one genuinely forgives someone, one must give it to God, let it go, and never bring it up again. Now, just because one extends forgiveness does not mean we must become unwise or a walkover.

In the ratherability of our discussion, forgiving others is the best way to gain or keep our power, our Wonderworking Power, to be exact. But repenting, fasting, and praying over whatever we are forgiving will determine whether we need to hold it, fold it, or walk away. In so many words, forgiveness does not make us foolish, nor does it dethrone us. It makes us WISE if we learn how to harness its power, *As It Pleases God.*

For example, I am quick to forgive myself and others. I am also quick to walk away when people take my kindness for a weakness, especially when they do not realize it is my GREATEST STRENGTH. Based on my mindset, I quickly learn, understand, and apply scripture. More importantly, if God allows it, there is a Nugget of Wisdom or Divine Understanding in need of extracting or converting, *As It Pleases Him.*

Listen, it does not matter where we are in life or what we are going through; experience is one of the greatest teachers known to man. Amid all the atrocities in my life, I was not stuck on stupid by a long shot regarding anything. I would not be able to speak on repenting, fasting, prayer, forgiving, and the Wonderworking Power we possess from within had I not lived it, lived through it, and depended upon it. After all of the jokes, laughs, humiliations, tauntings, and ridicule I have received regarding the God I serve, those are the same individuals depending upon Him right now or asking for Divine Revelation.

The 24-Hour Anointing Reloaded works, especially when our back is up against the wall. If it had not worked, one would not be reading this book. If one would take the opportunity to follow my lead, this book will empower them in ways they could only dream of, especially when getting rid of Toxic Influences.

CHAPTER 5

TOXIC INFLUENCES

The utter chaos we face today has tricked us into thinking it is the norm, or that we have it going on. The hustle of being so busy doing nothing has plagued us with distractions and detours blocking us from our Purpose or Divine Blueprint, *As It Pleases God*. Yet, we still pursue whatever we want while ignoring those we claim to love or devaluing those we think we do not need. Do we really think God will BLESS our toxic mess without us wholeheartedly attempting to do a clean sweep or Spiritually Till our own ground? Before answering this question, let us go deeper.

As we live our seemingly best lives, we find ourselves overlooking the valuable Biblical Principles on how to conduct ourselves, how to live *As It Pleases God*, and how to treat others using the Fruits of the Spirit and Christlike Character. In the Eye of God, by overlooking this information, we become toxic, we graft ourselves into toxic environments, and we toxify our legacy. How is this possible? Just look around. Are we adequately equipped to deal with the wiles of the enemy? Are we exhibiting Christlike Character in our daily relational living? Are we showing respect to God's Divine Creation?

When it comes down to the Bible, knowing it will not get it! We must learn to live by example and detoxify ourselves at the drop of a dime, *As It Pleases God*, not ourselves. How can I say such a thing, right? Here is what James 1:22 stated: *"Be doers of the word, and not hearers only, deceiving yourselves."*

"*All Scripture is given by inspiration of God, and is profitable for doctrine, for reproof, for correction, for instruction in righteousness that the man of God may be complete, thoroughly equipped for every good work.*" 2 Timothy 3:16-17. How do we know if we are not living it? We are known by our fruits, regardless of how well we camouflage them. So, I would prefer to take the answer from scripture:

- ☐ "*Beware of false prophets, who come to you in sheep's clothing, but inwardly they are ravenous wolves.*" Matthew 7:15.

- ☐ "*If anyone among you thinks he is religious, and does not bridle his tongue but deceives his own heart, this one's religion is useless.*" James 1:26.

- ☐ "*Therefore, the Lord said: Inasmuch as these people draw near with their mouths and honor Me with their lips, but have removed their hearts far from Me.*" Isaiah 29:13.

- ☐ "*He who says he is in the light, and hates his brother, is in darkness until now.*" 1 John 2:9.

- ☐ "*They profess to know God, but in works they deny Him, being abominable, disobedient, and disqualified for every good work.*" Titus 1:16.

- ☐ "*He who says, 'I know Him,' and does not keep His commandments, is a liar, and the truth is not in him.*" 1 John 2:4.

- ☐ "*But why do you call Me 'Lord, Lord,' and do not do the things which I say?*" Luke 6:46.

- ☐ "*First remove the plank from your own eye, and then you will see clearly to remove the speck from your brother's eye.*" Matthew 7:5.

- [ ] *"Therefore, when you do a charitable deed, do not sound a trumpet before you as the hypocrites do in the synagogues and in the streets, that they may have glory from men."* Matthew 6:2.

- [ ] *"For you pay tithe of mint and anise and cummin, and have neglected the weightier matters of the law: justice and mercy and faith. These you ought to have done, without leaving the others undone."* Matthew 23:23.

- [ ] *"He who works deceit shall not dwell within my house; He who tells lies shall not continue in my presence."* Psalm 101:7.

- [ ] *"But the hypocrites in heart store up wrath; They do not cry for help when He binds them."* Job 36:13.

Life has allowed free radical toxins to permeate the secret areas of our lives, instigating immorality of all sorts to yoke, soul tie, or zap our resilience. Why is this such a problem for us? If we cannot bounce back or become flexible, *As It Pleases God*, we create many avoidable issues, behaviors, or thoughts that complicate our lives further.

How do we recognize toxicity or a toxic environment? First, we must awaken ourselves from our slumber. Secondly, we must understand what God is expecting from us. Thirdly, we must immerse ourselves in the resilience of truth regarding our contribution to the toxins. Fourthly, we must decide to change the breeding ground for toxic growth. How do we go about doing so? The best way to develop our resilience in this area is to ask the right questions to avoid becoming led astray, soul-tied, yoked, or unusable.

What is the purpose of querying ourselves? Most often, a toxic individual does not realize they are toxic because we all appear right in our own eyes. Really? Yes, really! Without a Spiritual

Mirror, *As It Pleases God*, using the Fruits of the Spirit, Christlike Character, and the Word of God, we adapt to harmful or traumatized toxins when they become our normal. Moreover, we will become intensely paralyzed by Spiritual Blindness, Deafness, Muteness, or Dullness according to Kingdom Standards.

Furthermore, if we do not ask fact-finding questions, it is impossible to make the necessary corrections, *As It Pleases God*, making it easier to become negatively sifted. On the other hand, we have those who have conditioned themselves to beat the system.

How can someone beat the system? They have been trained to ask the right questions to point the finger or degrade others without correcting their own hidden biases. Then again, they may use the Word of God to browbeat others to make others feel inferior or unworthy to mimic how they feel about themselves. From a Spiritual Perspective, those are the ones who become the most traumatized, the insatiably toxic, or who produce the most damaged fruits.

Why does attempting to beat the system make us worse? When we know better and consciously choose not to do better, it silently instigates hidden disappointment, sludge, and trauma from within the human psyche with a slated conscience and a trail of rotten fruits. Nevertheless, regardless of where we are in life, there is hope for us; we just need to activate the Spirit of Resilience, *As It Pleases God*.

Spirit of Resilience

The human capacity to recover, adapt, save lives, and grow in the face of adversity and challenges is better known as the Spirit of Resilience. Confronting setbacks, overcoming trauma, and approaching difficult circumstances with courage, love, and determination is not a faint feat in the Eye of God.

Why does God like us operating in the Spirit of Resilience? It exudes an underlying faith that is cultivated and developed, even if we do not label it as such. Nonetheless, the Spiritual Rewards are the same as using our standalone faith. Why? Operating in the Spirit of Resilience PLEASES Him. Here is the Spiritual

Correlation: *"But without faith it is impossible to please Him, for he who comes to God must believe that He is, and that He is a rewarder of those who diligently seek Him."* Hebrews 11:6.

What does resilience have to do with Spirituality? The Spirit of Resilience has everything to do with breaking the chokehold of mediocrity through our adaptability, flexibility, and the ability to learn and glean from experiences to help others for the Greater Good.

Suppose we take a look at the word resilience for a moment. To me, it says, Re-Silence. If we take a moment to redo what we keep silent about, *As It Pleases God*, we can revolutionize our lives. What do resilience and Re-Silence mean for us in layman's terms? The moment we positively revamp our perceptions of the people, places, things, traumas, and pains in our lives, we can make our lives Spiritually Pliable and Usable. In this workable condition, we will most often find our Gifts, Talents, Calling, Creativity, or Purpose.

Moreover, if we overlook the revamping process of our perceptional edifices, we may also miss the hidden lessons, tests, or training we need for our Predestined Blueprint. More importantly, if our perceptions are negative or toxic, we will settle for failure instead of creating a win-win.

According to the Heavenly of Heavens, when our inner silence is ignored, it does not mean we cannot hear it instinctually. We hear the loud, inaudible wailing from within the psyche, but most often, we do not understand it. As a result, to avoid losing our minds, we use negative habits or temporary satisfaction to drown out its cry. Does it work? Absolutely not. Our soulish cries are a part of us, and when it is hungry or thirsty, we can silence them on the outside, but our inner voice does not shut up amid our silence, resulting in our disappointments or our desire for controllable dominance.

Listen, self-disappointment is the main contributor to our insecurities, where we focus more on outer adornment over inner adornment. In so many words, we complain about not having a pair of shoes to match our outfit when we already have 50 unworn pairs in our closet. While not giving a second thought about the human soul that does not have shoes at all.

Now, my question is, 'Who are we trying to impress?' Are we attempting to impress ourselves, others, or God? Clearly, I am not advocating not caring for ourselves because we must care for the Temple of God. However, I want us to become truly aware of the ultimate cause of our insecurities. What is the cause? Ungratefulness.

The purpose of *Toxic Influences Reloaded* is to learn how to ask the right questions at the right time, with the right motives. If we do not question ourselves, we can encounter a lot of nonsense on our journey through life, causing us to wallow unnecessarily. How is this possible? The stench of folly does not go away on its own. It will remain in our lives until we get to the root of it or locate our point of erring. How do I know? Jesus prided Himself on asking a lot of questions to provoke the element of thought. Regardless of whether we question ourselves, our lives, or others, if the refreshing or renewal of the mind does not take place regularly, negativity or evil practices can become routine.

Wailing Prayers To The Deep Reloaded is designed to flip the script on this mind germ, allowing us to embrace the power of living our best lives. But there is a catch. What is it? We must also become diligent in applying it without chasing people off with the 'HOLIER THAN THOU' façade. To do so, we must understand the *Toxic Influences* by reloading ourselves with a Spiritual Understanding to bring about contentment from within. What are they? Here are the 4 toxins:

- ☐ Mental Toxins
- ☐ Emotional Toxins
- ☐ Physical Toxins
- ☐ Spiritual Toxins

Spiritually Speaking, this is a very serious matter, and it cannot be taken lightly. According to the Heavenly of Heavens, we have a lot to lose, especially if we do not get a grip on what is really taking place right before our very eyes.

When our reality blinds us, we cannot see what is hidden in plain sight, no matter how hard we try. Why? We are VEILED. Therefore, we must understand the toxins keeping us bound or blinded by our Mental, Emotional, Physical, and Spiritual traumas. Trauma? Yes, I said trauma! The traumas that keep us judging the people, places, and things we do not understand. What do we not understand? The hidden truths buried beneath the surface and the mind germs that are taking over in broad daylight.

The power of social influence has created a wave of toxicity, taking us so far from our family and Spiritual Values. When we find ourselves becoming a little mentally unstable, it is an obvious indication that we need to repent, pray, and fast. We need to go through the formal process of putting our thoughts into captivity under the subjection of the Holy Spirit.

Most often, we do not think that repenting, praying, forgiving, and fasting apply to the mind. But let me say this: It is more of a reason to do so, to protect the mind from running wild. Without the mind, the body begins to die a slow and dreadful death, so we must protect it. Why must we protect the mind? We become what we think about all the time, positively or negatively. How is this possible? According to scripture, *"As a man thinketh in his heart, so is he."* Proverbs 23:7.

Let us briefly reflect on the Children of Israel before Moses came into the picture. From my understanding of the scriptures surrounding them in the Book of Genesis, they built temples and monuments for the Egyptians during their time of enslavement. Even though their enslavement seemed very harsh and abusive, it did not change God's heart toward them. Looking from the outside in, I think they were being TRAINED to take possession of the Promises of God. How is this possible when they were enslaved? They were being TAUGHT the invaluable mental, physical, and motor skills of how to build, when to build, where to build, and why they needed to repent, pray, forgive, and fast to get rid of the Toxic Influences. Nevertheless, let us go deeper.

Getting Rid of Mental Toxins

The Children of Israel previously lived in the desert in tents, in the scorching heat, getting lazy, talking about the past, getting into each other's business, and making babies they could not feed. They did not have any previous experience in building anything other than tents and altars. Nor did they pride themselves on gaining any more knowledge than what they already had from their Forefathers, Abraham, Isaac, and Jacob.

From my point of view, in all due respect, they were experienced in setting up things (tents and altars) with little or no stability. Also, they were not interested in proactiveness, creating a new life, or desiring more. As a result, they became conditioned to limitations. What type? The *'Follow the Leader'* and the *'Do no more than what we are told'* Slave Mentality.

What creates a Slave Mentality? With all due respect, it is the *"Yes sir boss"* mentality vs. *"What can I do to build us"* mentality. The two mentalities will **NEVER** be about being told what to do, when to do it, how to do it, why to do it, or where to do it. Why? As long as we have the Breath of Life in our bodies, we must listen to someone, follow instructions, or obey the rules. The real difference is about becoming proactive and knowing what to do without being told, manipulated, bullied, or forced.

But more importantly, it is gaining the skills, the know-how, the how-to, and the acquiescence to build an empire of our own with the information we have learned. How is this possible when we are enslaved? Here is the secret: We must understand that our knowledge, wisdom, skills, how-to, and know-how are not just about us or for us. It is about activating the Law of Reciprocity, helping someone else with what we have, helping someone else with the lessons we have learned, or helping someone else with the BLESSINGS we may have acquired to leave a LEGACY to build a better generation of people!

Regarding our *Toxic Influences Reloaded*, it is not what we learned or how we learned it that counts; it is what we DO with what we learn that makes the real difference! As a rule of thumb, we must leave people better off than when we met them, and if we cannot do this, then something is seriously wrong! Why does something need to be wrong with us? Whether we feel right or wrong, our positive attributes or fruits should always outweigh our negative ones, period. If our negative outweighs the positives, leaving a trail of victims, we must repent, pray, forgive, and fast, doing a clean sweep from the inside out, ushering in the Fruits of the Spirit and Christlike Character.

Okay, let us get back to the story at hand. The Children of Israel were piggybacking off of Abraham's Promise from God. What was the Promise? To BLESS him and make him a great Nation. However, to become a great Nation, they needed skills! I mean some real skills contending with the BLESSINGS God had so graciously bestowed upon them. From my perspective, the tent and altar-building skills would not get it!

They needed to get around people who already possessed the Empire Building skills instead of fighting with each other over who was more blessed, talented, or favored. Of course, this is my spin...but the truth is, we cannot expect to sit around and reap the BLESSINGS of God and not learn more than we did the day before. I do not care who we are or how Blessed we think we are; the Mind of God does not work like this! He holds us accountable for learning, understanding, and Spiritually Tilling our own ground, *As It Pleases Him*. In addition, He also holds us accountable for what we DO NOT learn, understand, do, or become, and the toxins we hold on to as well!

The moment we stop learning, we will have to go back to the classroom, Mentally, Physically, Emotionally, or Spiritually, through some form of enslavement. For me, it is an atrocity for God to place Divine Wisdom right in our hands for us not to soak it up while choosing to become enslaved, judgmental, and ungrateful.

Enslaved by what? It is more like by whom! We become our worst prison wardens through our thoughts, actions, reactions, words, ego, emotions, biases, materialism, greed, negativity, or selfishness. Then, we have the nerves, or better yet, we have the audacity to wonder why our tent is leaking or we are getting wet in the middle of a storm!

Have you ever put up a tent? Maybe or maybe not, but it takes little or no skills at all. A little child can figure out how to do it. Then, building an altar is like building a barbecue pit; come on! Can we become a great Nation from within if we are okay with not taking ourselves to the next level? Can we become a great Nation if we sit around waiting for a handout, gleaning the Blessings of others when we are entitled to our own? Can we?

The Children of Israel went from building tents to monuments and structured buildings. Still, they could not see their training because their enslavement blinded them, and their perception was traumatizingly keeled. How is this possible? Their perception of the situation was off. How often do we do this to ourselves? How often do we say woe unto me with a self-created victim mentality, especially when we are genuinely BLESSED with the God-Given skills to build or create something or someone?

Before I go any further, I am going to drop another secret. What is it? That something, that someone, or that great Nation, is within the depths of your soul, and it is wailing. Can you hear it? Or, have you blocked it? You are empty, and you know it! Your tent has fallen because you feel it!

The dust of famine has covered you, for the unquenchable enemy of thirst has caused you to become Publicly THIRSTY! Socially THIRSTY! Mentally THIRSTY! Emotionally THIRSTY! Physically THIRSTY! Spiritually THIRSTY! Or, Financially THIRSTY! Thirsty, Thirsty, Thirsty. Now the question is, "Thirsty for what or whom?"

Why do you have to be Thirsty, right? Who knows, but you! Let your conscience become your guide, searching for the hidden secrets that have caused you to lose your VIRTUE. Yes, those little hidden toxic secrets you cannot tell anyone about, or those little hidden toxic secrets you have not forgiven yourself for.

When there is no shame in your game, when you have lost your sense of integrity, when you cannot seem to find a way around your selfish behaviors, when you thrive to be in charge, and when you are on the take more than you give, this is an indication the mind-germ or the slave mentality is knocking on or has slipped into your back door. However, there is hope; it is time to gather up the skills necessary to build your Empire. The Empire is within you, it is around you, and it is all for Y.O.U. It awaits the wake-up call you have just received. Matthew 5:6 clearly tells us, *"Blessed are those who hunger and thirst for righteousness, for they will be filled."*

One can only wonder why I am talking about our thirsty little secrets when telling the story of the Children of Israel, right? My reason for doing so is that they were in a famine because of their hidden secrets. How is this possible when God chose them? Chosen or not, God held them to a higher standard. Why? *"For everyone to whom much is given, from him much will be required."* Luke 12:48.

Now, let me dig a little deep into this matter: Due to their tiptoeing around their unjustifiable waywardness, arrogance, ungratefulness, disrespectfulness, and unforgiveness, they put themselves on the chopping block of corruptible character. In my opinion, based on the actions, behaviors, and atrocities of Abraham, Isaac, and Jacob, as well as their descendants, they were in Egypt as enslaved people for a charactorial timeout. Even though they were in the classroom of Egypt for seasonal correction, God did not intend for them to stay for a lifetime.

There are times when our secret thirsts will delay our Promises or our Divine Blessings on our behalf, on our children's behalf, or on behalf of our descendants. How? God will bring about famine to protect us, He will send a generational curse as a slap on the hand, or we will experience a wrestling match within the soul. In my opinion, irresponsibly fighting against ourselves is one of the worst forms of correction. Why? We will not experience peace.

Listen, living on the edge of destruction due to a Spiritual Beatdown will cause us to seek God, even if we appear to be on top of the world. Remember, the longer we fight or resist, the longer it will take for the Spiritual Correction to occur. Hence, as a preventative method, we must become ever so mindful of the seeds we are sowing and our family secrets. Why? They will bear fruit when we least expect, positively or negatively.

Trickery, lies, waywardness, and the shedding of innocent blood will bring about a famine in the land. Why would we have famine as Believers? God will not allow anyone to bring shame to His name.

Does God care what we think about Him? Absolutely not, but He does care about Divine Purpose and Promises. He will shut us down by any means necessary when we get out of line, thinking we are above Him or above His Laws. How do we make this make sense when we are humble and obedient to Him? There are times when we are caught up in the issues of life, when we cannot see where we are going astray. So, if we do not have a routine of repenting, praying, and fasting for correction on our own, God will allow a predicament of our own choosing to provoke a **Forced Fast**.

When we are under enough pressure of our own choosing, we will repent, pray, fast, and do many things we never thought we would do, positively or negatively. For this reason, it is not wise to ridicule or judge others for the same things we are knowingly or unknowingly guilty of. Instead, we should always offer mercy, compassion, understanding, forgiveness, repenting, fasting, and prayer.

Why should we be merciful to all? It is our backup plan or our Plan B, because we never know when we will need it for ourselves, our loved ones, our friends, etc. For me, I use it as Spiritual Ammunition. How so? I can place a Spiritual Demand on MERCY to the Highest Degree based upon the Spiritual Notches on my Spiritual Armor.

Make no mistake about it; the Spiritual Warfare that I endured to get to this point, I would not wish upon my worst enemy. Amid all of my Battle Scars, I made sure I strategically planted a forest of merciful seeds along the way, used the Fruits of the Spirit, behaved Christlike, and remained in Purpose on purpose with my Predestined Blueprint in hand, *As It Pleased God*.

What is the purpose of approaching mercy in such a manner with God at the forefront? It is done to keep my Spiritual Covering of the Holy Trinity fully ENFORCABLE, JUSTIFIABLE, and POWERFUL while preventing the mental toxins from penetrating my psyche. How do we make this make sense? When we approach God, *As It Pleases Him*, He will make sure that the Holy Spirit provokes self-corrective measures to keep us properly aligned through our Spiritual Discernment Faculties, such as with the use of the conscience, senses, instincts, feelings, and dreams. Nonetheless, here is what Proverbs 3:5-6 tells us: *"Trust in the Lord with all your heart, And lean not on your own understanding; In all your ways acknowledge Him, And He shall direct your paths."*

On the other hand, if we approach God to please ourselves, it makes us dull, lukewarm, stiff-necked, and sometimes Kingdom-Unusable until repentance occurs. Blasphemy, right? Wrong. Spiritually, this is why God will use the most unlikely people to accomplish the greatest feats for the Kingdom. Why? Let us take this to scripture: *"But the Lord said to Samuel, 'Do not look at his appearance or at his physical stature, because I have refused him. For the Lord does not see as man sees; for man looks at the outward appearance, but the Lord looks at the heart.'"* 1 Samuel 16:7.

God weighs the HEART POSTURE of mankind. For this reason, Proverbs 4:23 reminds us to: *"Keep your heart with all diligence, For out of it spring the issues of life."*

How did the Children of Israel get into Egypt? Were they trapped in the issues of life? In a nutshell, it was their toxic mindset! Today, we follow the same pattern; we build our lives with a tent-building mentality, expecting it to endure the trials and tribulations of real life. And, when the issues of life sweep us off our feet and land us right on our faces, then who do we call? Do we call on God? Of course, we do, and rightfully so!

For this reason, I encourage repenting, forgiving, fasting (full, partial, or modified), and praying, in or out of our time of need. It is unwise to wait for problems to occur before we get in gear. It is best to get our brownie points early in the game by PAYING IT FORWARD. God has empowered us to help ourselves by preparing for life in advance, *As It Pleases Him*, not as it pleases us.

As we move through life, setting up permanent residence in something or with someone designed to be temporary is one of the quickest ways to find ourselves settling where we do not belong. If something or someone leaves, we must trust life, and we must trust God. We cannot lose our POWER over it or them, regardless of how bad it hurts. Here are a few things we need to do:

- ☐ Repent.
- ☐ Pray.
- ☐ Fast for guidance to break the yoke or to sever a soul tie.
- ☐ Grieve briefly, if necessary.
- ☐ Forgive them, ourselves, or both.
- ☐ Document the lesson learned.
- ☐ Document the Win-Win or the reversal effect.
- ☐ Give it to God and let Him deal with it.
- ☐ Let go and move on in the Spirit of Excellence.

We cannot waste time on something or someone hell-bent on breaking down our minds, playing mind games, or playing Russian roulette with our thoughts to set us off! Listen, our minds are indeed something of great VALUE! The moment we lose value in what we put in our minds, we become susceptible to the mind germs of deception and control. If one has never noticed where there is a lack of value, there will also be a lack of priority. Once this happens, the people, places, and things in our lives will not be placed in their proper perspective, which creates DISORDER!

Disorderly conduct, disorderly mentality, disorderly emotions, or disorderly anything on our behalf or someone else's behalf is a character trait God greatly frowns upon. It is written all over the Book of Proverbs under the word foolishness. What are the signs of disorderly conduct? Here are a few signs, but not limited to such:

- ☐ Rudeness.
- ☐ Uncontrollable tongues.
- ☐ Violation of privacy.
- ☐ Lying at the drop of a dime.
- ☐ Untrustworthiness.
- ☐ Setting intentional traps to appease our curiosity.
- ☐ Plotting the downfall of someone.
- ☐ Disobedience.
- ☐ Ego problems.
- ☐ Lack of self-control.
- ☐ Hatefulness.
- ☐ Looks down on other people's weaknesses.
- ☐ Thrives in chaos.
- ☐ Getting a rush from mocking others.

Unfortunately, disorderly behavior in the Eye of God is not cool. It does not make one superior and is not a characteristic that reaps bountiful blessings. So, we must become aware of the folly it brings into our lives. Trust me, this **SECRET** should last a Lifetime.

Listen, we do not often hear about how the Children of Israel FASTED by force to get into Egypt through famine. Yet, we hear much about how they voluntarily FASTED at Passover to escape Egypt. It is incredible how God protects them from death and destruction. But, here lies the dilemma: How often did they fast between entering and exiting Egypt? The mystery question, right? What I do know is that they did not forget to wail to God amid their atrocities, which accounted for something. How? God sent Moses to deliver them.

Wailing or not, we can agree that God is indeed very strategic. He took one of their own, a Hebrew enslaved person, and showed him favor with Pharaoh's daughter. God's plan put him into the palace as a part of the royal family to learn what the Children of Israel should have been learning all the time.

Moses was not the only Hebrew in the palace. The ones enslaved in the palace were just unwilling to learn because their environment still enslaved their minds. In comparison, Moses' mind was ushered into a mentality of freedom, a mentality of creativity, a mentality of greatness, a mentality of empowerment, and a mentality of teachability. These are all characteristics God could use to lead, build, create, overcome, and conquer.

Once the worldly classroom was over for Moses, and the right time presented itself, God took him into the desert by circumstance into a Spiritual Classroom. In my opinion, this was a **FORCED FAST**, depriving him of the lifestyle and the foods he was accustomed to eating back in Egypt.

In this wilderness setting, God taught Moses how to survive in the desert with a Kingdom-Building mentality. He also trained him to lead a flock of people through herding sheep! What an insult. But it worked! Then, He taught him how to listen to His Voice, follow instructions, repent, fast, pray, forgive, and use what he had in his hand, *As It Pleased Him.*

Although we are not Moses, the storms of life will come. Why do we have to go through storms? It is called the CYCLE OF LIFE. We have to suit up or get swept out! It is not a matter of IF a storm will come; it is a matter of WHEN! Having a Tent-Life mentality will not sustain a Storm, Hurricane, Tornado, etc.

If you follow my lead, I promise to give you a few Secrets of Wisdom that will last you a lifetime. Plus, I will show you how to take a tent-building mentality of your old mindset and transform it into a strategic empire-building one. Now, before we move on to the next section of how to Get Rid of Emotional Toxins, remember this: *"A man's heart plans his way, But the Lord directs his steps."* Proverbs 16:9.

Getting Rid of Emotional Toxins

Do you think you can hide your emotions from God? Do you think you can hide your emotions from yourself? Do you think your emotions will not affect you? Do you know how to eliminate emotional toxins? Well, this section is written just for you! The truth is that we all have emotions, and we all will deal with emotional toxins because they are a part of our DNA. However, the overload of toxins is what makes the best of the best fall short in the Eye of God.

Emotional toxins are derived or accumulated from stress, anxiety, anger, resentment, fear, unforgiveness, shame, guilt, hatefulness, abusiveness, and a host of other negative emotions. And, being that our bodies hold on to these pollutants, God has given us the Fruits of the Spirit (Love, Joy, Peace, Patience, Kindness, Goodness, Faithfulness, Gentleness, and Self-Control) to counteract the negative effects.

With this Spiritual Counter-Balancing System, we can reverse any negative into a positive, regardless of how it appears to the naked eye. However, there is a lot of science behind this. But we are going to keep it simple to ensure that we can MASTER the reversal of negative to positive, wrong to right, unjust to just, bad to good, and so on.

What is the big deal about the reversal process when we are dealing with emotions? The toxins of our emotions have caused our greatest pains, traumas, failures, losses, and mishaps, whether we admit it or not. All we have to do is look around and within us, and we will see that we are a byproduct of our emotions. It is sad to say, but we are being taught to cover up our emotions with pills, drugs, alcohol, smoking, sex, money, and now, social media. But let me say this, 'It is not the answer!' We are also persuaded that it is okay to be disrespectful and rude! What is the World coming to, right?

When we get in our own way, it usually disguises itself as SELF-SABOTAGE. It is amazing how fear immobilizes our minds and prepares us to create failure through our actions, reactions, words, thoughts, beliefs, and biases. We sometimes subconsciously set ourselves up for failure based on previous experiences. What does this mean in layman's terms? We screw things up, despite our intentions of doing right.

Why is it important to deal with our emotional toxins, *As It Pleases God*? It only takes a fraction of a second to ruin a good thing and less than that to lose control of ourselves, especially if self-control is not established or utilized with integrity.

According to the Heavenly of Heavens, we must think on our feet without allowing our emotions to rule and reign. Is it really possible to control our emotions? Absolutely. If we do not control our emotions, then our emotions will control us by default.

How do we get a grip on our emotions, *As It Pleases God*? Here are a few ways, but not limited to such:

- ☐ We must become aware of our emotions.
- ☐ We must determine if they are positive or negative.
- ☐ We must document what we are feeling.
- ☐ We must know what triggers us.
- ☐ We must be honest with ourselves about our feelings.
- ☐ We must find healthy ways to express ourselves.
- ☐ We must establish limits and boundaries.
- ☐ We must learn how to repent and forgive consistently.
- ☐ We must get into positive environments.
- ☐ We must pray and develop a *Spirit to Spirit* Relationship with God Almighty.

Why does God require us to get a grip on our emotions? According to scripture, *"Whoever has no rule over his own spirit is like a city broken down, without walls."* Proverbs 25:28. In essence, anything goes with a wishy-washy person. Proverbs 29:11 says, *"A fool vents all his feelings, But a wise man holds them back."*

Should we not express ourselves? We should, but we must choose our words carefully. But more importantly, in the Eye of God, we are required to PAUSE and REFLECT on the underlying causes to avoid popping off. Clearly, we are human, and it is natural to experience a range of emotions. However, reacting impulsively or irrationally can lead to undesirable outcomes, making a mess, ruining lives, causing trauma, and having to play cleanup. Here is what we must know about this matter: *"So then, my beloved brethren, let every man be swift to hear, slow to speak, slow to wrath; for the wrath of man does not produce the righteousness of God."* James 1:19-20.

When representing the Kingdom of God, it is not wise to have loose lips that sink ships. According to the Heavenly of Heavens, as Believers, we are the Anchors of the Kingdom, bringing life to His precious sheep and protecting them while they are in the Spiritual Fold. If we cannot control our emotions, we must step back into the Spiritual Classroom for Divine Updates. Why? We are consuming our own Spiritual Fruits, we have rotten fruits in need of Spiritual Regrafting, *As It Pleases God*, or we are consumed by some form of fear.

What does fear have to do with anything? Fear is a destructive and crippling emotion that will rob us Mentally, Physically, Emotionally, and Spiritually, causing us to unawaringly destroy ourselves, as well as the people, places, and things around us. Fear is created in the mind of an individual and is primarily triggered by low esteem, appearing as fear of failure, fear of being ridiculed, fear of rejection, fear of imperfections, fear of making mistakes, fear of loving again, fear of success, lack of faith, lack of confidence, or outright insecurity, which are all created within oneself, spreading outwardly.

The more we fear outside of our *Spiritual Relationship* with God, the more we become a product of it. How is this possible when we are devout Believers? When we fall out of a genuine relationship with our Creator, we will eventually become self-centered, insecure, unforgiving, tense, miserable, overbearing, and Spiritually Weak. Why would this happen to us? Fear has only as much power as we give it; therefore, when we doubt God, ourselves, or others and outright lack faith, fear is waiting on its turn to prove us right in our own eyes.

In addition, fear gains fuel by our skepticism, rotten fruits, and debauchery, getting our engine jump-started to bring in the recruits to complete the film of toxicity. What does this mean? Negativity fuels negativity. If we do not accept negative fear into our conscious mind while replacing it with a positive win-win perception, it will not have any power over us and cannot become a debilitating force.

We cannot hold on to fear and faith simultaneously regarding our wailing process. If we are going to believe in God, we need to believe. If we are going to fear life, then fear it. We have free will to choose.

How do we overcome the barriers of fear? We must be willing to admit it, repent if necessary, fast, pray, forgive, and expose ourselves to the very things we fear. Once we become accustomed to feeling the fear, getting over it, giving it to God, and moving on, we can better deal with or overcome the distractions sent to cause our emotions to jump the track.

We all have felt out of control or as if someone else is pulling our strings. But let me say this: Being out of control for too long will cause a person's emotions to run rampant. From a Spiritual Perspective, allowing our emotions to run rampant for too long can become detrimental to our well-being.

How do we get our lives under control? We need to find out what controls us. We must find out what or who is pulling our strings and who or what is trying to control or break us to the core. Once pinpointed, repent, pray, forgive, and fast, while detaching mentally and emotionally. Once we detach in this manner, the body will soon follow physically!

The key to making the detachment work on our behalf, we must prevent ourselves from negatively reacting in any way, shape, or form. And then, assume full responsibility for our role in the situation, circumstance, or event. Why would this work on our behalf? We are entitled to protect ourselves from anyone or anything attempting to lure us into bondage, have a desire to yoke us, or keep us soul-tied.

Amid all, know this: *"Be anxious for nothing, but in everything by prayer and supplication, with thanksgiving, let your requests be made known to God; and the peace of God, which surpasses all understanding, will guard your hearts and minds through Christ Jesus."* Philippians 4:6-7.

Getting Rid of Physical Toxins

If you have not noticed by now, there are restaurants on every corner; not one, but several. The love of food is consuming our inner beings. We do not cook anymore. We depend on restaurants to cook for our families; we depend on them to keep our families healthy because we do not have time to cook. THIS IS AN EPIDEMIC.

In my opinion, it is all a form of Mind Control. How? Simply look at the television, social media, and listen to the radio; there are food commercials galore provoking us to eat, eat, eat. There is food everywhere. Where am I taking this? The toxins from the foods we are consuming are killing us royally.

Can one imagine trusting our health to someone we have never met? Can one imagine consuming food we do not know what is in it? Yes, the food tastes good, but we cannot pronounce the ingredients on the label or know how long the item has been preserved before our consumption! Plus, we have no clue about how our food is being prepared and the sanitary conditions of it. Food contamination is everywhere, and we must take responsibility for what is going into our bodies and the sanitation factors of what we consume.

We need to commit to God, allowing Him to control our desire to overeat or under-eat, and allow us to get back into the kitchen and get our families healthy again. Through my journey, I have found that fasting and prayer make you more powerful. However, the first step to getting rid of the physical toxins is to find out why you eat or why you are not preparing healthy meals for yourself or your family. It may take a little bit of soul-searching on your behalf. Nonetheless, this statement is not applicable if one has physical limitations on preparing food.

We are all creatures of habit, and anything we do long enough will become and feel normal. Just remember, food cannot solve problems; however, it may make you feel better for the moment, but the pain will return, guaranteed!

Let us reflect on the Children of Israel as they wandered through the desert. As usual, they became hungry and complained to Moses about it. Nagging, nagging, and nagging! It behooves me that they were willing to go back into bondage and slavery just to fill their stomachs with fish, leeks, onions, garlic, melons, and cucumbers for free. They did not realize it was not free!

God was trying to deal with their slave mentality through a **FORCED FAST**, and they were focusing on their next meal, as opposed to their next step. They spoke of freedom and continually thought of slavery. In my opinion, this indicates that the price of bricks and mud was more valuable to them than the freedom to create a life of whatever they wanted. However, despite their vicious complaints, Moses prayed to God, and He rained bread from heaven, commonly known as Manna.

After the Children of Israel got what they wanted, they complained to Moses about having meat. Can one imagine encountering someone who is never satisfied or always complaining? Of course, we all know someone. Nevertheless, due to their ungratefulness, God gave them meat to feed their fleshly cravings. He did not give them meat for one day, as He does with the daily ration of manna; He gave them meat for a whole month. While giving in to the murmurs and the lust of their flesh, they overindulged. How? By partaking too much of something they were not supposed to have anyway.

By this one act of greed, overeating meat caused a parasitic plague, taking the lives of many. Since they were not carnivores, their bodies could not fight off infections and viruses caused by rotten meat stored in the desert heat. As a result, a lot of people lost their lives. But more importantly, this allows us to go right where they went wrong. Although this happened in the Bible, this is still happening right now in today's time, but with a slightly different up-to-date twist. We are still overindulging in food, our bodies are still not able to fight off infections, we are still getting infections from animals, we are still dealing with infestations, and the list goes on.

The wilderness experience is designed to purge us from the desires of wanting or giving in to our fleshly desires. When we overlook our bodies, live our lives out of purpose, or live our lives in bondage, it creates a life full of limitations and excuses, hindering our ability to embrace our Purpose or Passion.

To do this chapter justice regarding toxins, keep in mind that food is designed to energize and refresh us. If it makes us feel sluggish, sleepy, or lethargic, we are eating the wrong foods for our body type. Why? From a Spiritual Perspective, it is God's way of symbolically telling us to change what we are consuming. Our lifeline is in the seeds we plant in our Temple, Mentally, Physically, Emotionally, and Spiritually. Do not think for a minute we can supersede the Spiritual Laws of SEEDTIME and HARVEST.

If we are eating badly, the harvest will come with time, so it is imperative to detox our bodies frequently. If our body is full of toxins, it is definitely more challenging for us to lose weight, focus, heal, and frankly, it is harder for us to do a lot if we pay close attention. Why? Because our body is fighting us back, and when it does, it affects our Spiritual Relationship. How is this possible? If we are eating amiss, not knowing it, more than likely, we are praying amiss as well. Who am I to judge, right? No judgment intended; I am just the Messenger. However, we cannot separate the body from our Spiritual Journey. It is the Vessel God uses to accomplish His extraordinary tasks.

In the beginning of time, we were created from dust, and God has designed the earth to care for itself. So, if we eat what we are supposed to eat, our bodies would take care of themselves, right? From my perspective, this is not the case in today's time. We have a lot of toxins and processed foods to deal with, whether we understand toxins or not.

Consequently, our bodies will not work correctly, especially if we do not know what foods to eat or consume the wrong foods. For example, if we leave a building unmaintained, what will happen? Weeds, creatures, mold, spiders, etc., will come out of seemingly nowhere to take over. By doing so, the Cycle of Life is designed to bring the unused, abandoned, and lifeless building back to the dust from which it was created. Reclaiming its territory.

Now, getting back to the Spiritual Temple, we need nutrition, period. Our bodies need the natural vitamins found in living fruits and vegetables. Although we can use dietary supplements; however, we must eat our fruits and vegetables. They have the natural enzymes we need, as well as the ones man has not discovered as of yet. The manufactured fruit and vegetable drinks cannot replace all-natural fruits. So, do not be fooled by the hype. If you prefer to take a supplement, take it in addition to your fruits and vegetables, but never as a replacement.

Physical toxins contribute to other forms of toxins, such as Mental, Emotional, and Spiritual toxins. They are all linked together; therefore, we must find a way to balance all of them on a moment-by-moment basis. What is the most effective way to do so? Although we are all different, the best way to balance the toxins will be through a consistent regimen of repenting, fasting, prayer, and meditation.

What does our Spirituality have to do with toxins? The excessive buildup of toxins has everything to do with our Spirituality. For example, if our body does not feel right, if we are sick or weak, it has a domino effect in other areas of our lives, even if we are in denial.

More importantly, Spiritual Oppression uses our failing health as a way to control and possess our Mind, Body, and Soul without us realizing what is happening until it is too late. As a Child of the Most High God, I will show how they are directly, succinctly, and strategically linked. Besides, I will also share how to make it work together for our good and how it will work against us, especially if we do not get it together.

Getting Rid of Spiritual Toxins

The new wave of Spirituality is causing us to deviate from loving our neighbors as ourselves. It is a shame in the Eye of God regarding how we allow Spiritual Toxins to contaminate our Spiritual Fruits. How? We base our worthiness on appearance instead of developing Christlike Character, *As It Pleases Him.* Above all, what good is it to look all fly, and our heart is nasty, cruel, hateful, and our mouth is full of unkind, destructive, or negative words?

Let me take this a little further: In today's time, if someone appears not to have money or live a life of luxury, they are subjected to being mistreated, looked down upon, or ridiculed by those who appear as if they have more. Those who are turning up their nose are only two paychecks away from being homeless, and the bank holds the note on everything they proclaim to own. What nerves, right? So, who really has more when we cannot sleep at night or are worried about how we will keep up an image that keeps us bound and enslaved?

To add insult to injury, we cannot pursue our God-Given Purpose in life because we are trying to keep up a self-given image of being more than we truly are. Without a doubt, if left unchecked, we will not realize that it is leaving an empty hole within the depths of our souls with a super-tight vise grip on the psyche. Unfortunately, this is why we overindulge in drugs, alcohol, food, and sex to fill a void of superficial power over the next man, predicated on hidden seeds of jealousy, envy, pride, greed, covetousness, competitiveness, revenge, or unforgiveness.

Yet, we still have an image to keep up, and we cannot dare tell anyone we are not fulfilled or battling with hidden vices. So, what do we do? We put down those who appear less than to make ourselves feel better about our unfulfilled desires or the lies we feed ourselves.

Now, before we go any further, let me clear the air. From a Spiritual Perspective, if we are out of Purpose or have not tapped into our Gifts, Talents, or Calling, we have no right to judge the life of another or look down upon them, period! Do we not have free will to judge anyone or anything? Absolutely! However, if we are not fulfilling the reason God has placed us here, we are dealing with a void. How is this possible? When we are impoverished in a different area, if we are taking negative digs at another, or when we have not taken the time to develop ourselves from the inside out, our void becomes bigger and more toxic.

Spreading toxins everywhere to make ourselves feel better for only a minute is an atrocity to our Spirituality. A toxic minute man or woman is the epitome of self-destructive behavior. After a fleeting minute, the feeling of unfulfillment returns to bear more negative fruits. Listen, if we keep spewing out negativity all day, it leaves us feeling empty, looking for a quick fix from something or someone who cannot fill the void anyway. Once this happens, repenting, fasting, and prayer become viable options to correct the toxicity being spread abroad into the lives of others.

Before I move on, let us briefly talk about King David. According to scripture, He was not a perfect King; he was by far not the most sin-free, and he would kill his enemies in a heartbeat without batting an eye. However, he was indeed after God's own heart.

Why would God choose a man like King David? First and foremost, David was in Purpose on purpose. Secondly, he prided himself on using his God-Given Gifts, Calling, Creativity, and Talents while following his Calling with Spiritual Preciseness to further the Kingdom of God. Thirdly, he was after God's own heart because he was quick to repent, pray, fast, forgive, and worship. If one does not believe this, then read the Book of Psalms. It is riddled with:

- ☐ The Wailings From David.
- ☐ The Weaknesses Of David.
- ☐ The Convictions Of David.
- ☐ The Repentances Of David.
- ☐ The Fastings Of David.
- ☐ The Pleadings Of David.
- ☐ The Empowerments Of David.
- ☐ The Victories Of David.

As a Vessel of the Most High, here is a little **secret**; in my opinion, The Book of Psalms and Proverbs are the most influential books of the Bible. In essence, they help us through the process and reasons for building our relational Christlike Character to bridge the gap in the practicalities of everyday living. Listed below is what I have found in these two books:

- ☐ They paint a picture of how to exhibit the Fruits of the Spirit.
- ☐ They provide examples of the people whom we should keep in our lives.
- ☐ They provide a list of causes and effects.
- ☐ They provide instant Spiritual Principles.
- ☐ They provide the consequences of our actions, behaviors, thoughts, beliefs, words, and biases.
- ☐ They provide a daily Spiritual To-do list.
- ☐ They explain the enemy's tactics and how to position ourselves, *As It Pleases God.*

- ☐ They provide the Spiritual Backup Scriptures to make our wailing process effective.
- ☐ They share business ethics and how to MASTER our Predestined Blueprint, *As It Pleases God*.
- ☐ They explain how to treat others while behaving Christlike.
- ☐ They teach us how to pray, why to pray, where to pray, who to pray for, and who or what to avoid.
- ☐ They teach us the importance of having a *Spirit to Spirit* Relationship with God.

Beyond a shadow of a doubt, these two books have changed my life in ways only God can tell the true story. Had it not been for those two Books of the Bible, one would not be reading this one right now. I am living proof...I live by them because they have become my source of inspiration through which I can see, hear, think, speak, and become more Christlike in my daily walk with my Heavenly Father, *As It Pleases Him*.

Before I end this chapter, let me say this: When we are delivered from toxins, we must not return to them, period. We must find a way to stay as far away as possible; otherwise, we will get into a worse situation than the previous one. Please do not, and I mean do not, return to a dingy place of vomit like a dog. Why should we not return? Once something or someone is regurgitated out of our lives, we must let it go, or we will endure a hurt or an atrocity far worse than before.

According to scripture, *"He that is not with me is against me: and he that gathereth not with me scattereth. When the unclean spirit is gone out of a man, he walketh through dry places, seeking rest; and finding none, he saith, I will return unto my house whence I came out. And when he cometh, he findeth it swept and garnished. Then goeth he, and taketh to him seven other spirits more wicked than himself, and they enter in, and dwell there: and the last state of that man is worse than the first."* Luke 11:23-26.

Now, for the sake of *Wailing Prayers To The Deep **Reloaded**,* some things are better left alone, especially if it is TOXIC.

CHAPTER 6

WAILING PRAYERS TO THE DEEP RELOADED

In our everyday lives, we often find ourselves tiptoeing around who we are and the reasons why we do the things we do. We may try to deny or ignore certain truths about ourselves, but one Spiritual Connection that cannot be denied is the Divine Bond we share with our Heavenly Father. Symbolically, this Spiritual Connection can be likened to the wailing of a child being heard by their parents. When we are Spiritually Synced or tightly bonded, *Spirit to Spirit*, with our Heavenly Father, *As It Pleases Him*, our cries, our hopes, and our dreams are heard and understood in a way that is beyond human comprehension.

Unbeknown to most, a genuine *Spirit to Spirit* Relationship with God, our Heavenly Father, brings about an instinctual knowing, a source of comfort, guidance, strength, a profound sense of peace, and a Divine Sense of Purpose to our lives. However, we must cast aside our doubts, fears, rebelliousness, wavering faith, selfishness, rotten fruits, insecurities, or loose lips, to name a few.

In light of our desire to go to the next level, all is not lost. In this chapter, we will go DEEP into the Source of our strength and how to extract it, causing things to work in our favor without becoming weak, used, or abused. Plus, the *Wailing Prayers To The Deep Reloaded* is profound and a force to be reckoned with once we understand its power.

What is so unique about the wailing process? It is the direct connection to the Source, *As It Pleases Him*. Can we really connect to God, *Spirit to Spirit*? Absolutely. In all due respect, the only person we must go through to get to God is ourselves! Once we do, the *Holy Trinity* (The Father, Son, and Holy Spirit) is waiting for us with open arms to empower us with Divine Protocol and Principles to woo Him.

Wooing God

How do we woo God? We woo Him by operating *As It Pleases Him*. As a result of this WILLINGNESS, He will empower us with the ability to fine-tune our inaudible Inside Voice and Spiritual Voice from the Heavenly of Heavens. What does this mean in layman's terms? The Mouth or Language of God cannot be traced by man, regardless of how intellectual, religious, or scientific we become, unless He allows Divine Access. Thus, if we cannot follow instructions, *As It Pleases Him*, then Divine Access is DENIED!

When we think we have God pegged, He will outmaneuver us; therefore, we cannot put Him in a box nor limit His capacity or reach. According to the Heavenly of Heavens, it is best to get into the box with Him, *As It Pleases Him*.

How is it possible to get in the box with God when we are taught not to place Him in one? Is this not a direct contradiction? Maybe or maybe not! A Spiritual Box is limitless, and a manmade box has limits. If we decide to use a Spiritual Box, *As It Pleases God*, we will be contained within the Four Corners of the Earth for our Heaven on Earth Experience or the completion of our Spiritual Assignments with specific instructions. Is any of this Biblical? I would have it no other way. *"The workmanship of the wheels was like the workmanship of a chariot wheel; their axle pins, their rims, their spokes, and their hubs were all of cast bronze. And there were four supports at the four corners of each cart; its supports were part of the cart itself."* 1 Kings 7:33-34.

What if we are not a cart? In the Eye of God, the workmanship of a CART, VESSEL, or CONTAINER is one and the same. We can play on words all we like, but when the Hand of God is moving across this Earthen Vessel, He will not be playing around with us. *"But we have this treasure in earthen vessels, that the excellence of the power may be of God and not of us. We are hard-pressed on every side, yet not crushed;*

we are perplexed, but not in despair; persecuted, but not forsaken; struck down, but not destroyed—always carrying about in the body the dying of the Lord Jesus, that the life of Jesus also may be manifested in our body." 2 Corinthians 4:7-10.

How do we make this make sense? The sensibility of this will determine whether one is Veiled or Unveiled, *As It Pleases God*. How so? If one is not Spiritually Ready, things will be hidden from them for their protection. *"But even if our gospel is veiled, it is veiled to those who are perishing, whose minds the god of this age has blinded, who do not believe, lest the light of the gospel of the glory of Christ, who is the image of God, should shine on them."* 2 Corinthians 4:3-4. But do not worry, I am getting you prepared, *As It Pleases God*.

Now, to enter the place of Divine Unveiling, *As It Pleases God*, we must do a few things to shake the dust off our character, such as:

- ☐ Willingly follow Spiritual Rules and Principles.
- ☐ Exhibit the Fruits of the Spirit.
- ☐ Exhibit Christlike Character.
- ☐ Become Grateful.
- ☐ Exhibit Humility.
- ☐ Be Kind.
- ☐ Get in Purpose on purpose, Spiritually Tilling our own ground.
- ☐ Unearth and Use our Gifts, Talents, Creativity, or Heed the Calling according to our Predestined Blueprint.
- ☐ Forgive.
- ☐ Have Mercy.
- ☐ Stay Positive.
- ☐ Repent, Pray, Fast, and Meditate regularly.

God does not expect perfection; He expects discipline, obedience, and willingness. Even if we start with one step at a time, He will honor our diligence, but we cannot stop there; we must keep growing and improving with a work-in-progress mentality. Once we perfect the twelve steps listed above, we will be able to speak God's language, *As It Pleases Him*.

Just so we are clear, God hears all of us, but He will take care of His own first. Is this unfair? No. We all have the same opportunity. What opportunity? He wants us to honestly attempt to develop a *Spirit to Spirit* Relationship with Him and follow the Spiritual Rules and Principles without thinking we are above Him.

Wail of Dominion

The Language of God may contradict everything we have been taught by worldly means. The best way to paint this picture is to go to the Animal Kingdom for a moment. For example, are we able to hear animals speak? The answer is no; we can only speculate from a human perspective. However, they have effective communication on a level where they can understand each other, understand us, and most of all, understand God, as we remain aloof. In my opinion, if we give them enough time, they can outsmart us without being able to speak one word. How?

- ☐ They use their instincts.
- ☐ They pay attention to us.
- ☐ They study.
- ☐ They strategize.
- ☐ They adapt.
- ☐ They remember.
- ☐ They practice.
- ☐ They are precise.
- ☐ They do not rush.
- ☐ They know who they are.
- ☐ They understand their limits while finding creative ways to do or accomplish whatever.
- ☐ They use the tools God has blessed them to have.

The Animal Kingdom will continually amaze us in ways that will always supersede our understanding. They do not deviate from their Divine Design and are open to learning how to outsmart those to whom God has given dominion. How can I say such a thing, right? All we need to do is pay attention to their method of operation.

The moment they do not perfect their wail to communicate with each other, if they become weak, or if they do not reproduce after their own kind, the boogeyman, as we call it, will present itself to wipe out their bloodline with no mercy. Why? They have a role to play in the ecological system, and if they cannot live up to the terms or contribute to the Cycle of Life, they are soon replaced. So, what do they do? They develop a system to make us scratch our heads while we forget about our Wail of Dominion. By doing so, we focus more on the problem and not the solution, which causes us to become our worst enemy from the inside out.

What is a Wail of Dominion? It is the ability to recognize who God has created us to be and His reasons why. But more importantly, I am not here to recreate the wheel because all the answers to our Level of Dominion are in the Book of Genesis. I am here to help perfect and break down the wailing process from a Spiritual Perspective.

As we move on, we must understand our vocal abilities have nothing to do with our Spiritual Wail. How is this possible? God does not need our humanness to communicate! When God speaks to us, do we actually hear an audible voice? The answer is no. He may send an audible confirmation through another person, but for the most part, He speaks to our Spirit. The *Wailing Prayers To The Deep Reloaded* wants us to know that we can do likewise.

Spiritually Deep

When we begin to perfect our wail, we can use our Spiritual Tongue on a level that most cannot. But more importantly, we can remove our Spiritual Blinders and unclog our Spiritual Ears while anointing our Spiritual Tongue, *As It Pleases God*. What does this do for us? It enables us to see, hear, and speak beyond our actual, taking us into the Spiritual Depth of Divinity. Or, better yet, making us Spiritually Deep, allowing us to communicate *Spirit to Spirit* with our Heavenly Father!

How can we become Spiritually Deep? Our prayers reproduce after their own kind. Seedtime and harvest are predicated on the things of the DEEP, but it is often overlooked as such. As a form of deception, we think quoting scriptures, religiosity, or degrees determines our depth; yet, they can help, but it does not make the determination. Then, what determines it? The Holy Spirit determines it, and the Blood of Jesus covers it. Without them or using them correctly when becoming Spiritually Deep, *As It Pleases God*, we are only faking it or going with the flow. When doing so, we must be careful. Why must we exhibit caution? Because it is easy to flow into the wrong ditch, especially if we have dug it ourselves!

Regarding harvestable seeds, a plant or tree cannot reproduce unless the seed is planted in the soil, right? If a seed is planted on top of the soil, it may not reproduce or take root properly unless it is designed to be a surface plant with little or no stability. Our prayers are the same; we must plant, water, and cultivate our prayers rooted in the right environment and soil. But more importantly, there must be some form of sacrifice. Why must we submit a sacrifice? According to the Cycle of Life, something has to die to give life to another. As harsh as it may seem, we must understand this process and RESPECT it.

As we all know, Jesus died on the cross to redeem us, becoming our Spiritual Atonement; however, we must do our part. What is our part? We must become cautious about the seeds we are sowing. We must repent, pray, fast, forgive, and meditate to water our faith. Then, we must exhibit Christlike behavior and the Fruits of the Spirit. Why? To cultivate our seeds while positively motivating, encouraging, teaching, and mentoring.

Wailing Prayers To The Deep Reloaded wants us to understand that if we desire to change positively, we must give up the negative. We cannot think for a minute that we can possess the Promises of God, doing whatever we want, without accounting for the cost. Now, to appreciate the power of the wailing process, we must reflect on Daniel, the one who believed in discipline with a continual state of fasting in the Book of Daniel. Although Daniel was not an ordinary man, he was very Spiritual and took his relationship with God personally. More importantly, his name meant, 'God is my judge.'

Daniel interpreted dreams with a special anointing in prophecy. How did he interpret and prophesy without the Holy Spirit in that day and age? First, he prayed thrice daily, meaning he spent time with God. Secondly, he refused to worship pagan gods, even at the pain of death. Thirdly, he believed in a strict vegetarian diet. Fourthly, he exhibited Godly character, topped off with a lot of faith. By doing these four things, he could interpret dreams no one else could interpret, and he was wiser than the magicians and enchanters. The same favored anointing on Daniel is available to anyone. How? If we believe, repent, pray, fast, forgive, become teachable, exhibit the Fruits of the Spirit, and behave Christlike, the Holy Spirit will guide us the rest of the way.

What made Daniel so different? He did not eat certain types of foods, making him healthier than those who were eating the delicacies of King Nebuchadnezzar. Why is this? When we choose the right foods for our bodies, it will energize us, keeping us balanced. When we participate in eating foods, slowing down our digestion, it blocks us Mentally, Emotionally, Physically, and Spiritually. One must decide how much they will sacrifice to become and stay Spiritually Balanced and Alert.

From a Spiritual Perspective, food is the easiest way to become ensnared. If we desire to become or stay Spiritually Alert, we must become ever so conscious about what we are eating, who we are eating from, why we are eating, when we are eating, how we are eating, and where we are eating.

Most often, we think Daniel's story is just about him interpreting dreams, prophesying to Kings, or prophesying the coming of the King; however, it is much more than this. It is about letting us know that God is in control of everything. He is also letting us know we must follow specific protocols and exhibit certain character traits to invoke the following:

- ☐ Spirit of Discernment
- ☐ Spirit of Favor
- ☐ Spirit of Prophecy
- ☐ Spirit of Wisdom

- ☐ Spirit of Knowledge
- ☐ Spirit of Intellectualism
- ☐ Spirit of Good Judgment

If we want to be Spiritually different, positively maximizing our full potential, we cannot eat like everyone else. Why? We must fast, pray, and exhibit the Fruits of the Spirit, period! To clarify, I am NOT saying God cannot use us as Spiritual Vessels, or that we are exempt from His grace and mercy if we eat whatever we want. If we want to experience everything God has to offer, we must follow the proper Spiritual Protocols, pushing away the plate occasionally.

After years of preparation and understanding, I have concluded that we must protect ourselves from Spiritual Invasions. Why must we protect ourselves? Spiritual Invasions are designed to sift us, especially if we do not put on the Whole Armor of God or think we are above Spiritual Laws.

Resisting Spiritual Attacks

Sometimes, we think we are exempt from a Spiritual Attack because we attend church, pay tithes, participate in church activities, and pray. Whereas, in all actuality, we become more susceptible. How is this possible when the Blood of Jesus covers us? Please allow me to counteract this question with another. What do we think will happen if the Spiritual attacker knows about God's Spiritual Laws and Principles better than we do? We will become outsmarted, and they will use God's Word against us!

The Word of God works for the just and unjust alike, and if we leave an open door of known or unknown unrepentant sin, it gives the enemy leverage. Listed below are a few reasons how the Word of God can be used against us, but not limited to such:

- ☐ If we do not know the Word of God, it can be used against us.
- ☐ If we doubt the Word of God, it can be used against us.

- ☐ If we do not apply the Word of God, it can be used against us.
- ☐ If we do not cancel negativity or evil with the Word of God, it can be used against us.
- ☐ If we do not use the Word of God positively, it can be used against us.
- ☐ If we use the Word of God as a form of hate, it can be used against us.
- ☐ If we use the Word of God inappropriately or unjustifiably to divide, it can be used against us.
- ☐ If we misuse the Word of God, it can be used against us.
- ☐ If we use the Word of God to hurt others, it can be used against us.
- ☐ If we mock the Word of God, it can be used against us.
- ☐ If we bring shame to the Word of God, it can be used against us.
- ☐ If we do not stand under or cover ourselves with the Word of God, it can be used against us.

The *Wailing Prayers To The Deep Reloaded* wants to help us in this process. Why do we need help in this area? If we do not learn how to close the door to the enemy, they will find our weakness to secretly drive us insane, especially if we do not understand the true essence of who we are and why we are in the Spiritual Realm.

For example, the dream Daniel interpreted for King Nebuchadnezzar in Daniel 4 stated that he would go temporarily insane. Moreover, Daniel also said he would have the mind of a wild animal instead of the mind of a human, eating grass and living outside. Spiritually Speaking, this is considered humiliation by possession! According to scripture, this occurs after the King bragged about his greatness, thinking he was above God. For King Nebuchadnezzar to break the curse, he had to confess his sins, acknowledging God as being the Most High.

Later on down the line, when King Darius, a new King, came along, favoring Daniel, the player haters concocted a law against prayer to plot the annihilation of Daniel. Everyone knew Daniel would NOT pledge his allegiance to any other gods, allowing them to get him out of the way. It is only hate, envy, or greed that would make one plot the disgrace or death of another innocent person for serving God. In my opinion, it is an atrocity for one to manipulate, brainwash, or bully another to defy the core of their belief system for selfish gain.

Once King Darius realized the law was a plot to eradicate Daniel, he tried to find loopholes in the law to overrule it, but he could not do so. Therefore, the sentence had to be carried out. As a result of this concocted bogus law, Daniel was placed in the Lion's Den to be torn to smithereens. But God...yes, but God was with Daniel. He made the lions be at peace with Daniel.

It is amazing how God will cover us in ways beyond human comprehension when we are obedient to Him. I have no idea what those guys were thinking by throwing God's Chosen One out to the lions. From my perspective, if God can allow King Nebuchadnezzar to act like an animal, what makes them think He cannot make an animal exhibit human characteristics, or better yet, send a Legion of Angels to protect His Chosen One?

Let me expose another secret regarding a kinetic connection between animals and man. Animals understand, *"We are created a little lower than angels."* Hebrews 2:7. Therefore, they will automatically have a residing fear buried within them, similar to the way we fear God or His wrath. Not only this, but an animal can also see the Spirit of man better than we can, especially if we are Spiritually Blinded. How are they able to see better than Believers? Animals use their instincts because it is how they live and survive. We, on the other hand, use our emotions.

We are brainwashed not to use our instincts as we should. As a matter of fact, we are taught to fear them, and we are conditioned to depend on others for their abilities when we indeed have them within us. Why would God allow this story to become a notorious part of the Bible with the KING of the Jungle? I will tell you why...if an animal senses an evil spirit or evil presence within a person, it will react, attack, or flee! Now, with the presence of an Angel or the Holy Spirit, an animal will become calm, loving, and nurturing.

A lion is one of the most dangerous carnivores in the Animal Kingdom and the most courageous, but God is the Creator of everything. When we align ourselves with Him, everything else will line up with us, putting our enemies at bay.

When we are highly favored, we will encounter those who pride themselves on throwing others under the bus to make themselves feel superior. Now, if we arm ourselves with the Laws and Principles of the Spirit with a clean slate, exhibiting the Fruits of the Spirit, it invokes the Spirit of Justice to work on our behalf.

Halting Waywardness

On the other hand, if we are filled with waywardness, knowing nothing about Spiritual Laws or Principles, and committing all types of atrocities, God's grace may or may not cover us. How can I say such a thing, right? There are certain things we do not get to redo; however, God may have mercy on us, but we cannot determine His wrath.

Wailing or not, as individuals, we must determine if we would like to take the chance of engaging in negative debauchery. What is the purpose of doing so? We have free will to do whatever we want, but our decisions outside God's Divine Will may not SAVE us from the enemy's wiles, especially if justified.

A perfect example of the removal of God's grace and mercy is mimicked with King Saul in 1 Samuel 13, where Saul's deliberate act of disobedience resulted in the loss of his Kingdom. Now, in light of the decree, after Saul's continuous rampage of wickedness, he chose not to self-correct; therefore, the apparent rejection from God was pronounced in 1 Samuel 15.

Just so we are crystal clear, we are all saved by grace, where we are given a second chance. Nevertheless, once we set ill will, negativity, or destruction in motion, we must understand that the Universal Law of Seedtime and Harvest is still in full effect. Remember, cause and effect are written all over the Bible, and we are sadly mistaken when we think we are exempt from accounting for the cost. Our behavior can create a generational curse, affecting our innocent loved ones.

So, let us briefly return to the Book of Daniel. Do we think for a minute the officials who concocted the law against Daniel thought it would affect their families? Absolutely not! As a result of the officials losing their lives to the lions, God showed no mercy on their bloodline by totally wiping out their seed. How? Their families were fed to the lions as well. As harsh as it may seem, we must exercise extreme caution in how our actions, behaviors, character, or debauchery affect the innocent.

According to the Spiritual Law of Justice, seedtime and harvest apply to everyone, including companies or associations. How? One bad apple can spoil the whole bunch. Listen, when we set up intentional traps to expose the weaknesses of others without just cause, it will implode families, organizations, relationships, ventures, etc., so be very careful when operating in such a manner.

What do we do when we are under a Spiritual attack? We must pray, fast, repent, and become well-educated on God's Spiritual Laws. What are the Laws? The Laws are written throughout the Bible in the Old and New Testaments. Herein lies the tragedy; some say we are not under the Law, and we are saved by grace. Spiritually, they are absolutely correct! However, we must tell the whole truth about Spiritual Grace and not just grace alone. What does this mean? There is more to the story about grace.

Listen, we are saved by grace, which means we do not have to make the bloody sacrifices of animals to redeem ourselves. To ensure we do not miss the point here, Jesus took the place of animal sacrifices, but it does not make us above Spiritual Laws. Nor does it make us below them, and it does not exempt us from knowing or understanding them from the Old Testament perspective. Why? The New Testament is simply a rewrite or parallelization of the Old Testament with an updated understanding of human relations and Divine Intervention. What does this mean? It is designed to renew our minds on operating with Kingdom Principles instead of judging, condemning, or killing others for the same condemnatory factors lingering within each of us.

For example, regardless of how holy we think we are or how much grace is bestowed upon us, it does not exempt us from the Law of Gravity, right? Grace does not exempt us from the Laws of the Land, the Law of Seedtime and Harvest, or Universal Laws, especially if they are justifiably or unjustifiably broken.

Grace can cover us in many ways, and although we can repent, be restored, and be forgiven, we may not get away without recompense or a free pass. The secret behind grace is our Spiritual

Endurance or Covering when reaping the seeds we have sown amiss. From my perspective, it is always best to sow the right seeds from the start to ensure our reaping is positive, productive, and fruitful. It is only wise to make our best attempts to get it right the first time around without having to redo, restart, refresh, etc., wasting precious time.

When it comes down to the recompense process, it is for the just and unjust alike. How? In the same way, we cannot get away with our foul behaviors; we also must understand that the wiles of the enemy cannot get away. There is a form of recompense; however, we must know Spiritual Laws to enforce them, *As It Pleases God*. Unfortunately, grace alone cannot do this for us, especially in the wailing process.

Here is a secret: If our enemies unjustifiably send ill will at us, we are Spiritually Justified in asking for recompense. For this reason, I make it my business to tell everyone to do good will while always keeping their hands CLEAN and BLESSED. Why? If we do good, according to Psalm 110:1, we can *"sit at the right hand of God, while He makes our enemy our footstool."*

On the other hand, if we partake in evil debauchery, we become the footstool. Really? Yes, really! Let us take it to scripture, *"One who increases his possessions by usury and extortion gathers it for him who will pity the poor. One who turns away his ear from hearing the law, even his prayer is an abomination. Whoever causes the upright to go astray in an evil way, He himself will fall into his own pit; but the blameless will inherit good."* Proverbs 28:8-10.

If we desire the gift of *Eternal Life*, we cannot leave ourselves Spiritually Open, Unchecked, or Ungoverned. What if we do? We will not be able to recognize what is right before our very eyes. The GIFT of Life!

One proven way to take advantage of the *Wailing Prayers To The Deep Reloaded* is to create a Blessing List. Once we keep track of our Blessings, we are less likely to become distracted or discouraged. As a result, we are more apt to become grateful for the simple things in life. In addition, it also helps to prevent Spiritual Shortsightedness as well.

When the issues of life are upon us, we tend to forget the good by human default, focusing on the negative or reminiscing on the past. What is more, if self-correction does not take place, we will tend to wallow as opposed to '*Prayerfully Wailing to the Deep*,' which is our Divine Birthright.

Taking Action

When taking action to Spiritually Enforce our Divine Birthrights, a profound *Spirit to Spirit* Relationship with God is a must. Why must we jump through hoops to take action? First, we do not have to do anything we choose not to do. Secondly, if we do not listen to Him through the basic instructions He has outlined in scripture, is it fair for Him to drop everything for us? Thirdly, is it fair to Spiritually Enforce something that we have not taken the time to search and apply scripture to what we are wailing about?

When we go before God wailing, we should first equip ourselves with Biblical Scriptures as Spiritual Ammunition, Leverage, and Alignment. Why does it take all of this when praying? If we take the time to wail, we must do our part in knowing what we are wailing for and what the Bible says about our issues.

With all due respect, if we are clueless about our prayers, we set ourselves up for clueless results. If we do not have anything to Spiritually Enforce our prayers, then how can we enforce them in a wailing state? Is this not a bit insensitive? Let me say this: When the enemy places a chokehold on us, our families, or our destinies, do we think he is being kind? Absolutely not...he is going for the jugular regardless of how we feel, think, or believe.

In the Eye of God, we must suit up with our Spiritual Armor, *As It Pleases Him*. We must know what we are praying for and why with Bible verses to Spiritually Seal our prayers, *Spirit to Spirit*. The bottom line is that we must TAKE ACTION, period. Here is the Spiritual Seal: "*Ask, and it will be given to you; seek, and you will find; knock, and it will be opened to you. For everyone who asks receives, and he who seeks finds, and to him who knocks it will be opened.*" Matthew 7:7-8. Here is the Spiritual Query Process to help us take action, *As It Pleases God*:

- ☐ What are we asking for? Why? How? Where? When? Who? Scripture?

- ☐ What are we seeking? Why? How? Where? When? Who? Scripture?
- ☐ What are we knocking about? Why? How? Where? When? Who? Scripture?
- ☐ What should God open the door for? Why? How? Where? When? Who? Scripture?

Why do we need all of this? It makes the Spiritual Negotiation process easier and more effective in our *Spirit to Spirit* Relationship.

Spiritual Negotiation

When we think about negotiation, we often associate it with a tool of manipulation. Whereas, if we dare to shift our perceptions about negotiation as a means of intervention or intercession, we can revamp our world. In reality, we cannot always get our way, control circumstances, or violate the will of others. But, in light of our faithfulness, if we learn the value of Spiritual Negotiation, we can cause all things to work together for our good. Then again, our enemies can become our footstool, making us a Spiritual Cornerstone. Although man's and God's objectives may not align with our present-day experiences, we have leverage with God if we place Him first, operating *As It Pleases Him*.

How do we make Spiritual Negotiation make sense? For example, mind-eye coordination must be developed to calibrate with the Will of God. So, if one is a lawyer, and God's plan is for them to become a medical doctor. To consciously decide to align with His Divine Will, they must take alternate classes to transition into their Divine Purpose to become a doctor while still being a lawyer. The Spiritual Negotiating factor comes into play when one can use one's training as a lawyer to help other doctors in the medical field. Meanwhile, capitalizing on both to increase one's capacity and effectiveness while creating a win-win situation. Simply put, give God what He wants according to our Predestined Blueprint, and He will give us what we want as icing on the cake for our willful obedience.

From a Spiritual Perspective, Spiritual Negotiation is like an insurance policy. How is this possible? The Bible's Spiritual 'Just-in-Case' Clauses are our backup plan when relating to God and man. Just so we are clear, this does not mean we have to walk around quoting scriptures; it means we live our lives based on them and use them when needed.

We cannot use our own means of negotiation as a bargaining chip or to manipulate God. Although we are sinful by nature, and if we become narcissistic in our approach to God, He will shut us down, or He will develop a deaf ear to us, allowing us to pick up bad habits to our detriment. But more importantly, we cannot remain divided, so sometimes we must interject the Christlike Skills of Negotiation.

We must use Spiritual Negotiation as a means of intercession on behalf of our Purpose, Blueprint, Passion, Skills, Talents, and Creativity to benefit the lives of others. In the Eye of God, this plays a vital role in the wailing process. Due to conditioning, we often would not use the Word of God to Spiritually Negotiate. Regardless of what we use to reach the Heart of God, the goal is to become effective. So, if we need to Spiritually Negotiate using the Bible, then so be it.

Proverbs 2:3-5 says, *"Yes, if you cry out for discernment, and lift up your voice for understanding, if you seek her as silver, and search for her as for hidden treasures; then you will understand the fear of the Lord, and find the knowledge of God."* Does it work? Absolutely. Especially if we quote this scripture back to God in the midst of the searching process and doing His Divine Will.

Why do we have to do God's Divine Will when we have free will? Once again, if we give God what He wants, He will give us what we want. *"If anyone wants to do His will, he shall know concerning the doctrine, whether it is from God or whether I speak on My own authority."* John 7:17.

Our faith can become a tool of negotiation as well. According to scripture, *"If you have faith as small as a mustard seed, you can say to this mountain, Move from here to there, and it will move. Nothing will be impossible for you."* Matthew 14:20. Of course, the elements of the unknown can and will shake the best of us; however, amid our faith, we must learn how to activate our Supernatural Faith. This form of inner knowing is the type of faith that can and will put our enemies and naysayers at bay, causing the Spirit of God to intercede on our behalf.

Developing our faith in such a manner will come through as an instinctual confidence that is Spirit-Led in nature. Although this is an unexplainable faith to some, it is available to all who repent, fast, forgive, and pray for it. God is no respecter of persons. The same faith Jesus had is available to us through the Holy Spirit; all we have to do is invoke His presence in our lives. Is it this simple? Yes, it is simple for those who take action.

Beyond a shadow of a doubt, there is life and death in the power of our tongues. So, whatever proceeds out of the gateway of our mouths reveals our level of faith. In my opinion, there is no 100% perfect life or faith. Why? We are trapped in life, and the issues of it are designed to test, train, and prune us. However, amid anything, we can perfect our level of faith by repenting, fasting, forgiving, and praying with the right motives while using the Fruits of the Spirit and behaving Christlike. What is the purpose of doing so? It is done to obtain favor with the Lord. Really? Yes, really! Psalm 5:12 says, *"For You, O Lord, will bless the righteous; with favor You will surround him as with a shield."*

Divine Favor

How do we receive favor? The best way is to ask for it. How do we ask? Recite to God daily, *"Teach me Your ways, so I may know You and continue to find favor with You."* Exodus 33:13. Is favor fair? No. Favor is not fair, but it is JUST! God has set in motion certain Laws reigning on the just and the unjust alike, swaying favor in our direction, especially if we learn the secrets of how favoritism works. Seedtime and Harvest happen to be one of them, while repenting, fasting, forgiving, and prayer are the other half.

Clearly, God is not partial; He loves us all regardless of who gave birth to us, and He stands for righteousness regardless of who we are or what we have. He loves us whether we are rich or poor, successful or unsuccessful, smart or not smart, healthy or sick, talented or untalented, etc.

But let me say this before ending this chapter: Favor is up for grabs! If we learn how to grab hold of it, how to use it, and how to sway God's heart in our direction, *As It Pleases Him*, there is nothing we cannot achieve. Trust me, when we exhibit the Fruits of the Spirit in our daily lives, it will get us a lot of favorable brownie points, keeping us glowing with BLESSINGS on high, opening our Spiritual Negev of Divine Provisions. Not only this, if we align ourselves with the Spirit of Obedience, we will also become unstoppable with favor as well.

www.DrYBur.com

CHAPTER 7

ETERNAL LIFE NOW

Our lives can become whatever we desire; however, if we want *Eternal Life*, we must align ourselves with God's Divine Will, *As It Pleases Him*. According to the Heavenly of Heavens, the bliss of *Eternal Life* is NOW, and it is not for the faint of heart. Spiritually Speaking, if we do not accomplish our Divine Mission, *As It Pleases Him*, we are destined to repeat it. Then again, we may get dragged through the dirt in a cycle of déjà vu until we get it right, unveiling our Predestined Blueprint or reason for being.

When it comes down to *Eternal Life*, most would think it is some mystical experience, but it is not. What is it then? It is an experience of having a real *Spirit to Spirit* Relationship with God, our Heavenly Father. How is it possible to engage *Spirit to Spirit* with Him? First, we are Spiritual Beings. Secondly, this is how we were created from the beginning, way before our Heaven on Earth Experience. Thirdly, we had to get His permission, *Spirit to Spirit*, before taking our first breath of life.

Sadly, we look for life in the tangibles of people, places, and things around us. Yet, we do not realize the true GIFT lies in how we perceive our intangible relational experiences from God's point of view, and *As It Pleases Him*. Here is what we must know about this matter: *"And the Father Himself, who sent Me, has testified of Me. You have neither heard His voice at any time, nor seen His form. But you do not have His word abiding in you, because whom He sent, Him you do not believe. You search the Scriptures, for in them you think you have eternal life; and these are* they which testify of Me. But you are not willing to come to Me that you may have life." John 5:37-40.

Contrary to our exposure, our *Eternal Life* is a right NOW experience. For whom? It is for those who have chosen to use their Gifts, Creativity, or Talents to pursue their Divine Purpose according to the Will of God and their Predestined Blueprint. Instead of living life on our terms, doing what pleases us, leaving Him out of the equation, or only using Him as a backup, we can place Him at the forefront as our Spiritual Compass.

According to scripture, *"Very truly I tell you, whoever hears my word and believes him who sent me has eternal life and will not be judged but has crossed over from death into life. Most assuredly, I say to you, the hour is coming, and now is, when the dead will hear the voice of the Son of God; and those who hear will live."* John 5:24-25.

Regarding understanding *Eternal Life*, we must know that everyone's experience is different. So, we cannot place ourselves or others in a box of traditional rationalism. If we do, we will experience a longing from within searching for a quick fix, jumping from pillar to post in unsurety.

The *Wailing Prayers To The Deep Reloaded* profoundly impacts our ability to grasp our lives beyond our limitations. Yes, the limitations as they relate to our sinful natures or our negative mindsets.

As a rule of thumb, we cannot discount one man for his sinful nature when our minds are plagued with negativity against ourselves or others. According to the Heavenly of Heavens, they carry the same penalty or weight in the Realm of the Spirit. Why? We are human, and we were created to embrace *Eternal Life* through our ability to relate to each other positively, compassionately, mercifully, lovingly, and gratefully. Besides, we DO NOT know what God is using to train, test, polish, prune, propel, or protect them for their Divine Mission, Purpose, or Blueprint.

As humans, we all have issues or something to work on. So, we should never spitefully or negatively point the finger at anyone, especially when we have a bend in our finger as well. For example, if we have a finger, it will also have a knuckle connecting it to our hand, right? If we have a hand, we also have a wrist, elbow, arm, and shoulder connecting to the body. The connection of joints and marrow comprises seen or unseen bends and curves (life issues), regardless of who we are. Yet, they are designed to work together to function for the BENEFIT of God, ourselves, and others with shareable good fruits, *As It Pleases Him.*

As a Body of Christ, we are designed to work together, period! Everything is connected and designed to function according to God's Divine Will with each individual's unique Blueprint. How would we know when we are Divinely Guided by God Almighty? Everyone is different, but know this: *"My sheep hear My voice, and I know them, and they follow Me. And I give them eternal life, and they shall never perish; neither shall anyone snatch them out of My hand. My Father, who has given them to Me, is greater than all; and no one is able to snatch them out of My Father's hand. I and My Father are one."* John 10:27-30.

Unbeknown to most, if we CANNOT be snatched, it indicates Divine Purpose or a Predestined Blueprint is involved. However, the key is that we need to KNOW and WALK in it, *As It Pleases God.* If not, we can 'get got' when operating in self-indulgence without any regard for our Blueprinted Mission!

For our *Eternal Life* to yield on our behalf, *As It Pleases God*, we need our God-Given Purpose or Divine Blueprint attached to it. If we create a disconnect within ourselves or instigate havoc to prevent another from discovering their reason for being, we will have a problem with God. Once we have a problem with God, we may have a problem with our Gifts, Calling, Talents, or Purpose, jumping from one person, place, or thing to the next. Now, with this sort of disconnect, we will find ourselves going to the dark side while secretly destroying ourselves, others, as well as our Bloodline while thinking we are right in our own eyes.

With all due respect, accepting or following Jesus as our Lord and Savior is NOT enough, especially when we camouflage our misbehaviors or intentionally destroy the innocent. Blasphemy, right? Wrong again. God needs our OBEDIENCE in following the truth without giving way to false doctrine, idolatry, player hating, or a lack of compassion. Why? The Blood of Jesus can act as a Spiritual Covering or Atonement, and it can also become an element of Spiritual Crucifixion if it is not used correctly. According to scripture, *"Put your sword back in its place,"* Jesus said to him, 'for all who draw the sword will die by the sword.' " Matthew 26:52. Willfully destroying people, places, and things out of selfishness is a big no-no, especially if we are out of control, Mentally, Physically, Emotionally, or Spiritually, knowing nothing about our reason for being, *As It Pleases God.*

The Doorpost

Listen, our known and unknown sins must be repented, period. When we set the Blood of Jesus in motion without the Holy Spirit involved, we must be careful about the doorpost we are placing it on. What is the reason for such caution? If we have unrepentant innocent blood on our hands or if we are outright wicked, it can unknowingly create a curse for us or our Bloodline, especially if we are contending with a Spiritual Elite or a Chosen One. Whereas, if the Holy Spirit were present and active, He would have advised one to self-correct instead of self-destructing. What is the difference? It is a matter of Pleasing God or pleasing ourselves..."*Choose this day whom you will serve.*" Joshua 24:15.

What is so special about a Spiritual Elite or God's Chosen Elect? They understand the Power of Spiritual Laws, Protocols, Principles, and Repentance. If we are praying for ill will against this type of person, and we are not in a repented state, our emotions are all over the place, or our minds are contaminated with all types of filth, our prayers will backfire. How can I say such a thing, right? According to scripture, *"For whoever finds Me finds life, and obtains favor from the Lord; but he who sins against me wrongs his own soul; all those who hate me love death."* Proverbs 8:35-36. Therefore, we must exercise extreme caution when justifying and rationalizing our negative behaviors. In addition, we must also be careful about trying to get God to come to our level instead of coming up to His Spiritual Standards with outright humility and obedience.

Just so we are clear, no one is without sin. We are all born into a sinful world. If we are not repenting or becoming transparent about our wrongness or rightness, we will become affected or traumatized when we are outed publicly or privately. For this reason, we need to take this chapter up a notch to perfect our ability to operate in the elements of damage or image control Spiritually without being provoked Physically, Mentally, or Emotionally.

Building Others

Our *Eternal Life* is not found in our ability to discredit but within our ability to build, motivate, and encourage the fallen. Why must we encourage others? Our Spiritual Battles are created from the inside out. When we struggle with ourselves or broadcast the struggles of another, having nothing to do with us or our point of reference, this is a tell-tale sign of an inner Spiritual Battle. For this reason, we must take it to God immediately. If not, we will fall prey to our weaknesses, causing us to become a victim.

How is it possible to become a victim, especially when we are devout Believers? Although victimization can be physical, it is also a mindset. If we do not pump the brakes on our thoughts, *As It Pleases God*, they can get the best of us, even if we are Believers. Without counteracting negativity with positivity and the Word of God, we can become open game for the enemy to slip into our lives to sift us as wheat or broadcast our sins to provoke a reaction. Why would they do such a thing? To create a distraction, and if we are not Spiritually Astute, our attempted damage or image control can become a seeming admission of guilt, especially when we should have taken it to God in the first place.

If we have been Eternally Invested, *As It Pleases God*, let us go to the next level. What does this mean for us? It means we are in Purpose on purpose with our Gifts, Creativity, or Talents in use, and we are Spiritually Tilling our own ground. How do we get to this point if we are not in Purpose or do not know our Gifts, Creativity, or Talents? If we find our Passion in life, we can find our Purpose. Are they not the same? No. Passion is an inner experience of joy, peace, contentment, and bliss. Whereas our Purpose is an outer experience in ACTION to provide a service, fill a need, or solve a problem.

The Experience

Once we combine our Divine Passion with Divine Purpose, the experience of *Eternal Life* begins here on earth. Am I pulling for straws? Absolutely not. We all have a reason for existing, and if we do not know why we are here, we will find ourselves searching for inner meaning, regardless of who we are or what we have. And all we need to do is to stop lying to ourselves.

Here is the deal: If one has never had a near-death experience, they would not truly understand the Afterlife or the true meaning of Purpose. However, once we have experienced almost losing our lives, or we are faced with a choice of crossing over to the next life while making a conscious choice to come back, the articulation of Eternal is profound.

Some would say the *Afterlife* and *Eternal Life* are the same, whereas, from my perspective, they are different. How so? The *Afterlife* is a completed Mission, Purpose, or Spiritual Crossover. *Eternal Life* is in action, moving, or evolving toward the completion of our Divine Mission, seemingly trapped in time. If this is above our heads, do not worry; I will break it down. Doing so will ensure we do not miss the mark or continue to repeat the same cycles of déjà vu with different characters without developing our Spiritual Language.

Spiritual Language

The *Wailing Prayers To The Deep* *Reloaded* has a built-in Spiritual Language that the human ear cannot hear. More importantly, it is powerful beyond what we can imagine; however, we must perfect the art of exhibiting the Fruits of the Spirit, mastering the differences between Blessings and curses, and operating in Christlike Character. Why must we know the difference? Spiritually, everything is an illusion.

Please allow me to Spiritually Align: *"Therefore we do not lose heart. Even though our outward man is perishing, yet the inward man is being renewed day by day. For our light affliction, which is but for a moment, is working for us a far more exceeding and eternal weight of glory, while we do not look at the things which are seen, but at the things which are not seen. For the* things which are seen are temporary, but the things which are not seen are eternal." 2 Corinthians 4:16-18.

In layman's terms, when it comes down to Spirituality, we must think inside, outside, around, through, over, under, and around the box of what we can and cannot see. Nevertheless, before moving on, please allow me to ask a few questions: Are we not a mere compilation of atoms and molecules? Yes, we are. Can we see atoms and molecules with the naked eye? No, we cannot. Do atoms and molecules die? No, they do not. Are atoms and molecules bonded together? Yes, they are. As we move on, for the sake of our wailing process, we need to know this for our Spiritual Edification.

Why do we need to know about atoms and molecules? Most of the issues we are wailing to God about are not real, or they are self-created or self-induced. Who am I to judge? No judgment is intended; however, it is our PERCEPTION of the issue that makes it seemingly real.

Regardless of what we see physically, it may have a different meaning or purpose, scientifically or Spiritually. Moreover, we cannot see the hidden components of our Spiritual Genetic makeup with our natural eyes. Why? It would scare us to the core, traumatizing us in ways that would have us shaking or doubting in our boots. For this reason, God will withhold certain Spiritual Information if we are not ready. Once we are ready, He will usher us through viable Levels of Spirituality.

Why does God use such caution? If mishandled, it can become detrimental to the well-being of ourselves, others, or our Bloodline. Conversely, we can also become Spiritually Reckless.

When we are overwhelmed with our fleshly wants, the craving will only become stronger over time, especially if it is not put under the subjection of the Holy Spirit while repenting, fasting, and praying. Spiritually, this is precisely why we compromise in areas God has given us power over.

The most critical question today lies in our understanding of *Eternal Life*. When we think about Eternity, we must understand the elements of life beyond ourselves into Purpose. This is similar to how we paint superficial mental pictures of what we desire without having specific details of how to bring the picture into reality. Nor do we know or understand what we will experience along the way or the training needed to prepare us. Nevertheless, as Spiritual Ambassadors of the Kingdom, this should not be a problem for us. Why? We have the Holy Spirit to assist us in our journey toward Greatness and the Blood of Jesus to cover us.

As a part of our evolutional process, our lives are designed by God as an experience of love, relationship, and community to create human bonds. In light of this, with the little glitch in our Matrix from the Garden of Eden, we decided to take over, doing our own thing, not realizing the true components of our Divine Design or who is really in charge. As a result, the bonds of our relationship with God, ourselves, and others are broken until we come to ourselves or experience a Spiritual Awakening.

Regarding our wailing process, our **Internal Life** is just as important as our **External Life**, and if we have an imbalance in these areas, our *Eternal Life* is put on pause. In all simplicity, we will be put in a Spiritual Timeout, allowing us the opportunity to go back into the Spiritual Classroom willingly. If not, the issues of life will eventually force us back in.

Just keep in mind that the more we become resistant, disobedient, disrespectful, or a hellion on wheels, the more complex our lessons will become while we pick up more bad habits to coax the hidden pain. Will the coax work? Yes. They will temporarily work, spiraling us into a deeper cycle of déjà vu.

It is a red flag when we experience inconsistencies in our character or an imbalance where our mouth is saying one thing, but we are doing another. I am not impressed by what people do or say in front of me; I am impressed by what they do or say behind my back. Why? Anyone can put on a front, but the actual character emerges when our back is turned. I am always amazed by the masks people assume, thinking I cannot see beyond the mask.

How can I see beyond the mask of others? I pay attention to their People Skills and the Fruits of the Spirit. They do not lie. Matthew 7:20 says, *"Therefore by their fruits you will know them."*

With our *Eternal Life Reloaded*, to effectively wail on a level where we can dispatch a Legion of Angels to assist us at the drop of a dime, we must become cautious, compassionate, and concerned about the lives of others. For sure, if we desire *Eternal Life* now, and we have no regard for the life or safety of another, we have work to do.

When we enter into God's presence wailing, He wants to know what we are doing with the Gifts, Talents, Creativity, and Resources of our External Blessings to make an Internal Impact on His sheep. He should already know this information, right? Of course, He does; however, He wants us to know as well, and He wants to ensure our wailing is not all about us.

Why does God require us to be in the know? If we are clueless about what we are doing or the reasons why, then we are only deceiving ourselves or playing the blaming game, similar to the 'Adam and Eve Experience' in the Book of Genesis.

The endless Spiritual Provision is here and now; however, we cannot equate it to worldly standards. If we do, we will become involved in the negligence of Spiritual Laws. How so? Let us take it to scripture, "*You give a tenth of your spices—mint, dill, and cumin. But you have neglected the more important matters of the law—justice, mercy, and faithfulness. You should have practiced the latter, without neglecting the former.*" Matthew 23:23. If we selfishly give while crucifying, complaining, or cursing them simultaneously, it will cause a Spiritual Disconnect.

Divine Expectations

According to the Heavenly of Heavens, helping others does not give us a license to destroy them, Mentally, Physically, Emotionally, Spiritually, or Financially. Nor does it give us the right to treat people like junkyard dogs or throw them under the bus because they have less in comparison to our more.

How do we readjust our behaviors? We need to repent, pray, or fast to jumpstart ourselves, then exhibit the Fruits of the Spirit (Love, Joy, Peace, Patience, Kindness, Goodness, Faithfulness, Gentleness, and Self-Control). Once perfected, we need to usher in the Holy Spirit to guide us in Spiritual Protocols, Principles, and Laws through reading Biblical Scriptures.

Spiritual Laws set forth by God are overlooked daily due to Spiritual Blindness, Deafness, and Muteness. How is this possible, especially as Believers? We focus on Spiritual Works such as tithing, giving, or caring for someone without having the Spiritual Illumination of Godly Expectations, *As It Pleases Him*. Simply put, we may overlook the importance of exhibiting Christlike Character or using the Fruits of the Spirit when it comes down to unveiling our *Eternal Life*.

Our walk with God has more to do with the contents of our hearts than works. Why are we taught to put in the work for the Kingdom, Spiritually Tilling our own ground? The proactive works will come naturally with no strings attached if our hearts are right with our Heavenly Father. If we focus on works only to prove our Godliness, our motives can become swayed or pompous based on our conditioning, biases, or traumas. How do we know if our works have the wrong motives?

- ☐ If we give with conditions.
- ☐ If we are expecting something in return.
- ☐ If we keep track of our giving to use it as leverage to control, manipulate, or use someone.
- ☐ If we are always reminding someone of what we have done for them.
- ☐ If we set expectations for others based on what we gave them.
- ☐ If we manipulate someone by what we do, give, or say.
- ☐ If we make someone feel guilty about what we have done.
- ☐ If we focus on how much it will cost us without considering the sincere need.
- ☐ If we make promises of giving, knowing we cannot keep the promise.
- ☐ If we are always on the take.
- ☐ If we lie about what we have to paint a picture of being more than we are.
- ☐ If we hoard or hide to prevent people from begging.

Before we move on, remember that possessing some of these characteristics may not make us bad, evil, or unusable in the Eye of God. We can simply be uninformed, brainwashed, deprived, aloof, or misunderstood as I once was. Really? Yes, really! Our conditioning, traumas, abandonment, or unresolved hurts play a vital role in these character traits; however, all is not lost; it can be reversed, *As It Pleases God*.

It Is A Wrap

Once again, my Spiritual Training was so fierce that I would not wish it upon my worst enemy! Still, in the Eye of God, the Battle Scars were necessary for me to become Spiritually Anointed, Appointed, and Accurate, *As It Pleased Him*. Why was it necessary? When the enemy comes for Believers, he will not be playing around with us; he will hang us, our children, families, and Bloodlines out to dry. And if our game is not tight, our motives are not right, we have rotten fruits all over the place, and our character sucks, justification can be warranted or allowed by God to do the teaching for Him.

Plus, I am not willing to lose one precious sheep on my watch; thus, I am not going to sugarcoat the TRUTH. Why such passion about this matter? I wish someone had given me this information back then. But now that I have it, *As It Pleases God*, it is a wrap! So, no excuses!

How can we reverse our ungodly motives to perfect our wailing process? Here are a few steps, but not limited to such:

- ☐ First, we must become aware of our behaviors, thoughts, beliefs, desires, biases, words, and mindsets. We cannot deal with what we ignore, deny, or lie about.

- ☐ Secondly, we must make the appropriate changes or corrections, *As It Pleases God*, and use the Fruits of the Spirit consistently. In my opinion, it is best to get in writing what we need to change or correct. Doing so gives us an opportunity to reflect on what we have written, especially when our minds or emotions jump the track.

- ☐ Thirdly, we must surrender them to God through repentance, prayer, forgiveness, or fasting. Even if they are difficult to give up, we must become willing to release them without giving up on ourselves.

- ☐ Fourthly, whenever they present themselves, we must cancel them, replace them with positive affirmations, and back them up with Biblical Scriptures.

Will the above four steps work for anyone? Absolutely, but let us take it to scripture, *"Be sober, be vigilant, because your adversary the devil walks about like a roaring lion, seeking whom he may devour. Resist him, steadfast in the faith, knowing that the same sufferings are experienced by your brotherhood in the world. But may the God of all grace, who called us to His eternal glory by Christ Jesus, after you have suffered a while, perfect, establish, strengthen, and settle you."* 1 Peter 5:9-10.

Why must we go through this process when the fight is already fixed? Our unresolved selfishness or waywardness can become our downfall if we are not careful. Unfortunately, it can leave an open door for Spiritual Invasions and generational curses to attach themselves to our lives, generational seeds, or Legacy.

From the Ancient of Days until now, if we want all God has for us, *As It Pleases Him*, we cannot neglect to have mercy, do the right thing, share, exhibit the Fruits of the Spirit, and behave Christlike. Frankly, the same things we expect from God, we must exhibit to others with no strings attached. What makes this so important? Excuses for our selfishness cannot override the Spiritual Laws of God, regardless of how we try to buy our way through life. As Believers, if we persist in having our way in pleasing ourselves, we will become Spiritually Lethargic in due time.

Overcoming Spiritual Lethargy

Spiritual Restlessness and Lethargy will affect the psyche in ways we do not fully understand. Therefore, let us not get caught up in debilitating Spiritual Matters that cause us to get a SIDE EYE from God Almighty. What can we do to help ourselves? Once again, the Fruits of the Spirit work very well in rectifying a troubled Spirit. Secondly, we must stop lying to ourselves about our attitudes, behaviors, thoughts, emotions, or disrespectfulness. Thirdly, we must seek the Holy Spirit for WISE counsel.

How can the Holy Spirit help us? Let us take it to scripture, *"However, when He, the Spirit of truth, has come, He will guide you into all truth; for He will not speak on His own authority, but whatever He hears He will speak; and He will tell you things to come."* John 16:13.

There are wolves in sheep's clothing all around us, so we must seek God for Divine Counsel and Guidance to ensure we are going in the right direction. If one wants to continue to repeat their lessons in a cycle of déjà vu, then kudos to them; however, I do not like to return to the classroom, especially a Spiritual Classroom. Why? Spiritual Correction, or the Rod of Correction, can do a number on us from the inside out. So, I prefer to get it right the first time around, moving on to bigger and better things, *As It Pleases God*.

Wasting precious time is not in my repertoire; thus, when I am in question about something or someone, and I need a little Spiritual Guidance, I do not hesitate to wail to the DEEP, fast, and pray while invoking the Holy Spirit. Why is this so important? My PERCEPTION is indeed everything. I cannot afford to get it wrong or miss the Spiritual Lesson, Cue, or Wisdom. Therefore, I must learn, appreciate, and glean from everything to heighten my Spiritual View, Understanding, and Stature, DOCUMENTING my findings, *As It Pleases God*.

As a Vessel of the Most High, my *Eternal Life* resides in my ability to provide a Spiritual Benefit for the Kingdom of God, myself, and others with no strings attached. What is the big deal, especially when we are all dealing with the same things? I have been ordained to point God's sheep in the right direction, place them in a fold, bring them out of a fold, and extract the Gifts, Talents, Creativity, Calling, and Blueprint of those who have been Destined for a time such as this. Simply put, I am responsible for reloading them with the opportunity to embrace Divine Illumination, *As It Pleases God*.

Divine Illumination

When it comes to Divine Illumination, most Believers do not think that it is attainable, nor do they think it is a real commodity. Yet, they go with the flow of it with residing doubt. As of this moment, the secret doubt must cease as Divine Illumination becomes our Heavenly Bread and Butter.

Here is the deal: We must Divinely Illuminate ourselves to become Spiritually Transparent without sugarcoating, justifying, or rationalizing our Spirituality, thinking we are more righteous than we really are.

What is the purpose of Divine Illumination? We have light and darkness all around us, and as a Child of God, we want to stay in the LIGHT. Why? To become Christlike, we need it. So, it is best to take this to scripture, *"Then Jesus spoke to them again, saying, 'I am the light of the world. He who follows Me shall not walk in darkness, but have the light of life.'"* John 8:12.

In the act of walking in light, we must take action. How? Let us take it to scripture, *"Walk while you have the light, lest darkness overtakes you; he who walks in darkness does not know where he is going. While you have the light, believe in the light, that you may become sons of light. These things Jesus spoke, and departed, and was hidden from them."* John 12:35-36.

We must set the scriptures in motion in our lives, *As It Pleases God.* For example, we should use scriptures to reinforce our prayers. When we go about our daily lives, we should also align them with scripture, using the Fruits of the Spirit as backup. How can this work on our behalf? What we do not get right as it relates to scripture, our Fruits of the Spirit (Love, Joy, Peace, Patience, Kindness, Goodness, Faithfulness, Gentleness, and Self-Control) will give us grace for trying. Also, it allows us to redo or revamp our point of erring as long as we own up to our issues without whitewashing them.

How do we enlighten ourselves? When we understand the problem, solution, strategy, and what God has to say about it, *As It Pleases Him,* our dullness becomes Divinely Illuminated by default. According to the Heavenly of Heavens, we must also ask for Divine Illumination. Why? It is a free-will offering requiring our willingness and participation.

How do we ask for Divine Illumination, *As It Pleases God*? In the wailing process, quote this scripture to God, *Spirit to Spirit*: "Open my eyes, that I may see Wondrous things from Your law. I am a stranger in the earth; do not hide Your commandments from me." Psalm 119:18-19. What is the purpose of asking? It helps to open our Spiritual Eyes, Ears, and Mouth, giving us the ability to:

- ☐ Spiritually Analyze.
- ☐ Spiritually Focus.
- ☐ Spiritually Think.
- ☐ Spiritually See.
- ☐ Spiritually Hear.
- ☐ Spiritually Speak.
- ☐ Spiritually Control.
- ☐ Spiritually Change.
- ☐ Spiritually Divide.
- ☐ Spiritually Infuse.
- ☐ Spiritually Decree.
- ☐ Spiritually Wail.
- ☐ Place a Spiritual Demand.
- ☐ Fine-tune our Spiritual Language.

Our Divine Illumination is predicated on our developmental abilities. According to the Heavenly of Heavens, we cannot expect to become Divinely Illuminated with the Presence of God and remain the same with rotten fruits. We must enter the Spiritual Classroom to purify worldly debris from the psyche. *"For whom the Lord loves He chastens, and scourges every son whom He receives."* Hebrews 12:6.

On the other hand, if we desire to enlighten ourselves without God, we still have free will to do so. However, I would NOT suggest it. Remember, neither God nor I will violate man's free will. He did not create us as robots; therefore, we must choose the Kingdom of God for ourselves.

For a time such as this, we must understand that the Word of God is our Spiritual Tool of Enlightenment, taking us to the next level. We can start with the Book of Revelation. What is the purpose of using this book? According to scripture, "*Blessed is he who reads and those who hear the words of this prophecy, and keep those things which are written in it; for the time is near.*" Revelation 1:3.

Why not start with the Book of Genesis? We can start where we prefer; however, if we lack an understanding of the Spiritual Protocol of God's Chosen Elect, we will do things our way. What does this mean? Let me give an example from a writer's perspective. When writing, we do not begin a book at the beginning. We must perfect the ending, outcome, or Purpose of the book to make all of the other chapters fall into alignment. If not, the chapters will be unsynced without any form of correlation, or better yet, they will be all over the place.

To know what God wants, we must align ourselves with what He has in mind, right? The same applies to our Divine Purpose or Blueprint. If we know what it is or have an idea, then we will know what to cast down, cast out, or reverse.

Most often, we associate casting out a Spirit with an exorcist experience. Although there are some cases as such, that is so far from what I am talking about here. I am referring to casting down, casting out, or reversing the negative thoughts, words, habits, characteristics, or behaviors causing Mental, Physical, and Emotional problems or disruptions within the human psyche designed to thwart our DESTINY.

As life would have it, there is good and evil in everyone. The goal is to have our good outweigh the evil buried within the depths of our souls. I would definitely disagree if one were to say evil does not reside within them.

Why would I disagree, especially when I do not know the person? According to the Heavenly of Heavens, we know good and evil based upon the Adam and Eve Experience. If we did not, we would not be able to recognize the difference between the two, we would not be able to exercise discipline, we would not have a reason to repent, we would not have a reason to seek forgiveness, we would not have a reason to pray, Jesus would not have become our Spiritual Atonement, and we would not need the Holy Spirit. For those reasons, we must find a way to shed light on the negative Spiritual Matters to ensure they do not overtake the good inside us.

The moment we think we are not possessed by something, we are wrong. Even if we think we are right, perfect, or pristinely polished, we are all dealing with some sort of Spiritual Issue from within. Although lusts, habits, weaknesses, flaws, disabilities, idiosyncrasies, power, money, pompousness, or whatever may camouflage them, they still exist. How do I know? It is the training ground God uses for our Predestined Blueprint or invokes our Gifts, Calling, Talents, Creativity, Skills, Passion, or Purpose. Really? Yes, really!

If we have any form of negative habit, rest assured, it is Spiritual. If one does not believe this, then try to give up the habit cold turkey and watch how it will fight back. We do not have to wait for someone to cast out the Spirit of Negativity; we can do this ourselves, *As It Pleases God*. The scripture says, "*If I with the finger of God cast out devils, no doubt the kingdom of God is come upon you.*" Luke 11:20.

When dealing with Divine Illumination, to effectively cast out Devils, we need God Almighty involved in our equational efforts first. Secondly, we must be able to repent, fast, forgive, and pray. Thirdly, we need the Blood of Jesus for our Spiritual Atonement. Fourthly, we need the presence of the Holy Spirit. Lastly, we must make our best attempts to exhibit the Fruits of the Spirit and behave Christlike. Without them, we are limited in what we can do, say, become, cast out, or illuminate in our own strength.

Why do we become limited as Believers? Please allow me to answer this question with another. If we behave like the enemy, how is it possible to judge, condemn, or cast out what we are in partnership with? Then again, with all due respect, would this not make us look like hypocrites?

Above all, if we do not prepare ourselves, *As It Pleases God*, here is what can happen: The exorcists attempt to cast out the evil spirit by invoking the name of the Lord Jesus, whom Paul preaches. "*And the evil spirit answered and said, 'Jesus I know, and Paul I know; but who are you?' Then the man in whom the evil spirit was leaped on them, overpowered them, and prevailed against them, so that they fled out of that house naked and wounded.*" Acts 19:15-16.

Unfortunately, this illustrates the danger of engaging in Spiritual Warfare unequipped and without a genuine and personal relationship with our Heavenly Father, *Spirit to Spirit*. Meanwhile, in any event, it is only wise to cover ourselves with the Blood of Jesus and have the Holy Spirit on full alert at all times to help us become a Cornerstone of Greatness.

The Divine Cornerstone

In building Divine Cornerstones, *As It Pleases God*, we never want to reap into our lives the very things we are passing judgment on. What can we do about this matter? We are all different; therefore, what to do exactly is not set in stone. Nevertheless, exhibiting responsibility, *As It Pleases Him*, ensures we can see ourselves and our faults clearly so we are not crucifying others on the same things we are, have been, or will be guilty of.

According to the Heavenly of Heavens, we must become responsible without exhibiting recklessness, irresponsibility, or twisting the truth with lies or deflection. Why is this so important in the Eye of God? We must think proactively to fulfill a need before the desire presents itself. If we are consumed with judgmentalism, lies, debauchery, and blaming, we become exempt from being Kingdomly Commissioned to feed His sheep, *As It Pleases Him*.

What is the big deal, as long as His sheep get fed? Of course, God will use anyone or anything to feed His sheep. Just because He allows us to participate does not mean we are in Purpose on purpose or are properly aligned with our Predestined Blueprint, *As It Pleases Him*. Nor does it mean we are Spiritually Sealed, Anointed, or Appointed. For this reason, we must become accountable and responsible for our fruits and character, period. How? Use the Fruits of the Spirit and behave Christlike while Spiritually Tilling our own ground.

Spiritually Speaking, why would we opt to be the stepping stone instead of becoming the CORNERSTONE? We have free will to choose the Spiritual Path we so desire. Well, what is the difference? The only difference is that a Divine Cornerstone is being in Purpose on purpose, *As It pleases God*. Whereas, when we become stepping stones, we are usually out of purpose, pleasing ourselves. However, in the Eye of God, we should be proactively learning, developing, and using both.

When we own our truth, admit we have made a mistake, confess when we are wrong, forgive quickly, sincerely apologize, or acknowledge our shortcomings, we open ourselves up to God's Classroom of Divine Wisdom to learn the Kingdomly Lessons linked to our Predestined Blueprint or Cornerstone of Greatness. Now, just so we are clear about this Spiritual Protocol, let us take it to scripture: *"If we confess our sins, he is faithful and just to forgive us of our sins, and to cleanse us from all unrighteousness."* 1 John 1:9.

On the other hand, when we are in denial about our truth, we automatically place limits on our growth, deceiving ourselves and others. In my opinion, we do not have to tell the world about our sins; however, if we repent, fast, and confess our sins to God in our prayer closet while learning our life lessons and exhibiting Divine Integrity, we will become a victorious POWERHOUSE that Wisdom and Favor will chase down.

Spiritual Integrity

When we speak of integrity, we all think we have it without truly understanding the fundamental principles associated. Whereas, in all actuality, our level of integrity is different based upon our perceptional conditioning, mindsets, and traumas. If we bring God into the equation, regardless of which side of the tracks we live on, Spiritual Integrity does not change, period.

The highest or most beneficial bidder should not determine our integrity's unction. If it does, it brings an inner conviction, filling us with greed and lasciviousness. What does this mean in layman's terms? We desire to do right, but our thoughts, actions, words, attitudes, biases, and behaviors rope us into ungodliness, no matter how hard we try to do right. However, to break the soul tie, bondage, or yoke, we must first understand whatever it is, repent, fast, forgive ourselves, and pray until it breaks.

When it comes to fasting, we must consult our doctor first, especially if we have medical issues. However, when fasting over a severe issue, we may have to do a modified fast after the full fast, which we will review in the next chapter.

In light of our faithfulness, if we want to polish our integrity according to what God has in mind for us, we should consider mastering the Book of Proverbs. Why would we use this book? It gives perfect scenarios and lessons about what or who can trap us and how to prevent ourselves from getting caught up.

Integrity is essential in building a solid foundation structured according to the Will of God, *As It Pleases Him*. We must learn how to live daily with the reality of good fruits instead of creating an illusion of goodness or living a fake life!

According to the Heavenly of Heavens, we are equipped with the right tools to practice what we preach. If we exhibit the Fruits of the Spirit, we can better keep ourselves in alignment with what God has in mind for us, others, and our Purpose.

As we move on, here is what integrity means to me...it means getting 'Into The Gritty.' When we can exfoliate the gritty areas of our lives, we can own our truth with transparency, transcending what people think of us into what we think of ourselves, according to the Will of God, *As It Pleases Him*. Once we understand our dirt (our issues) while creating a win-win for God, ourselves, and others, He will begin to trust us with more. More of what? More of what we need while protecting us from what we do not need.

In the Eye of God, integrity is a seed, and we will reap accordingly. Unbeknown to most, Godly Integrity is also considered a Spiritual Fruit. What type of fruit is this, especially when not listed in the Fruits of the Spirit? Integrity is one of the Fruits of the Spirit; it is hidden in plain sight under what we call Faithfulness. We cannot divide integrity and faithfulness because they are the same. But more importantly, it is the backbone of the Fruits of the Spirit. How is this possible?

- ☐ If we have LOVE without integrity, our relationships will be destroyed due to the lack of trust.

- ☐ If we have JOY without integrity, our selfishness will squander it with the issues of life, causing us to become materialistic. Or, we will confuse our inner joy with temporary happiness obtained in conjunction with our soulish nature, creating self-destructive habits.

- ☐ If we have PEACE without integrity, it is only short-lived because it is only a matter of time before pandemonium erupts.

- ☐ If we have PATIENCE without integrity, it brings about conditional patience when we are getting what we want. And, when we do not get what we desire, we become a hellion on wheels.

- ☐ If we have KINDNESS without integrity, it causes us to assume masks of deception, becoming unkind to those we think we do not need.

- ☐ If we have GOODNESS without integrity, it is only a matter of time before someone triggers our sore spot.

- ☐ If we have GENTLENESS without integrity, we will pick and choose where it is exhibited based on our conditioning, biases, and traumas. As a result, we become abrasive to the people, places, and things we look down on or turn up our noses at.

- ☐ If we have SELF-CONTROL without integrity, it is only a façade of manipulation to get what we want. When people, places, and things are not in our favor, we lose our grip with uncontrollable actions, thoughts, and words.

Regardless of how we view our integrity, it bridges a significant gap in our communicative skills, making it vital in our wailing process as well. How so? It helps us with our motives before wailing amiss to God. Just so we are clear with the Fruits of the Spirit, even if we do not possess them right now, we can work on them one at a time until we master them. The key is to recognize their use of them and then perfect the practice of their use until we become a master. Why does it take all of this? Once again, we are known by our fruits. Of course, we are all a work-in-progress...so, if we fall short, repent, forgive, correct, and keep it moving in the Spirit of Excellence.

If we take a moment to focus on becoming an expert on the Fruits of the Spirit, we will find the Spirit of Wisdom will come knocking at our door, granting us a triple portion of God's Divine Favor on high. It will also heighten our Spiritual Instincts and Connection with a natural GPS written on the Tablet of the Heart, consisting of God's Divine Will and Ways.

Are the Fruits of the Spirit essential in the Eye of God? Yes. *"Now are ye light in the Lord: walk as children of light: For the fruit of the Spirit is in all goodness, righteousness, and truth; proving what is acceptable unto the Lord."* Ephesians 5:8-10. If one does not take anything from this book, please understand the Fruits of the Spirit are the essential ingredients in living a fulfilled lifestyle, *As It Pleases God*.

When I meet someone who proclaims to be righteous, I look for the Fruits of the Spirit. Why? The fruits will tell me everything I need to know about the individual. Please understand I do not use this to discriminate against anyone because I exhibit love and kindness to all; however, it does help me to weed out the wolves in sheep's clothing. In addition, the Fruits of the Spirit help me to protect myself and my Gifted Anointing and to self-correct, *As It Pleases God*.

In all due respect, regardless of who we are or why we are, the flesh creeps up on us when we are not on guard or when we least expect it. When we are doing wrong, we know it! When we are doing the right thing, we can feel it! For this reason, we must find a way to take justification of our wayward behaviors, thoughts, beliefs, and biases out of the equation, while focusing our attention on using the Fruits of the Spirit, *As It Pleases God*. Even if some of our fruits have spoiled, we still have hope. Repenting, fasting, forgiving, and praying can indeed prune our lives in a way that will begin to bear good fruit, especially if we desire to put our flesh under the subjection of the Holy Spirit.

According to the Heavenly of Heavens, if God is not in the center of whatever it is, it may not be of Him. According to scripture, *"See to it that no one takes you captive through hollow and deceptive philosophy, which depends on human tradition and the elemental spiritual forces of this world rather than on Christ."* Colossians 2:8. Now, if we feel ourselves getting caught up, leading us away from the Will of God, we have the power to change the trajectory.

CHAPTER 8

USEFUL EXPECTATIONS

In life, we must become useful in the things we do, say, and become. In the Eye of God, we cannot settle for mediocrity, period. Nor should we sit around twiddling our thumbs, waiting for others to do what we are not willing to do for ourselves. Above all, in our usefulness, God is expecting more from us, and we should also expect more from ourselves.

When we exhibit childlike humility in and out of the Spiritual Classroom and share the Good News with outright kindness, *As It Pleases God*, we have the upper hand on those who are too arrogant for their own good. Here is what God expects from us: "*Let your speech always be with grace, seasoned with salt, that you may know how you ought to answer each one.*" Colossians 4:6. And, "*Let no corrupt word proceed out of your mouth, but what is good for necessary edification, that it may impart grace to the hearers.*" Ephesians 4:29.

With all due respect, as I look around, I see many Bible Toters who are not willing to exhibit the Fruits of the Spirit. Then again, they may know nothing about them at all. To add insult to injury, they refuse to put their bodies under subjection in any way, shape, or form. They even treat others like junkyard dogs, speak negativity about everyone, and refuse to lend a helping hand to those in need. Plus, they use the Bible to manipulate others and pimp God out for their selfish benefit. Yet, they proclaim to be truly powerful, filled with the Holy Spirit that can shake Heaven and Earth, but behind closed doors, there is a different story.

Spiritually, I cannot speak against the power they possess; however, I can only wonder about the power they would truly possess if they would only repent, fast, humble themselves, *As It Pleases God*, exhibit the Fruits of the Spirit, and behave Christlike! Nonetheless, here is what I know: *"Assuredly, I say to you, unless you are converted and become as little children, you will by no means enter the Kingdom of Heaven. Therefore whoever humbles himself as this little child is the greatest in the Kingdom of Heaven. Whoever receives one little child like this in My name receives Me."* Matthew 18:3-5.

Breaking The Spirit of Coveting

Before we go any further, we must also understand what makes us ineffective. When we compare ourselves with others, it is one of the quickest ways to fall into the coveting status. Coveting others, coveting things, or when we covet period, we set ourselves up for demise from within the human psyche.

If we dare to tell the truth, the Spirit of Coveting torments our Mind, Body, and Soul, causing us to contemplate our secret waywardness. Or, it causes us to think we are better than others based on our material gain, status, or title. Unfortunately, this is a deep-rooted Spiritual matter that must be reckoned with immediately.

Why must we deal with the matters of the heart as Believers? It plagues the human psyche like cancer, without us realizing it is eating us alive.

Now, if one does not believe they are coveting, it is okay by me. I am only here to expose the truth or the seed of our mishaps. To break the Spirit of Coveting, *As It Pleases God*, we must own our truth, period. Nobody can do this for us due to our free will to choose. Listen, if we keep lying to ourselves while feeling the hidden sting of jealousy, envy, arrogance, and competitiveness, we create a disservice to ourselves and others.

Why must we deal with the Spirit of Coveting immediately? Competing with others for what does not belong to us will keep us on a mental and emotional rollercoaster, causing us to break down from within, spreading outwardly. It is amazing how coveting is linked with many negative characteristics plaguing us to this very day.

But there is hope for us all. According to the Heavenly of Heavens, we can uproot and eliminate the seed of coveting. How so? By owning our truth, repenting, fasting, praying, forgiving, canceling the negative and replacing it with scripture or positive affirmations, and willfully using the Fruits of the Spirit. Will this work for us? Absolutely.

Although it is a journey to undo the lies we feed ourselves, it is still doable. Yet, if we desire to become impactfully effective, *As It Pleases God*, utilizing this process can break this malicious Spirit faster than anything I have encountered.

If we are at war from within, we will not be able to understand the true elements of who we are or the power residing within us due to Spiritual Blindness, Deafness, or Muteness. Just so we are clear, it does not mean it is unavailable; it means we must clear the path. How do we go about doing so? It is in our wailing process or *Wailing Prayer*, but not limited to this process only. Remember that everyone's journey is different, making the Spiritual Requirements different as well. Some of us may have more work to do and some less, depending upon our level of waywardness, conditioning, resistance, or trauma.

Understanding a Wailing Prayer

A Wailing Prayer is a deeply emotional and heartfelt cry out to God, our Heavenly Father. This type of bellowing of prayer is when an individual expresses intense grief, pain, or desperation to Him, seeking comfort, understanding, and help in a time of great need. In addition, it is often characterized by a sense of urgency and authentic emotions, expressing our innermost thoughts and grievances while releasing pent-up feelings. To be clear, a Wailing Prayer is not a griping session. It is to be viewed as an act of faith with a profound belief that God is listening and will respond to our heartfelt cries, *Spirit to Spirit*.

Even in our darkest moments, we must understand that we are never alone. What if we are not alone, but feel alone in our struggles? We can usher in the Presence of the Holy Spirit or connect to God, *Spirit to Spirit*, through worshipping Him, removing the cloud of loneliness, giving us the courage and determination to move forward in the Spirit of Excellence. What if it is not working? We must begin to change how we think, reversing all negative words, thoughts, beliefs, and ideologies into positives, using positive affirmations, and creating a win-win, regardless of how it appears to the naked eye.

Becoming Spiritually Deep

Developing a DEEP Spiritual Life requires an authentic and willing desire to grow closer to God, *As It Pleases Him*. If we desire to please ourselves, we will remain on the surface level of Spirituality. Why must we remain on the surface? First, it is for our safety. Secondly, we cannot handle Divine Power, especially when we are Spiritually Blind, Deaf, and Mute, not realizing we are in such a state.

For the record, remaining on the surface level of Spirituality does not mean that it is a bad thing; it only means that we can only handle Spiritual Milk, and not Spiritual Meat. According to the Heavenly of Heavens, we must become Spiritually Trained and Tested to handle the Deep Elements of Spirituality, *As It Pleases Him*.

If one is not well-versed in Spiritual Laws and Principles, they may miss the mark with their prayer due to the lack of knowledge or understanding. As with everything in life, we must follow specific rules and regulations. When calling out to God, we must ensure we come with clean hands and a pure heart, or it may unawaringly affect us or leave an open door for the enemy to sift us.

When we have a problem, we often run to someone else for answers or to obtain their opinion. Not realizing we have become oblivious to the fact that we have the power to run to God in Prayer with a repented and fasted State of Mind.

For example, in Biblical times, any vessel of God would not hesitate to repent, fast, and pray. Look at David, a man after God's Own Heart; amid his sin with Bathsheba, he fasted and prayed for his child to live. Although the child did not live, after he realized

God's Divine Will was done, and it was not His Divine Will for the child to live, David got up and ate a meal, letting bygones be bygones. Spiritually, this is how we must take on issues; we must repent, fast, and pray, leaving the issue in God's hands and moving on, knowing all things work together for our good.

When pleading our case to God, we should present what He likes out of RESPECT. From my perspective, it is best to go to Him in total humility, with a repented, fasted, and prayed-up heart, as opposed to the gimme, gimme, gimme attitude. By far, this is one of my biggest secrets, and I keep repeating it over and over in this book because we must get it.

Clearly, I am not saying God will allow us to have our way when repenting, fasting, and praying, but He will definitely make sure our ways will not have us. Trust me, if we give God what He desires, He will give us what we need or desire according to His Divine Will and Ways.

Wailing Prayers To The Deep Reloaded is what brings about a Spiritual Power and Alertness we cannot or will not receive otherwise. Of course, this very well may not be what we want to do. Still, to reap the Heavenly Benefits of our Birthrights, *As It Pleases God*, we must faithfully surrender our bodies as a living sacrifice, HOLY and ACCEPTABLE unto Him.

Expectations of the Holy Spirit

As long as we have breath in our bodies, we will always have a ray of hope left, sparking a greater hope from within, based on this one scripture: *"Faith is the substance of things hoped for, the evidence of things not seen."* Hebrews 11:1.

The filling of the Holy Spirit and the Fruits of the Spirit are what we need to bridge the gap between what we do not have and where we fall short. Most of us want to be guided by the Holy Spirit, but we do not know how to do so. Therefore, I am going to make it really simple with this checklist, but not limited to such:

- ☐ Become ONE with the Holy Trinity. Doing so helps us establish *Spirit to Spirit* Unity for our Heaven on Earth Experience.

- [ ] Cover ourselves and the doorpost of our homes with the Blood of Jesus as Spiritual Atonement. Even if we think that we do not need it, we do! Plus, we should not take this lightly because the Realm of the Unseen can be plotting against us, positively or negatively.

- [ ] Become AWARE or AWAKENED to the situation, circumstance, issue, or event by asking ourselves, 'What is the problem, issue, or trauma?' This question is the acknowledgment or the admission phase we must come to terms with. Without it, there is no solution, resulting in buried whatever, unlearned lessons, and unresolved brokenness.

- [ ] Repent of all known or unknown sins by assuming responsibility for our role, regardless of how significant or insignificant it is. Apologizing to God, ourselves, and others can make a big difference in our lives, putting the icing on our People Skills.

- [ ] Choose the type or level of fasting needed based on the situation at hand. The details of the types of fasting are included in '*The Fasting Chambers Reloaded*,' Chapter 9.

- [ ] Get into our Prayer Closet, quiet corner, or space for *Spirit to Spirit* Relations. When having a meeting place with God, He will open up more to us when we find the time to Spiritually Connect to Him. Thus, it grants us the peace, clarity, understanding, and guidance that the psyche needs or seeks. By doing so, it helps to establish reverence and obedience in the Eye of God.

- [ ] Give Thanks. Gratefulness is one of the most beneficial Spiritual Bonding Commodities known to mankind and the Realm of the Spirit. The lack of it divides them both. So, do not operate without it!

- ☐ Ask for the presence of the Holy Spirit. Doing so turns on our Spiritual Discerning Faculties, helping us to understand the promptings of the Holy Spirit. Plus, it allows us to download Divine Information, *Spirit to Spirit*.

- ☐ Ask the Holy Spirit to speak. It allows us to become open and receptive to the promptings, utterances, and guidance of the Holy Spirit while acknowledging our belief (faith) in His Divine Presence. For Spiritual Elites, we call this Spiritual Readiness.

- ☐ Tell the Holy Spirit that His Voice is desired as the DEEP CALLETH UNTO THE DEEP.

- ☐ Repeat selected psalms or songs. Worshipping in the Spirit can help us rid ourselves of negative debris and distractions.

- ☐ Listen to what the Spirit speaks to our hearts. The Holy Spirit pays close attention to our attentiveness and alignment of worldliness or Spirituality.

- ☐ Document in our Spiritual Journal. If we do not document the instructions or information, we may forget it, even if we have a good memory. The Holy Spirit will give us more if we become good stewards of the little.

- ☐ Seal our *Spirit to Spirit* Relations with an AMEN as a formal agreement. Without this agreement, we can leave ourselves open to the wiles of the enemy.

Is it this simple? Yes, it is simple once we get accustomed to this process! But, at first, we may need to use this checklist. As a word of caution, if one is not ready for the leading of the Holy Spirit, *Spirit to Spirit*, then one must leave it alone. He will convict, evict, and shut down our waywardness because He is not someone with whom we should play around in any way, shape, or form. Is any of this scriptural? I would have it no other way.

- ☐ "But you, when you pray, go into your room, and when you have shut your door, pray to your Father who is in the secret place; and your Father who sees in secret will reward you openly." Matthew 6:6.

- ☐ "Be filled with the Spirit; speaking to yourselves in psalms and hymns and spiritual songs, singing and making melody in your heart to the Lord; giving thanks always for all things unto God and the Father in the name of our Lord Jesus Christ; submitting yourselves one to another in the fear of God." Ephesians 5:18-21.

Once we step up our Spiritual Game with this wailing process of approach, God will guide and protect us. Plus, He will not suffer our foot to be moved, especially if we are humbly obedient, *As It Pleases Him*. Spiritually Speaking, God does not play when it comes down to protecting those who exhibit the Fruits of the Spirit. Nor does He play around with His anointed ones who are 'Spiritually Marked' for a specific purpose. According to scripture, here is the Spiritual Seal on this matter: *"If a son shall ask bread of any of you that is a father, will he give him a stone? If he asks a fish, will he for a fish give him a serpent? If he shall ask for an egg, will he offer him a scorpion? If ye then, being evil, know how to give good gifts unto your children: how much more shall your Heavenly Father give the Holy Spirit to them that ask him?"* Luke 11:11-13. God will provide for those who diligently seek Him.

There are times when trusting God is challenging, especially when dealing with the elements of the great unknown, when storms are raging in our lives, or when we are in a famine. Still, we cannot leave room for doubt, especially if we have not sought out the bigger picture, looked for the positive, or created a win-win.

Of course, I do not expect one to become a pro at removing doubt overnight. With a bit of work with the Fasting Chambers, a few blessings under our belts, a little favor in our repertoires, and a few miracles, the removal of doubt will be on autopilot as we become well-versed in how God operates, *As It Pleases Him*.

CHAPTER 9

THE FASTING CHAMBERS

Wailing Prayers To The Deep Reloaded is designed to bring us into the truth of our reality today, empowering us with the rational Spiritual Tools that have somehow become buried by the issues of life. Meanwhile, the Fasting Chambers are designed to cleanse our Mind, Body, Soul, and Spirit, preventing us from becoming clogged or contaminated with all types of known and unknown toxins.

As a formal disclaimer: I am not a medical doctor, nor do I proclaim to be. If one has a health issue, please consult a Licensed Doctor before embarking upon any food-restricted fast. This book is not designed to diagnose any health conditions; it is only used to bring about awareness of the Power of Fasting from a Spiritual Perspective and its benefits.

The Bible speaks about fasting frequently, yet we overlook it constantly. Why is it overlooked? Fasting hurts; no one likes giving up what they like or what brings them comfort! We always want the easy way out, not realizing we contribute to our own hurt or detriment. In all due respect, it is hard to see how we are doing so when our reality blinds us.

For example, we often cringe when speaking of the devil or use him as a crutch to avoid assuming responsibility. But if we dare to take a moment to spell devil backward, it reads the word lived! From my perspective, it is indeed the past tense of living. When we live in the past, it is the one thing that provokes the devil or evil inside us like no other, leaving all types of doors of deception open.

We cannot deny that evil lurks within the depths of our souls. Why must we deal with this as Believers? We are Spiritual Beings having a human experience, knowing the difference between good and evil. Now, if we constantly live in the past, it becomes the WRITING ON THE WALL for the evil to override the good inside us. At the same time, it gives us an excuse to crucify or point the finger at others for our unresolved or hidden issues from the past. In my opinion, this is the very reason why we need to exhibit self-control, repent, fast, and pray. If we do not, we will become a victim of the atrocities buried within the depths of our soul, overriding the good it should bring forth.

Fasting has a way of healing the inner trauma of our past, bringing forth peace from within. Contrary to what most would think, inner tranquility is not something we should take for granted. Here is why, according to Ephesians 6:12: *"We wrestle not against flesh and blood but principalities and wickedness and rulers in high places."* Fasting needs to become a lifestyle, and our lifestyle needs to consist of fasting. If we have not noticed by now, we must pray to continue to build our faith in God. For our prayers to become POWERFUL and EFFECTIVE, we must understand what it takes.

Selfless sacrifice has a way of enhancing the wailing process. I am not saying our prayers alone will not get us what we desire. All I am saying is our prayers alone will not be as powerful and effective as possible without a combination of fasting, forgiving, and repenting.

Regarding the *Wailing Prayers To The Deep Reloaded*, when we opt for Spiritual Nourishment over the physical, it brings forth the inner-bred humility needed to woo God. Can we possibly woo God? Absolutely. First, developing a genuine *Spirit to Spirit* Relationship with Him is a great way to get our Spiritual Woo on. Secondly, using lovable humility with the Fruits of the Spirit and behaving Christlike creates a double woo. Thirdly, approaching all things *As It Pleases Him* with the Holy Trinity at the forefront gets the triple woo. Fourthly, using our Gifts, Calling, Talents, and Creativity according to our Predestined Blueprint invokes the quadruple woo. Wooing God like this gives us a Spiritual Unction, breaking our selfishness to the core. More importantly, it also gives us Spiritual Access to Divine Wisdom, Understanding, Secrets, and Treasures of the Kingdom.

As a child of the Most High God, we cannot expect a one-night stand with a fast or with God, expecting results for a lifetime! Unfortunately, it does not work in this manner! Fasting is a part of our Spiritual Relationship with our bodies, bringing us closer to God for many different reasons.

Can we obtain things without fasting? Yes, we can have some things, but we will not get the full benefits as we would if we had an ongoing, interactive *Spirit to Spirit* Relationship with God. In my opinion, having partial benefits will not provide the substance we need in a time of Spiritual Warfare. I would rather have the benefits and not need them than need the benefits and not have them!

When Not To Fast

Fasting is good, but it can become detrimental if we use it to control, manipulate, and deceive others. Here are a few ways fasting will work against us:

- ☐ When we fast to hurt someone. Spiritually, this is a quick way to get hurt or create a generational curse. To fast unjustly to cause harm is very wicked, and one must repent of this sort of wayward behavior.

- ☐ When we fast to force God's hand on a matter, without allowing His will to be done.

- ☐ When we fast out of selfishness. Selfish gain has a way of cursing our hand instead of BLESSING it.

- ☐ When we fast to show off. Using God as a pawning tool will cause us to bring shame to our name quicker than just not fasting at all. Trust me, God knows the intent of the heart; if we think we can fool Him, we are only fooling ourselves instead.

When We Fast

Fasting is our business! We are not supposed to broadcast our fasting to the World. As scripture would have it, *"When we fast, do not look gloomy like the hypocrites, for they disfigure their faces that their fasting may be seen by others. Truly, I say to you; they have received their reward. But when you fast, anoint your head and wash your face, that your fasting may not be seen by others but by your Father who is in secret. And your Father who sees in secret will reward you."* Matthew 6:16-18. We cannot get any clearer than this, right? Keep it simple; there is no need to boast about what we are doing, especially when our faith should consider it already done.

Here is another **secret**: it is important not to tell others when we are fasting to ensure our fasting is not contaminated by their spoken or unspoken thoughts, prayers, words, or behaviors. Always remember, Satan walks to and fro seeking whom he shall devour; therefore, we do not know who he is trying to use to sift us, distract us, or prevent us from fasting as we should. Fasting is our power tool; if we give it away or do not maximize it, we cannot blame anyone but ourselves.

As one gains a grip on fasting, remember there are many different forms. Find one or a few that work to keep the Spiritual Toxins at bay. What can repenting, praying, and fasting do for us?

- ☐ Repenting, fasting, and praying will help us get into an Egypt or a Spiritual Fold to save, nurture, train, or protect us.

- ☐ Repenting, fasting, and praying will help deliver us out of any Egypt, bondage, or soul tie we have in our lives.

- ☐ Repenting, fasting, and praying will help us through our Desert Experiences, equipping us with the essential tools needed to grab hold of the Promise.

- ☐ Repenting, fasting, and praying help us to overcome the Slave or Negative Mentality.

- ☐ Repenting, fasting, and praying will help us create a win-win or reverse negative situations into favorable ones.

- ☐ Repenting, fasting, and praying help us to develop a Positive Mental Attitude.

- ☐ Repenting, fasting, and praying help us to gain the courage and know-how to overcome, create, and pursue.

- ☐ Repenting, fasting, and praying help us to unveil our hidden Gifts, Talents, Calling, Purpose, or the HOW-TO.

- ☐ Repenting, fasting, and praying can cause our enemies to create footstools for us.

- ☐ Repenting, fasting, and praying can remove the debris covering our instinctual nature.

- ☐ Repenting, fasting, and praying help to bring oneness and peace to our weary hearts.

- ☐ Repenting, fasting, and praying bridge the gap between God, ourselves, and others.

In Deuteronomy 9, Moses fasted before receiving the Ten Commandments. We are often taught we are not under the law because we are saved by grace. Now, this is partially true; however, it is also through the Spiritual Laws that save us by grace. But let me say this before I go any further, Moses fasted for this LAW! So, it does account for something, whether we realize it or not.

In so many words, being that Moses made a sacrifice of himself for 40 days and 40 nights for those GUIDELINES set forth by God, there is a hidden impact we are overlooking. Am I pulling for straws here? No, I am not. How many of us can fast for 40 hours, not even to speak of 40 days straight?

Regarding the *Wailing Prayers To The Deep Reloaded*, we will take this up a notch. If the truth is told, the Ten Commandments are also listed in the New Testament. Nevertheless, we must put this into proper perspective; if not, we will not possess what we need Spiritually to deal with the enemy's wiles.

To clarify, I am not here to discredit anyone's take on the Ten Commandments. We have free will to do or think whatever we like, but we cannot expect the Treasures of Heaven without following the Spiritual Rules of the Kingdom. More importantly, we should never develop the nerve to fall on grace without breaking a sweat to FAST on our own, choosing to wallow in our folly to our detriment! We have to do better than this! We cannot put ourselves in a box regarding repenting, fasting, and prayer. Here are a few reasons, but not limited to such:

- ☐ It is vital to use it for our Spiritual Growth.
- ☐ It is vital to use it when we have messed up.
- ☐ It is vital to use it before making any major decisions.
- ☐ It is vital to use it when we encounter negative situations.
- ☐ It is vital to use it when we have been shifted to the core.
- ☐ It is vital to use it when we are sick.
- ☐ It is vital to use it when dealing with difficult people.
- ☐ It is vital to use it when fine-tuning our approaches.
- ☐ It is vital to use it when we are interceding.
- ☐ It is vital to use it when we are clueless.
- ☐ It is vital to use it when we are Spiritually tested.
- ☐ It is vital to use it when suffering from challenges.
- ☐ It is vital to use it when being chastened.
- ☐ It is vital to use it when seeking Spiritual Instructions.
- ☐ It is vital to use it when needing Divine Intervention.
- ☐ It is vital to use it when feeling tempted or lured.
- ☐ It is vital to use it to become better as opposed to bitter.

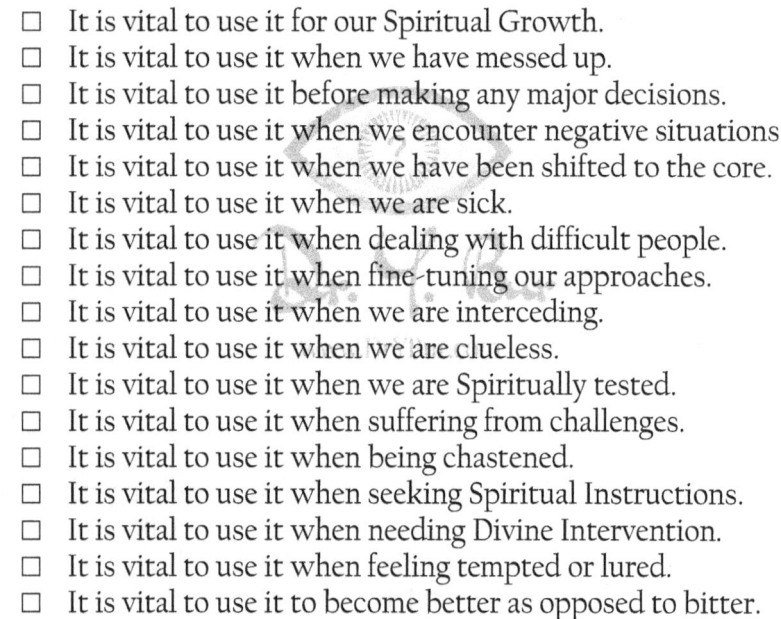

Our relationship with God is suffering, and our People Skills are declining. The hardcore judging law is of no effect, but the soft-core Spiritual Law is in FULL EFFECT regardless of whether we use grace as a platform or an excuse. This is blasphemy, right? Wrong again.

Let us take it to scripture in two parts. First, Jesus shared how to relate to God in Matthew 22:34-40, *"But when the Pharisees had heard that he had put the Sadducees to silence, they were gathered* together. Then one of them, a lawyer, asked Him a question, testing Him, and saying, 'Teacher, which is the great commandment in the law?' Jesus said to him, 'You shall love the Lord your God with all your heart, with all your soul, with all your mind.' This is the first and great commandment. And the second is like it: 'You shall love your neighbor as yourself.' On these two commandments hang all the Law of the Prophets."

The second part is when Jesus responded to the Young Rich Ruler in Mark 10:17-19 regarding his People Skills, "Now as He was going out on the road, one came running, knelt before Him, and asked Him, 'Good Teacher, what shall I do that I may inherit Eternal Life?' So, Jesus said to him, 'Why do you call Me good?' No one is good but One, that is, God. You know the commandments: 'Do not commit adultery,' 'Do not steal,' 'Do not bear false witness,' 'Do not defraud,' 'Honor your father and your mother.' "

According to scripture, he had not fallen short in this area. But, if we dig a little deeper, Mark 10:20-22, it says, "And he answered and said to Him, 'Teacher, all these things I have kept from my youth.' Then Jesus, looking at him, loved him, and said to him, 'One thing you lack: Go your way, sell whatever you have and give to the poor, and you will have treasures in heaven; and come, take up the cross, and follow Me.' But he was sad at this word, and went away sorrowful, for he had great possessions."

So, what was this man's problem? There were two issues here with the Young Rich Ruler. **First Issue**: He was bound by materialism and pompousness. He was unwilling to let go of his image to obtain the glory of wealth from the inside out. How do we get arrogance out of this story? It is wrapped in two words: sad and sorrowful.

In all reality, we cannot become sad or sorrowful unless our expectations are unmet or we have set false expectations. In all simplicity, our motives were not authentic, resulting in a crushed ego. Unfortunately, this is similar to what happens to us when we are praying amiss to God.

Second Issue: He was bound by coveting, which clouded his ability to make the necessary sacrifice, to share with people in need, and to follow out of obedience. Frankly, his identity was wrapped in his possessions, and not *Eternal Life*. Being that he was rich, he assumed he could buy what Jesus possessed or buy his way into the Kingdom. Whereas, when it comes down to the Realm of the Spirit, there are certain things money cannot buy, and *Eternal Life* is one of them. We must put in the work, perfecting our People Skills, period.

Regardless of whether we follow the Commandments or not, there are certain things we would not have to FAST about, especially if we would just heed the Commandments God gave Moses. Am I a little insensitive? Maybe or maybe not, but we know right from wrong, and if we continue in our folly just because we are saved by grace, it is an atrocity for ourselves and the victims of our waywardness. For this reason, we must FAST continuously to drive out the temptation of the flesh.

If something was not right in Moses' sight, he was quick to fast for up to 40 days, according to Deuteronomy 9:9,18 and Exodus 34:28. In my opinion, He was considered a professional faster. He even fasted on behalf of the Children of Israel because of their impatience, their lack of faith, their constant complaining, and their slave mentality. Why would he need to fast for them? Their mind was stuck in the past, reminiscing on having fish, cucumbers, melons, leeks, and onions from Egypt (the place of bondage).

If Moses fasted on behalf of someone else regarding issues disrupting the God-Given Mission set forth, so can we. If we have a situation we cannot seem to leave behind, it is driving us insane, or it is hindering our progress, the first thing we need to do before we complain is to declare a Spiritual Fast!

What are the Spiritual Benefits of fasting? Matthew 17:21 says, *"Some things only come out through fasting and praying."* There are times when we cannot get our breakthrough without putting our flesh under the subjection of the Holy Spirit. Why do we need to place our flesh under subjection? For the Spiritual Purification process.

The sacrificial need to allow our flesh to hunger, thirst, or desire will bring forth Spiritual Discipline. Why is discipline so important? Our outer discipline determines or sets the stage for our inner discipline. For example, if someone proclaims to be a Spiritual Elite, I consider their discipline from the outside in. I pay attention to their method of operation as it relates to immaterial things, such as:

- ☐ Their level of respect for God, themselves, and others.
- ☐ Their level of proactiveness, filling a need beforehand.

- ☐ Their level of follow-through or follow-up.
- ☐ Their level of helpfulness.
- ☐ Their level of selflessness.
- ☐ How they manage their time.
- ☐ How they manage their emotions.
- ☐ How well they follow instructions.
- ☐ How well they deal with a crisis.
- ☐ How they exhibit self-control under pressure.
- ☐ How they respond to whom they do not need.
- ☐ How well they resolve conflict.
- ☐ How well they reverse negatives into positives.
- ☐ How committed they are to their spoken words.
- ☐ How dedicated they are to their God-Given Mission in life.

In the Realm of the Spirit, in or out of our fasting state, our People Skills set precedence over many mind-controlling innuendoes.

The most common innuendo I have heard that we can all relate to is, 'Cleanliness is next to Godliness.' Well, from my perspective, first and foremost, it is not Biblical. Secondly, it is a form of manipulation, dividing us based on appearance. And thirdly, cleanliness or purification scriptures in the Bible refer to cleansing the inside of ourselves via the Mind, Body, and Soul.

Why is inner cleansing so important? From experience, I have met the most organized people, who are nasty and outright evil, squashing anyone who appears beneath them. Yet, they were haunted by their hidden inner demons while calling me for help as their life continued to spiral downward into the abyss. And, until they changed their perception of life and toward people in general, they could not break the yoke. Why am I telling this story? If we clean the outside, forgetting about cleansing the soul, we can become easily defiled, Mentally, Physically, Emotionally, and Spiritually. And, in due time, the joke will be on us.

Just so we are clear, cleanliness is essential for proper hygiene, but when we incorporate God into the equation, we must target the heart first. Why the heart first? Because God will send His Chosen Vessel into some dirty, stinky places to pull out His sheep. If we get into the mindset of turning up our noses at something or someone without lending a helping hand. Then, we have a sincere issue from within in need of reckoning.

What is the big deal? God may require us to get our hands dirty, *As It Pleases Him*. If we are afraid of a bit of dirt, we are not fit for the Kingdom. How is this possible? If we cannot deal with dirt, it is a possibility that we cannot deal with ourselves due to some form of known or unknown identity crisis.

The moment we forget who we are or how we got here, this is the moment the digression process starts to bring us back home to the dirt from the inside out. Really? Yes, really...let us take it to scripture, *"By the sweat of your face you shall eat bread, till you return to the ground, for out of it you were taken; for you are dust, and to dust you shall return."* Genesis 1:27. So, we should never become ungrateful regarding our point of origin or the way God is using the lives of others to accomplish His purpose, especially if we are not doing our part.

Here me and hear me well, God will never place our treasures in plain sight. For example, diamonds are hidden in the dirt, and gold must be purified. Why? If we want it, we have to put in the work to get it, period.

When we allow God to become our Bread of Life for a particular need, want, desire, or stronghold, our hidden weaknesses become apparent strengths due to our willingness to place whatever it is under the subjection of the Holy Spirit. The Bible states clearly, *"For when we are weak, then we become strong,"* according to 2 Corinthians 12:10. When we awaken the Holy Spirit through repentance, fasting, and praying, it will rout anything we are going through.

Just keep in mind that fasting alone will not do it! Repenting, fasting, praying, forgiving, and invoking the Holy Spirit are the vital ingredients of a truly healthy lifestyle to keep the Mind, Body, Soul, and Spirit in top condition. Once again, there are many different types of fasts, but it is our responsibility to pray for the type of fast needed while considering our medical conditions, which may require a modified fast.

Often, we confuse ordinary dietary fasting with Biblical fasting when they are indeed two different entities. Fasting to lose weight and fasting for Spiritual purposes are like apples and oranges!

When we confuse the two, we deceive ourselves and lose the Spiritual Benefits of what a Biblical fast can offer.

Regarding the *Wailing Prayers To The Deep Reloaded*, we should not fear fasting. Why should we not fear being deprived? God has created our bodies in a certain way that complements fasting. On the other hand, if we do not fast, we can cause the body to work against itself. For example, when animals get sick, they will instinctually stop eating. Even though they have never been taught about fasting, they will do it to heal their bodies naturally.

Is it hard to subject our bodies to a fast? The first time, maybe, but the results are well worth it! Do we have to be religious to fast? Absolutely not! Fasting for God does not require religion but a relationship with Him. If we are willing to repent, pray, forgive, and expect in conjunction with a fast, then He has something to work with.

We have all types of information at our fingertips about fasting, yet we couldn't care less about it. We do not want to experience the hunger pains that come with fasting. Anything painful or challenging...we tend to avoid it. What is the reason for this? Food and the pleasures of life have become our pride and joy, not realizing that it is killing us from the inside out. Am I pulling for straws again? Absolutely not.

Let us take it to scripture, *"Cry aloud, spare not; lift up your voice like a trumpet; tell My people their transgression, and the house of Jacob their sins. Yet they seek Me daily, and delight to know My ways, as a nation that did righteousness, and did not forsake the ordinance of their God. They ask of Me the ordinances of justice; they take delight in approaching God. Why have we fasted, they say, and You have not seen? Why have we afflicted our souls, and You take no notice? In fact, in the day of your fast you find pleasure, and exploit all your laborers. Indeed you fast for strife and debate, and to strike with the fist of wickedness. You will not fast as you do this day, to make your voice heard on high. Is it a fast that I have chosen, a day for a man to afflict his soul? Is it to bow down his head like a bulrush, and to spread out sackcloth and ashes? Would you call this a fast, and an acceptable day to the Lord? Is this not the fast that I have chosen: to loose the bonds of wickedness, to undo the heavy burdens, to let the oppressed go free, and that you break every yoke? Is it not to share your bread with the hungry, and that you bring to your house the poor* who are cast out; when you see the naked, that you cover him, and not hide yourself from your own flesh? Then your light shall break forth like the morning, your healing shall spring forth speedily, and your righteousness shall go before you; the glory of the Lord shall be your rear guard. Then you shall call, and the Lord will answer; you shall cry, and He will say, 'Here I am.' If you take away the yoke from your midst, the pointing of the finger, and speaking wickedness, if you extend your soul to the hungry and satisfy the afflicted soul, then your light shall dawn in the darkness, and your darkness shall be as the noonday. The Lord will guide you continually, and satisfy your soul in drought, and strengthen your bones; you shall be like a watered garden, and like a spring of water, whose waters do not fail. Those from among you shall build the old waste places; you shall raise up the foundations of many generations; and you shall be called the Repairer of the Breach, the Restorer of Streets to Dwell In. If you turn away your foot from the Sabbath, from doing your pleasure on My holy day, and call the Sabbath a delight, the holy day of the Lord honorable, and shall honor Him, not doing your own ways, nor finding your own pleasure, nor speaking your own words, then you shall delight yourself in the Lord; and I will cause you to ride on the high hills of the earth, and feed you with the heritage of Jacob your father. The mouth of the Lord has spoken." Isaiah 58.

Denying our flesh is becoming more and more a thing of the past, and if we do not refocus, putting our fleshly desires into their proper perspectives, we will self-destruct. Even if we are battling with some sort of health issue, we should not make this an excuse for not fasting. There are so many abridged versions of fasting, appeasing God all the same, regardless of our condition.

In my opinion, it very well may be a possibility that we are sick due to the buildup of toxins in our bodies because we do not fast. However, other forms of fasting provide meaningful benefits; therefore, it is best to check with our Doctors regarding which food fast would best suit our health condition.

There have been many instances in the Bible where there was **FORCED FASTING** by means of famine or circumstance. Still, for this book, our primary focus will be on voluntary fasting, but not limited to such.

The Hidden Secrets of Jonah

Although the Book of Jonah is very short, it is packed full of awesome information that will revamp the way we think about life and our ability to fast. Fasting is not often spoken about in the Book of Jonah because we are so focused on Jonah's faith; however, my spin will take us in a direction that will revolutionize how we perceive Jonah from now on.

As we all know, Jonah ran from God because he did not want to save the people of Nineveh, whom he presumed to be heathens due to their idol worship. The people of Nineveh did not know anything about the true God. They only knew what they were taught by their Forefathers, which was to worship idols, as well as to war and conquer, capitalizing on their wickedness daily.

Nevertheless, due to their perplexed waywardness, Jonah decides to do the opposite of what God instructed him to do. So, he runs away from his God-Given Mission, boarding a ship headed to Tarshish.

Due to his disobedience by not following God's instructions to go to Nineveh, a big storm arose, tossing the ship to and fro. It is funny how God has a way of turning our lives and those of the people supporting our rebellious behaviors upside down. Then again, it is mind-boggling how He brings certain things to a complete halt until we align with His Divine Will and Ways of doing things.

Okay, let me take that back...it is not funny when it is happening to us, but it is definitely an eye-opener when it does happen. From my many experiences, God will shake Heaven and Earth to get us in place or align us with our God-Given Purpose to keep us on schedule as He did with Jonah.

Now, getting back to the story, the sailors felt like someone on the ship was to blame as the storm continued to rage out of control. As they panicked, fearing the ship being torn to smithereens, Jonah was on the ship SLEEP. Can one imagine sleeping on a ship when it is about to capsize?

Was Jonah sleeping out of depression, sleep out of fear, sleep out of neglect, sleep because he did not want to pray, or sleep because he did not want to deal with his acts of disobedience? This brings me to a scripture in Proverbs 20:13, *"Do not love sleep or you* will grow poor; stay awake, and you will have food to spare." Jonah, being able to sleep through this ordeal comfortably, is a prime example of how we can grow poor, Mentally, Physically, Emotionally, and Spiritually in a state of mediocrity, running from doing what we were called to do.

Jonah was a Man of God; if God told him to go to Nineveh, do we think for a minute, he did not know the storm was coming? Or do we think he did not know God would track him down? He knew! In my opinion, this is why he was sleeping! Regardless of the reason why he was sleeping in a storm as such, when he was confronted with praying for God's help, he refused to do so. Now, that was a dead giveaway regarding Jonah's motives and heart posture.

For the most part, as a Woman of Wisdom, it was totally disrespectful for Jonah to get innocent people involved in his mess. When a man is guilty, and their conscience is convicting them, it is definitely more comfortable to sleep on people, places, and things deserving our attention. For this reason, if we are wrong or disobedient regarding something or someone, we need to OWN IT! Trust that the truth always has a way of surfacing when we least expect it.

After the sailors had cast lots to their false gods to find out who was the cause of their dilemma, they realized it was Jonah running from God Almighty. This ordeal shook the sailors up more so than the storm itself; as a result, they tried to spare him, but there was no use; the storm kept raging. Eventually, Jonah was thrown overboard to save the lives of the innocent. But lo and behold, the God he was running from rescued him.

What did God really rescue him from? Did God rescue him from drowning? Did God rescue him from the predators of the sea? Or did God rescue Jonah from himself? Wait, wait, wait, let me ask this question: 'Did Jonah bring this upon himself?' 'Was this self-inflicted?' The true answer to these questions will forever remain between Jonah and God.

Now, as we pick up on the known details, God allowed him to be swallowed up in the belly of a fish for three days and three nights. Which, in my opinion, was a **FORCED FAST**. This experience was God's way of saving him from himself by giving him time to think about a few things and an opportunity to change his perception of people. Here are a few things we can glean from Jonah:

- ☐ It gave him time to realize he could not run away from God, nor could he run away from his God-Given PURPOSE.

- ☐ It gave him time to think about his acts of disobedience or his acts of sin, which made him no better than the next person.

- ☐ It gave him time to recognize his selfishness, and he was not operating in the Spirit of Love, nor was he exhibiting the Fruits of the Spirit.

- ☐ It allowed him to repent, ask for mercy, and pray.

- ☐ It gave him time to think about whether or not God was going to save him.

- ☐ It gave him time to think about how he was thrown overboard and abandoned, similar to the way he ran off, abandoning the people of Nineveh.

- ☐ It gave him a bird's eye view of how the people of Nineveh needed to be saved from their sins, similar to the way God was saving him from his.

- ☐ It gave him an understanding that we have all sinned and fallen short.

- ☐ It gave him an opportunity not to judge God's Divine Will and Ways of delivering His people from destruction.

- ☐ It gave him the opportunity to OWN his issues and not run from them.

- ☐ It gave him the ability to understand the power of God's grace and mercy.

- ☐ It gave him the opportunity to wake up to the reality of understanding we all deserve the Love of God.

As Jonah cried out in the belly of the fish, he renewed his relationship with God, and the fish spewed him out on dry land. He went to Nineveh to preach and proclaimed a fast to prevent their obliteration in forty days. As a result, they repented, wore sackcloth, fasted, and cried out to God.

According to scripture, God saved them; however, Jonah secretly wanted their demise. But, due to their ability to fast, repent, and turn from their wicked ways, God's grace and mercy fell upon them regardless of how Jonah felt.

It is amazing that when Jonah was in need of God's help, he repented, prayed, and did what God asked him to do after a three-day **FORCED FAST**. Then he turns around and gets upset about God not destroying Nineveh, when they went on a **VOLUNTARY FAST**. In my opinion, this was a double standard for Jonah! God forced him to fast for deliverance out of the belly of the fish. Whereas the people of Nineveh voluntarily fasted for their deliverance. Were they not entitled to the same grace and mercy extended to him? Absolutely, a fast is a fast as long as we repent and pray.

God is a just God, regardless of how we feel or how others feel about us. He rewards our sacrifices, whether in the belly of a fish, partaking in the idolatry of our Forefathers, or when battling for our faith. It does not matter where we are, where we are from, or what we have going on; our Heavenly Father is the same yesterday, today, and forever.

Now, to add insult to injury, Jonah had the nerve to get upset about a plant dying overnight, as opposed to the obliteration of human lives. The mindset of Jonah was irreversibly tainted beyond human comprehension. Jonah failed the PEOPLE TEST God sent him. After this, unfortunately, we do not hear anything else about Jonah.

The mind-germ of religion can indeed taint our relationship with our Heavenly Father and His prized creation, which is human life. Remember, *"We are created a little lower than Angels, and we are crowned with glory and honor."* Psalms 8:5.

According to the Heavenly of Heavens, we must always wish our enemies well, regardless of whether we feel they deserve God's grace and mercy. Spiritually Speaking, He loves everyone, regardless of our creed, deed, or need, and He will test the contents of our hearts through how we treat and relate to ourselves and others, especially when no one is looking.

So, stay with me as we go through the different details, levels, and chambers of fasting to ensure we can take our People Skills to the next level, *As It Pleases God*.

Details of Fasting

In today's time, we are not educated on how food dramatically impacts Spirituality. So, we become accustomed to putting anything in our bodies as long as it tastes good. But let me say this: Everything that tastes good is not suitable for our bodies. We are the Temples of God, and we must become ever so cognizant about what we consume daily and when fasting. Here is what we need to know about this process:

- ☐ When fasting, we must define our objective. The **WHY**. We need to know our perception of fasting, regardless of how significant or insignificant it may seem. Our perception of fasting has been the one thing that has held us back from doing so.

- ☐ We must know what we are petitioning before we embark upon the fast. The **WHAT**. If we are fasting for no reason, then why are we fasting? Are we fasting to lose weight, detox, or get into a pair of jeans? In my opinion, this keeps us from lying to ourselves. Plus, approaching God with lies is a big no-no.

- ☐ It is best to document our fasting in a journal, writing our petitions. By far, this will help us stay on track, understanding the rational results of our sacrifices. The **HOW**.

- ☐ We must know the moment to start and end the fast, setting a Spiritual Marker. The *WHEN*. It is not wise to aim for a target without setting the goal from beginning to end, creating a distinctive marker. Nevertheless, we will learn more about this later in this chapter.

- ☐ We must know the location or restrictions of the fast to eliminate any form of confusion, justification, or rationalizing. The *WHERE*.

Indulging from time to time is not what I am speaking about; I am referring to indulging all the time without any form of discipline whatsoever. Can we get away with treating our bodies like this? The answer is NO. How we treat our bodies will become evident sooner or later; therefore, we must find a way to undo some of the damage we may have already caused by fasting our way out.

Food bondage has wreaked havoc on our bodies, preventing us from taking responsibility for our behaviors. Why is food bondage plaguing Believers? Let us take it to scripture, *"Every kingdom divided against itself is brought to desolation, and a house divided against itself falleth."* Luke 11:17. In so many words, we become divided from our own house (the body) by what we are putting in it. When we become enslaved by food, it consumes our every thought. When this happens, we must find a way to break this sort of stronghold.

Although we are taught not to miss a meal, missing a meal to fast and pray will help us more than the meal itself. How is this possible? After the meal, we will hunger again; however, giving up a few meals could help us in ways we cannot imagine. Society has set us up to fail in our Spiritual Lives, and now it is left up to us to gain control over our bellies. When we get to the point where we choose man-made foods over God-made foods, we know we have a problem. A deep-rooted problem, of course!

Even though we may not be Jesus, fasting for forty days and forty nights. Still, if we cannot push the plate away for forty hours, our bodies are doomed!

I am not saying we should become perfect in fasting. All in all, we should become aware of the power encapsulated in the ability to do so. Even if we start slowly, eliminating one type of food, activity, or behavior at a time, it is a sacrifice, and it is better than nothing at all.

Cleaning up the dust and debris in our lives will help us find peace from within, and it will also help keep the baggage of life from getting too heavy for us. Furthermore, we must find a way to appreciate everything we have and everything around us, the good, the bad, the right, and the wrong. As we very well know, life is full of surprises, and there is no reason for us to settle for a life of mediocrity when our breakthroughs are knocking on our door through our ability to repent, fast, and pray.

The most common form of fasting is replacing a meal or several meals with prayer for a designated length of time. However, this is not the only form of fasting—there are indeed many different types of fasting. Here are a few:

- ☐ A liquid fast, which allows only water or juice.
- ☐ A fast consisting of only fruits and vegetables.
- ☐ Abstaining from eating meat only.
- ☐ Eating one meal a day.
- ☐ Sacrificing a meal a day.
- ☐ Sacrificing Television.
- ☐ Sacrificing extracurricular activities.
- ☐ Sacrificing sexual relations.
- ☐ Sacrificing any type of habit.
- ☐ Sacrificing social media.
- ☐ Sacrificing talking on the phone.
- ☐ Sacrificing eating out.

Fasting is to be used to receive the fullness, guidance, and power of the Holy Spirit. Once again, fasting is not to be used as a weapon to get money, houses, cars, or worldly possessions. These things may come from the result of a fast, but fasting primarily for material gain is considered a fast for the wrong reason. Once again, we must become ever so cognizant of the reason why we are fasting. Why? To ensure we do not focus on material gain as opposed to inner gain or our inner wealth.

Fasting has a lot of benefits. I will give the Biblical benefits first, and then I will give my opinionated benefits secondly.

Biblical Benefits

- ☐ Fasting enhances the power of our prayers or the wailing process.
- ☐ Fasting enhances the healing process, Mentally, Physically, Emotionally, and Spiritually.
- ☐ Fasting enhances our humility.
- ☐ Fasting enhances our Spiritual Gifts.
- ☐ Fasting enhances our ability to radiate the Fruits of the Spirit (Love, Joy, Peace, Patience, Kindness, Goodness, Faithfulness, Gentleness, and Self-Control).
- ☐ Fasting enhances our Spiritual Alertness.
- ☐ Fasting enhances our understanding of the things of the unknown.
- ☐ Fasting enhances our ability to ask for mercy or receive it.
- ☐ Fasting enhances our discipline.
- ☐ Fasting enhances our ability to plead our case with God to change His mind about something or someone.
- ☐ Fasting helps us to rout demons in Spiritual Warfare.
- ☐ Fasting helps us to overcome Spiritual Blindness, Deafness, or Muteness.
- ☐ Fasting helps us to place our worldly rudiments, fleshly ways, or naughty behaviors under the subjection of the Holy Spirit.
- ☐ Fasting helps to set Biblical Scriptures in motion.
- ☐ Fasting helps tame the ego.
- ☐ Fasting helps to enhance our People Skills.
- ☐ Fasting will cause the Angel of Death to PASS OVER our loved ones or us.
- ☐ Fasting helps us to consecrate our bodies.

My Opinionated Benefits

- ☐ Fasting helps us appreciate eating, period!
- ☐ Fasting helps us to curb our eating habits.
- ☐ Fasting helps us lose unwanted weight.

- ☐ Fasting cleanses our blood.
- ☐ Fasting gives us energy.
- ☐ Fasting gets rid of toxic waste in the body.
- ☐ Fasting helps us to gain a new outlook on life.

When fasting, here are a few things to avoid:

- ☐ Avoid having tempting foods around.
- ☐ Avoid social events as much as possible.
- ☐ Avoid fasting during major holidays.
- ☐ Avoid going out to dinner.
- ☐ Avoid group settings that involve food.
- ☐ Avoid discussing your fast with anyone except for your family.
- ☐ Avoid watching television. The food commercials are designed to entice you to eat or crave a particular food.
- ☐ Avoid stressful situations that provoke the desire to eat.

When to start a fast?

A fast is designed to teach discipline. Therefore, if we would like our fast to become effective, we must set a marker, which is a designated time to renew our fasting vows through prayer.

As it relates to the wailing process, fasting alone without prayer is basically going without something with no target or destination Spiritually. The fast we are dealing with in this book requires repentance and prayer.

The overall Spiritual Goal is to go without to bring forth or take down. To do so, we must learn the powerful secrets of fasting. Listed below are a few Spiritual Markers to allow us to realign ourselves with God:

The Sunset Marker: This is a fast from 6 a.m. to 6 a.m. or p.m., lasting in 12 or 24-hour increments. This fast can be renewed daily at 6 a.m. or p.m. with an option to vary the fast if needed. This is done for Spiritual Elevation, if we need more of something, such as favor, provision, etc. This viable option is designed to bring more of whatever we so desire **INTO** our lives.

The Noonday Marker: This is a fast from 12 p.m. to 12 a.m. or p.m. lasting in 12 or 24-hour increments. This fast is done to bring down something. If we need to rid ourselves of something or someone, it is best to choose this fast. This viable option is designed to remove whatever we so desire **OUT** of our lives.

The 7th Hour Marker: These **THREE FASTS** are from 6 a.m. to 12:59 p.m. to bring forth, 12:00 p.m. to 6:59 p.m. to take down or remove, or 6 p.m. to 12:59 p.m. to bring forth and remove. This fast only allows you to consume foods going into the 7th hour. What this means is that you would consume a meal at 1 p.m., 7 p.m., or 1:00 a.m. The 6 p.m. to 12:59 a.m. **7th Hour Marker** is the most popular. It is also said to be the easiest, because most people fall asleep at around 10-11 p.m.; therefore, they do not feel deprived while getting the same amount of benefits. Plus, they are not going to break their sleep to get up at 1:00 a.m. to eat. However, one must decide what works best and stick to it!

Why the 7th hour and not at 6:00 p.m.? I am basing this on the principle of the 7th Heaven. Is 7th Heaven Biblical? Of course, Heavenly Places are real, often referred to as the Kingdom of Heaven. However, let us take it to scripture anyway: *"And God called the firmaments Heaven. And there was evening and there was morning, the second day."* Genesis 1:8. Spiritually, this is a Realm of the Spirit for Him, *As It Pleases Him*, and being that we are trapped in time, we must RESPECT the Heavenly of Heavens. *"For by Him all things were created that are in heaven and that are on earth, visible and invisible, whether thrones or dominions or principalities or powers. All things were created through Him and for Him."* Colossians 1:16.

We are mere Vessels of Spirituality, regardless of our deed, creed, or breed. Contrary to what most would think, we are not of ourselves. So, if we desire to become divided from something or someone, or bring forth something or someone, in the holiest, purest, and happiest state of mind with extreme JOY, any one of the three Spiritual Markers will work. The ultimate bliss of having an unexplainable inner joy and peace is food for the soul. We do not need to make this complicated; the goal is to get closer to God, period!

Types of Fasting

So, as we move along, in addition to the Spiritual Marker, we must determine the type of fast needed. Listed below are **THREE** types of Food Fasts and **ONE** type of Behavioral Fast the Bible speaks about:

- ☐ **Absolute Fast.** This type of fast consists of no food or water. However, I would not suggest this fast due to all of the toxins in our food today. If one does partake of this fast, it should not be for more than three days.

- ☐ **Normal Fast.** This type of fast consists of water or juice.

- ☐ **Partial Fast.** This is a restricted food fast, which is called a Chamber Fast, which we will learn more about later in this chapter. In all due respect, I suggest that if one is partaking of a fast for more than seven days and is not well-versed in fasting, this is a viable option. My goal is to empower everyone to succeed. To do so, we must strategically plan in levels until our Spiritual Staminas are developed.

The Bible speaks about **ONE** Behavioral Fast:

- ☐ **Sexual Fast.** In Exodus 19:15, the Children of Israel were restrained from having sexual relations for three days to prepare for their encounter with the Lord at Mt. Sinai. However, before going on a sexual fast, one must discuss it with their husband or wife before doing so.

Choices of Fasting

Instead of waiting for a once-a-year Day of Fasting, create a once-a-week *Day of Fasting*, a *Monthly Fast*, or a *Chamber Fast*. Our soul is considered to be the lifeline. If we can sacrifice 24-25 hours, from sundown to sundown of the following day, to put our flesh under subjection, we would be amazed at the results we would have. As scripture would have it, *"The words of the Lord in the ears of the people in the Lord's house upon the fasting day: and also thou shalt read them in the ears of all Judah that come out of their cities."* Jeremiah 36:6.

Whatever we are going through or going to, our one-day fasting will help us in ways we could not imagine. It will also bring things to the light regarding what we may have consciously or subconsciously blocked out or suppressed. But more importantly, when we become true to ourselves, we are better able to deal with life and people, and we are better able to take the good with the bad and keep it moving in the Spirit of Excellence.

☐ WEEKLY ⸺FAST

This particular fast is where you stop eating one day a week at sundown on Friday at 6 p.m. On Saturday, you can only have juice, broth, smoothies, and water until 6 p.m., and back to normal from Sunday through Thursday. This fast gives your digestive system a break weekly. Why not 7 p.m., according to the 7th Hour Marker Fast? We can choose any of them, but the goal of this fast is more for the long-term, and the 7th Hour is primarily for short-term use to usher in or bring down something.

Above all, we can develop our own schedule, simply take it to God in prayer, *Spirit to Spirit*, seeking what is best for the situation at hand, *As It Pleases Him*. We do not need to overcomplicate this fast; it is between our Heavenly Father and us; therefore, allow the Spirit of the Lord to lead, according to our Predestined Blueprinted Mission.

☐ MONTHLY ⸺FAST

The Monthly Fast is the First Fruits fast. This fast is where we sacrifice the first three days of the month to Spiritually Atone the rest of the month, similar to Spiritually Anointing our homes with the Blood of Jesus, but this is for the body. When we give our system a break, we can only have juice, water, smoothies, or vegetable broth. Those with a medical condition must engage in an abridged version according to their doctor's advisory.

☐ CHAMBER FAST

The Chamber Fast is the 3, 7, 21, or 40-day absolute, normal, partial, or behavioral fast. However, the length of time is not set in stone. Seek God, *Spirit to Spirit*, regarding the length of time for the fast, *As It Pleases Him*.

The Chamber Of Fasting

There are many different chambers of fasting we do not understand; therefore, we give up after only a few hours of trying to fast. However, in this chapter, each chamber will be broken down accordingly.

What is a chamber? I consider a chamber to be a certain place or room of fasting. If we put our house (the body) on a cold-turkey fast, it may work against us; therefore, if we section the fast off into certain chambers, we can work our way up to the ultimate fast. Remember, each chamber of fasting is still a fast; therefore, God will reward our efforts until we become a pro at this.

Once we have graduated through the chambers, we cannot give God Chamber 1 when we are at Chamber 5. Or, if we are in Chamber 7 and we want to play in Chamber 1. It does not work like that...once we get through the chambers, it increases our Spirituality to the next level. God will not tolerate us begging Him for His DIVINE BLESSINGS, especially when we are half-stepping in our sacrifices!

When first embarking upon a fast for the first time, one must start slowly. If we have never fasted before, there is a lot of toxic sludge in the body that will make us very sick if we move too fast. To maximize the benefits of fasting, I suggest starting gradually, with each chamber lasting seven days. Please check with your doctor before beginning any sort of fast.

☐ CHAMBER 1

Removing caffeine first. Yes, this includes soda, coffee, tea, and chocolate. Why? Caffeine keeps our bodies stimulated. If we take out the stimulant in addition to food, we may not survive a fast. Therefore, we must take it very slow....removing a few things at a time to ensure our bodies can adjust to each chamber of the fast. We may experience headaches or dizziness due to the withdrawal of caffeine, but it will subside.

☐ CHAMBER 2

Remove all dairy products, including Chamber 1. We may experience a bad taste in our mouths. All we need to do is brush our teeth and move on.

☐ CHAMBER 3

Remove all forms of meat, including Chambers 1 and 2. It includes all fish, poultry, beef, pork, turkey, and eggs. Yes, I said eggs. Any animal products or anything from an animal must be eliminated in this chamber. However, we may have protein powdered supplements. Once we eliminate meat products, the body will start purifying itself.

☐ CHAMBER 4

Remove all bread, pasta, wheat, cookies, crackers, processed foods, and any inconspicuous gluten, including Chambers 1, 2, and 3.

☐ CHAMBER 5

Remove all sugar and starchy products, including Chambers 1, 2, 3, and 4. Sugary products include candy, gum, artificial sweeteners, etc. Starchy products include all types of rice, potatoes, yams, etc. At this point, we are limited to just fruits and non-starchy vegetables.

☐ CHAMBER 6

Remove all fruits, including Chambers 1, 2, 3, 4, and 5. Edible fruits must be eliminated at this point. At this stage of the fast, eat only vegetables and drink juice or water.

- ## CHAMBER 7
Remove all vegetables, including Chambers 1, 2, 3, 4, 5, and 6. Drink only juice or water.

How To Break A Fast

When we break our fast, we must regulate ourselves. We must limit the intake of food, taming the monster of gluttony unleashed when we start eating again. Why must we move slowly when breaking a fast? We do not want to overeat or get sick. Plus, the goal is to exercise discipline, so we must adjust our bodies to eating again.

The best way I would suggest is to reverse the chambers, adding food back into our diet in reverse order. For example, if we are in Chamber 7, when we break our fast, we must introduce Chamber 6 back in, then Chamber 5, Chamber 4, Chamber 3, etc. We do not need to introduce all the chambers back in. We have the option to exclude the ones we are comfortable leaving out.

Just so we are clear, regardless of which one we choose when fasting, here are a few things we may encounter at first:

- We may experience a headache.
- We may experience a little tiredness.
- We may experience feeling light-headed or dizzy at times.
- We may experience aches, cramps, or pains in our bodies.
- We may experience a body odor change.
- We may experience constipation.
- We may go to the bathroom a lot.
- We may experience bad breath.
- We may get a little disoriented.
- We may experience inner or outer chaos.
- We may experience lucid dreams.
- We may experience a desire to explore life outside of ourselves.

Nevertheless, we must not give up; these are all the signs of a fast working to purify our bodies of the toxins sitting around hanging out. If we persist, the side effects will go away after three days, but we will have to stay on top of the bad breath issue and drink lots of water. As a simple reminder, we need water to ensure we do not become dehydrated. Now, here are a few things we need to do when fasting:

- ☐ Limit distractions.
- ☐ Limit noise.
- ☐ Limit Television and Radio.
- ☐ Build a system around your fasting to keep you on track.
- ☐ Follow God's instructional or instinctual nudges.
- ☐ Take notes while praying, and be ready to take notes at any given moment when fasting.
- ☐ Engage in stimulating conversations only.
- ☐ Engage in things you enjoy doing.
- ☐ Do not debate over people, places, and things you cannot change.
- ☐ Keep everything simple and to the point.
- ☐ Create a No-Fight Zone. Focus on peace, love, and happiness.
- ☐ Keep a smile on your face even if you feel as if you have nothing to smile about...smile anyway.

In or out of our wailing process, the *Eternal Plan* of God is established; therefore, we must master creating a win-win situation out of everything.

We are a part of the Divine Plan, so the wailing process should not be prolonged. If we need to head into the Spiritual Classroom, do it. If we need to change our perceptions, do it.

We are on a Spiritual Mission to set the captives free through Spiritual Empowerment, opening doors that would not have opened otherwise. What doors? The door to the Divine Secrets of Spirituality, or the door to our Secret Place. It is basically the place we have set aside to have a one-on-one with God Himself, *Spirit to Spirit*.

CHAPTER 10

THE SECRET PLACE

The face-to-face encounter with God is not a natural phenomenon, as most would think or fabricate. According to scripture, *"No one has ever seen God, but the one and only Son, who is himself God and is in closest relationship with the Father, has made him known."* John 1:18. The truth is that God must take on human form or a vessel for us to see Him visually.

In the same way, He used Jesus as a Spiritual Vessel to save us; He uses us to save others as well, as a Jesus Prototype. Blasphemy, right? Wrong again. *"For you died, and your life is hidden with Christ in God."* Colossians 3:3. Now, my question is, 'Does this apply to you?' 'Does this apply to me?' Or, 'Does this apply to all who are Baptized in the Blood of Jesus?' *"For in Him we live and move and have our being, as also some of your own poets have said, 'For we are also His offspring.'"*

God is SPIRIT and will not violate Spiritual Laws to satiate our fancies; thus, we must come to Him for a one-on-one, or better yet, a *Spirit-to-Spirit* Divine Encounter. However, when wailing, know this: *"For in the time of trouble He shall hide me in His pavilion; In the secret place of His tabernacle He shall hide me; He shall set me high upon a rock."* Psalm 27:5.

To get to this Spiritual Rock, we must develop a Lord-Will-Provide Mindset. Why? If you were able to provide Spiritual Means for yourself, you would not need Him. What if we are complete without Him? Woe unto the lies we tell ourselves...unfortunately, this is how we 'get got' by the wiles of the enemy. But, do not take my word for it, let us take it to scripture: "*And you are complete in Him, who is the head of all principality and power.*" Colossians 2:10.

If we think for a minute, God is playing around with us, we need to think again! How do I know? I do not know, but the psyche surely does! Plus, if we are doing things without Him to strengthen ourselves, it means that we have not tapped into our Divine Completeness. In fact, here is what we must know: "*In Him we have redemption through His blood, the forgiveness of sins, according to the riches of His grace.*" Ephesians 1:7.

The Secret Place *Reloaded* is indeed our place of grace. So, it does not matter if we call this zone our *Secret Place, Meeting Place, or Prayer Closet;* God will deal with each of us individually, *Spirit to Spirit*. Why do we need a zone for Him? We are all unique with different wants, needs, desires, and traumas; therefore, we must come to Him, *Spirit to Spirit*, and *As It Pleases Him*, arranging the point of Spiritual Contact.

For example, when going to bed, we do not go to the kitchen to sleep. When cooking, we do not go to the bedroom to cook. When bathing, we do not go to the pantry to cleanse our bodies. More importantly, I cannot do this for anyone. Nor can anyone do it for us; it is a personalized experience, not a community one, regardless of what we are deceived into believing.

How will God speak to us personally? He speaks to us through live or current events, testimonial stories, illustrated examples in the Bible, matters of the heart, and so on. But more importantly, we cannot limit our teachable moments because God can use anything or anyone to get our attention. Plus, this is the reason for having a zone of reconciliation, giving us the time to focus, forgive, and forget. What will this do for us? It gives us time to listen from the inside out, not from the outside in, keeping the negative confusion or chatter at bay or refining it accordingly.

Divine Refinement

Godly refinement of the human soul is our Spiritual Grace to get whatever it is right. What does this mean for us? Wailing souls, empty stomachs, open humility, and owning our truth will open up our ear gates to God! How? Let us take it to scripture, "*You who are trying to be justified by the law have been alienated from Christ; you have fallen away from grace. For through the Spirit we eagerly await by faith the righteousness for which we hope.*" Galatians 5:4-5.

The true meaning of grace has become aloof to most; therefore, let me put my spin on grace for a minute. Our place of REFINEMENT cannot become confused with man's reasoning for grace. We often think grace gives us an excuse to commit willful, sinful acts and get away with it. From a Spiritual Perspective, this is not the case at all.

Here is the deal: We often confuse grace with mercy. Why would God say His grace is sufficient? Grace is used for the regrafting, refining, reseeding, fine-tuning, or enhancing of our Spiritual Relationship to combat our human weaknesses. How do I know? According to 2 Corinthians 12:9, "*And He said to me, 'My grace is sufficient for you, for My strength is made perfect in weakness.' Therefore most gladly I will rather boast in my infirmities, that the power of Christ may rest upon me.*"

Now, with mercy, it is a completed act, result, or pending decree based upon one's behaviors, attitude, character, conditioning, mindset, or Bloodline. According to *The Secret Place Reloaded*, we must combine both. Why do we need both as Believers? Actually, we need more than that, but for the sake of this chapter, we will use the two for now. God has MERCY on our souls so we can live in His GRACE of becoming better according to His Divine Purpose.

According to the Ancient of Days, we sit around, doing nothing about our hidden flaws or frailties, especially when we must become more Christlike to mentor those coming behind us. Why is this so important? Let us take it to scripture, "*But you are a chosen generation, a royal priesthood, a holy nation, His own special people, that you may proclaim the praises of Him who called you out of darkness into His marvelous light; who once were not a people but are now the people of God, who had not obtained mercy but now have obtained mercy.*" 1 Peter 2:9-10.

From my perspective, the grace God wants us to have is a positioning, stance, confidence, knowing, or poise, such as girding up our loins with a '*Whatever I lack, You will fix me*' attitude, transforming it into Divine Grace. Really? Yes, really? Whether we settle for regular or Divine is our choice.

God will always put us to the test; whether we ace or fail it, it does not deprive us of the hidden WISDOM. The grab-and-go wisdom can become Divine once we learn how to use it, *As It Pleases Him*. So, it is always best to approach Him with the 'Fix Me' attitude and work-in-progress mentality. Is this Biblical? *"The refining pot is for silver and the furnace for gold, but the Lord tests the heart."* Proverbs 17:3.

Why do we need to go through the refining process? It makes us better, stronger, and wiser. Here is what we must know: *"I counsel you to buy from Me gold refined in the fire, that you may be rich; and white garments, that you may be clothed, that the shame of your nakedness may not be revealed; and anoint your eyes with eye salve that you may see. As many as I love, I rebuke and chasten. Therefore be zealous and repent."* Revelations 3:18-19.

When a person is covered by the Grace of God or the Positioning of God, they will have a supernatural covering over them, with unshakeable confidence and heart posture, defying human understanding. But more importantly, they will also possess a level of humility, fooling the prideful. By far, this is a position one would never want to compromise. Why? A fall from grace, a fall from our position, or a fall from our calling will result in a blow to our esteem. What would cause such a fall? Disobedience, rebellion, idolatry, and the denial of the refinement process are often the culprits of the forfeiture of grace.

How is it possible to lose the grace of God? When one loses their covering, as Saul did in 1 Samuel of the Bible, they will become tormented by something or someone, publicly or privately. Here is a big **secret** Saul left behind for us to glean. He would not have lost his covering, or he would not have lost his grace with God if he had just repented, fasted, prayed, and obeyed the Voice of God.

Although we all make mistakes, God viewed this issue as a Spiritual Disconnect. How? Let us take this one to scripture: *"Rebuke is more effective for a wise man than a hundred blows on a fool. An evil man seeks only rebellion; therefore, a cruel messenger will be sent against him."* Proverbs 17:11-12. Unfortunately, this is what happens when we get out of control, doing our own thing, especially when holding a Crown of Grace.

As the issues of life are upon us, when it comes down to GRACE, fasting alone is not going to get it, praying alone is not going to get it, repenting alone is not going to get it, and obeying alone is not going to get it, we need to incorporate everything, and then get into our *Secret Place, Meeting Place, or Prayer Closet, 'Wailing To The Deep.'*

Why must we seek solace with God, *Spirit to Spirit*? First, the regrafting of the heart, *As It Pleases Him*, must become Christlike using the Fruits of the Spirit. Secondly, we can only become refined properly, *As It Pleases Him*, through the Holy Spirit as our Comforter and the Blood of Jesus as our Spiritual Atonement.

Why do we need a *Secret Place, Meeting Place, or Prayer Closet*? God takes our *Spirit to Spirit* Relationship seriously. If we cannot get into His face, *As It Pleases Him*. Then, we must ask ourselves, 'Whose face are we in to please ourselves, or whose approval are we seeking to satisfy our own desires?' This answer may frighten us, but the question must be asked and answered.

What is the purpose of querying ourselves as Believers on this matter? Idolatry is real, and if we create space for this...then creating a zone for God Almighty should never be an issue for anyone, anytime, or for any reason.

We cannot truly obey God if we cannot hear His voice, and we cannot hear His voice if we do not pray. Here is the catch: We cannot hear His voice clearly if we do not fast, repent, or forgive!

Our communication gets really fuzzy, or the inner chatter will take over if we are not repenting, fasting, forgiving, and praying, in conjunction with obeying the Voice of God via the Holy Spirit to safeguard the grace on our lives, regardless of whether it is regular or Divine.

Divine Grace

When Divine Grace is on a person whom God has refined, *As It Pleases Him*, they will light up the room. They can bring light to any situation, circumstance, event, or person. Although grace is taken for granted, without grace in our lives, it removes our covering, subjecting us to worldly reasonings or standards.

If we lose the Covering of God, we will fall prey to the wiles of the enemy by default, like the biblical character named Job. Now, we can look down on Job due to his condition or state of poverty. Nevertheless, he knew he was Blessed, he knew God's grace was on his life, he knew he was protected, he knew he was being tested, he knew he was being refined, and he knew God was going to restore him. How did he know? Because he was outright OBEDIENT, and his character was in ALIGNMENT with God, *As It Pleased Him.*

The only time Job wavered in his faith was when he started listening to the opinions of those who did not know or understand the value of God's Divine Grace, the value of God's Divine Covering, or the value of the Divine Positioning God had on his life.

Of course, we will all have a moment where we will waver in our faith when faced with the atrocities of being sucker-punched, when we are blindsided, or outright thrown under the bus. However, listening to the negativity of others will cause us to curse our hands while doubting God. If the people, places, and things in our lives are not contributing to the positive aspects of our gracefulness, then we need to rethink who we are hanging with or what we are becoming involved in.

If we need grace or refinement in an area where we have fallen short or have lost our covering, it is best to repent, fast, pray, and obey. It will work wonders. How do we get started? Spiritually, it is better to start with repenting and praying on an empty stomach, as opposed to ending our day repenting and praying on a full belly.

How often do we need to repent and pray? It is good to repent and pray in the morning, at noon, and in the evening. What makes this so ideal? By the end of the day, we are tired, and sometimes we fall asleep on God. Therefore, eating very lightly in the evening is always good to ensure it does not affect our prayers to the point where we fall asleep on the One who BLESSES us to wake up in the morning.

Why do we need to go through this process? It is a form of sacrifice. For example, if we want to love, we make a sacrifice by giving it. If we have an anger problem, we must sacrifice something not to become angry. If we have a problem arguing, make a sacrifice of not arguing. If the urge comes, we must go to our *Secret Place, Meeting Place, or Prayer Closet* to repent, pray, and put our flesh under the subjection of the Holy Spirit.

What is the *Secret Place, Meeting Place, or Prayer Closet*? According to the *Wailing Prayers To The Deep Reloaded*, it is a place designated just for communing with God, *Spirit to Spirit*. This zone is where the *Wailing Prayers To The Deep* takes place, where your prayers will become the most powerful. You will meet there for your daily instructions or strategies to build faith beyond human understanding. You will also meet there for your daily confessions, prayers, and meditation.

In this place, you represent the Arc of the Covenant, with the 10 commandments written on the tablet of your heart. Matthew 6:5-6 explains how we should keep our prayers in secret: *And when thou prayest, thou shalt not be as the hypocrites are: for they love to pray standing in the synagogues and in the corners of the streets, that they may be seen of men. Verily I say unto you; They have their reward. But thou, when thou prayest, enter into thy closet, and when thou hast shut thy door, pray to thy Father which is in secret; and thy Father, which seeth in secret, shall reward thee openly.*

For the most part, now is not the time to get your prayers caught up in the wrong hands, as every moment allows you the opportunity to manifest your Destiny! You are in control over the lessons you learn and the lessons you do not. If your day is not going the way you anticipate, change your expectations and go to your *Secret Place, Meeting Place, or Prayer Closet*. Remember, every day is a BLESSING in itself, and you create your own miracles by how you think, how you pray, and the PLACE where you pray. Of course, you can pray anywhere, as well as on the go, and I do encourage this; however, you must designate a specific place you call your very own *Secret Place, Meeting Place, or Prayer Closet*.

If you want to hear God speak, go to your *Secret Place, Meeting Place, or Prayer Closet* at the same time every day when fasting and say, "*Speak Lord, your servant is listening.*" In God weighing our hearts, ensure you are equipped with your Bible, notepad, and pen. While attentively listening, capture what is being said regardless of whether you understand it or not.

Why must we document? Once again, it ensures you do not forget what is being said; it may become relevant later. If your mind is all over the place, keep a note of where it is going.

How do we pinpoint the ideal place to meet with God, *Spirit to Spirit*? It should be where you can find peace of mind, resting in His stillness, *As It Pleases Him*. In this place, He will speak to you, renewing your mind, thoughts, perception, soulish nature, and Spiritual Connection, recharging you in ways the human mind cannot conceive. Does it really work? Absolutely. Frankly, this is how I got it, and I continue to get it, *As It Pleases God*!

On behalf of the Heavenly of Heavens, this is precisely how I am giving it to you. *Spirit to Spirit*, this is not a place of bargaining...one has to take it or leave it. Why is this such a non-negotiable spot? Spiritually, this is how God allowed me to perfect my Gifts, Calling, Creativity, and Talents. Meanwhile, the naysayers laughed, cracked jokes, called me names, sabotaged me, confused me, bullied me, abandoned me, and dragged me through the dirt, trying to detour me by any means possible.

But more importantly, I did not stop the refining process; I was determined to get through it to activate the Law of Reciprocity. And now, here we are due to God's Divine Grace and Mercy. Yet, after all the years of preparation, my GIVE BACK is available to all.

Our prayer life is not set in stone; therefore, we can adjust it according to our schedule or the leading of the Holy Spirit. Sometimes, our prayers cannot wait until a designated time; we may have to pray during an ordeal, crisis, or whatever. In this situation, God is not picky when it comes to our right now prayers; we can pray sitting down, on our knees, in the car, in bed, or wherever. As long as we get our prayers in or make our requests known to God, that is what really counts the most. When praying or wailing, here is a checklist, but not limited to such:

- ☐ Direct the prayer to our Heavenly Father.
- ☐ Give thanks.
- ☐ Do a little praise and worship session.
- ☐ Find a scripture, personalize it, meditate on it, and quote it back to God.

- ☐ Invite the Holy Spirit into your presence to speak.
- ☐ Repent of known and unknown sins.
- ☐ Say a prayer from the heart.
- ☐ Ask for God's will to be done.
- ☐ Intercede on someone's behalf for a special need if necessary.
- ☐ Bless oneself and others.
- ☐ Pray for guidance and protection.
- ☐ Pray for deliverance if necessary.
- ☐ Ask for the leading of the Holy Spirit with the covering of the Blood of Jesus, along with another THANK YOU and AMEN.

Instead of running to alcohol, cigarettes, pills, food, or sex for comfort, we should run to our *Secret Place, Meeting Place, or Prayer Closet*, seeking the *Spirit to Spirit* consultation for Divine Solutions, *As It Pleases God*.

Here is a Model Prayer that will help you if you do not have one: *Examine me, O' LORD, and try me; test my mind and my heart as You search my hidden motives, making them pure as gold. I pray for favor, health, wealth, and good success over my life, my finances, my family, my job, and all those I come in contact with. I repent of all of my known and unknown sins. Allow the Love of Christ to flow through my veins, giving me the Breath of Life to empower and inspire myself, as well as those around me. I am fasting for unity and wholeness from within the depths of my loins to bring forth Your will and Your way in my life. For I am seeking You with all my heart as I use my body as a Living Sacrifice that is holy and acceptable unto You. As I invoke Your presence in this phase of fasting, I am asking that You lead me to a place that's higher than this fleshly realm of life. In the name of Jesus. Thank you. Amen.*

Understanding the Bow

When we repent, fast, and pray, *As It Pleases God* without murmuring, while using the Fruits of the Spirit and behaving Christlike, Divine Wisdom will bow down to us. Spiritual Enlightenment will bow down. Spiritual Favor will bow down.

The Spiritual Veil will bow down to cover us. And the Holy Spirit will bow down to guide us in the right direction, GUARANTEED.

Is having the Elements of the Spirit bow down to us blasphemy? Bowing down is not used negatively or disrespectfully, but *As It Pleases God*. Life is designed to serve us; we simply need to know it and follow the Spiritual Principles associated with it doing so. But more importantly, it is used as a form of a yielding process or process of RESPECT.

There are LEVELS in Spirituality, even if we pretend there are not. We cannot expect God to move Heaven and Earth for us if we do whatever we want with whomever to please ourselves. On the other hand, if we Spiritually Align, *As It Pleases Him*, He will move Heaven and Earth for us and through us.

In the ratherability of what we are discussing, if we think we are getting away with ungodliness, think again; one is only the FOOTSTOOL for the higher Spiritual Ranker who is in Purpose on purpose! How is this possible? As this is a touchy subject, let us take it to scripture: "*A good man leaves an inheritance to his children's children, but the wealth of the sinner is stored up for the righteous.*" Proverbs 13:22.

What do we do when life pounces on us while doing the right thing? Let us take it to scripture again: "*The LORD said to my Lord, Sit at My right hand, till I make Your enemies Your footstool.*" Psalm 110:1.

Humbly thinking ahead, if we desire for the unseen Spiritual Forces of the Nature of God to bow down or Spiritually YIELD to us, we must bow down in repenting, fasting, forgiving, and praying, *As It Pleases Him*. Also, getting into our *Secret Place, Meeting Place, or Prayer Closet* to extract our Gifts, Talents, Purpose, Creativity, or Instructions according to our Predestined Blueprint is required.

If we give God what He wants by walking according to His Divine Will and Ways for the Kingdom of Heaven, using the Fruits of the Spirit with Christlike Character, He will COVER us or PLACE us in a Spiritual Fold. By willfully being in Purpose on purpose, *As It Pleases Him*, He will also usher us through the Spiritual Classroom with Divine Protection. Is this real? Absolutely! I am living proof!

How do we get into a Spiritual Classroom? Fortunately, there are many ways with God Almighty. However, the easiest way is by becoming humble first. Secondly, getting a *Secret Place, Meeting Place, or Prayer Closet*, putting our fleshly desires under subjection in PRIVATE. Thirdly, show up for class every day, ready, willing, and able to grow through the REGRAFTING process while documenting our encounters. Fourthly, we must follow instructions.

Who is the Teacher of this Spiritual Classroom? The Holy Spirit becomes the Teacher, using Spiritual Vessels such as myself to assist until we can effectively become the Real Prophet from a Biblical Perspective, holding our own, *Spirit to Spirit* with our Heavenly Father. In addition, in our Secret Place, He helps us to proactively put on our Spiritual Armor, ensuring we are suited up and ready to go.

Spiritual Armor

In order to get a better understanding of the Whole Armor of God, let us talk about the mind for a moment. When the enemy has a desire to sift us as wheat, he will come for the mind first through our senses. What we see, hear, taste, touch, and smell will affect what we think, and it creates paranoia or a gateway to brainwashing from within the depths of our souls. If we allow our minds to run wild or become ungoverned with unwarranted, superficial thoughts, we will not notice when negativity slips in to affect how we are feeling.

Once our Emotional or Mental rollercoasters are left unchecked, negativity gets into the psyche, affecting what comes out of the mouth. Regardless of our upbringings or backgrounds, an ungoverned tongue creates strife, envy, or coveting, which confirms the negative mindset.

How can we get a negative mindset out of negative behaviors? Negativity breeds negativity if it is never corrected into a positive or controlled positively. If we do not find positive ways to deflect the negative, it will create an inner battle that is secretly ignited between the soul and mind to place doubt in our faith, instigating a warring psyche where we begin to question the Truth of God.

Here is an example question: *"Did God really say that you must not eat from any tree in the garden?"* Genesis 3:1.

Once it gets to this point of doubtfulness, it becomes a deal breaker, and temptation, rationalization, or justification begins to take root, affecting our peace. Plus, it is extremely hard to pick up the Sword of the Spirit to fight a battle with the enemy if we are secretly or openly fighting against ourselves.

The Whole Armor of God and you are encapsulated in the same package; even if you cannot see it—trust me, it is there. God has given us the tools to WIN, whether we are Believers or not. The Power of our Armor resides in our Spiritual Relationship with Him, *Spirit to Spirit*. In addition, it also resides in the ability to gain access to our Tools of Combat to break the yoke of bondage while embracing our Birthright to Freedom. So, in our Secret Place, we need to put on:

- ☐ The Belt of Truth.
- ☐ The Breastplate of Righteousness.
- ☐ The Sandals of Peace.
- ☐ The Shield of Faith.
- ☐ The Helmet of Salvation.
- ☐ The Sword of the Spirit.

When we find ourselves between a rock and a hard place, responding with the Word of God is one of the quickest ways to jumpstart the Mind, Body, Soul, and Spirit. Yes, God's grace is sufficient, but we must have Spiritual Muscle Power to go toe-to-toe with the wiles of the enemy, especially when we have become negatively yoked, enslaved, or soul-tied. Hence, if you desire for the Real Prophet to come forth, then make sure you are ARMORED UP, *As It Pleases God*.

CHAPTER 11

THE REAL PROPHET

The *Wailing Prayers To The Deep Reloaded* is for all who are willing to avail themselves to the Kingdom of God, embracing their Heaven on Earth Experiences to bring forth The Real Prophet. From the Ancient of Days, prophesying continues to be a subject of interest and debates full of misinterpretation, misinformation, miscalculations, and misunderstanding. For this reason, in this chapter, we are going to lift the Spiritual Veil on this matter to ensure an understanding is established from a Divine Perspective, *As It Pleases God.*

It does not matter where we are, what we have done, or what we are going through; the Spiritual Q and A sessions with God are available to all, *Spirit to Spirit,* to bring forth what is already with a fully enforceable Spiritual Covenant. Here is the Spiritual Seal: "But this is the covenant that I will make with the house of Israel after those days, says the Lord: I will put My law in their minds, and write it on their hearts; and I will be their God, and they shall be My people." Jeremiah 31:33.

The Real Prophet and everything you need in Earthin Vessel from within is already! Ezekiel 36:27 says, "*I will put My Spirit within you and cause you to walk in My statutes, and you will keep My judgments and do them.*" All it boils down to is having things your way or doing things God's Divine Way, *As It Pleases Him.*

According to the Heavenly of Heavens, we all have a PROPHET from within in need of training. For example, in order to get a fake or false prophet, there must be some sort of prophet to begin with.

Simply put, the fakeness or falseness must have something to work with or attach itself to in order to establish elements of deception. Thus, in the Eye of God, it is our responsibility to perfect *The Real Prophet* from within. Then again, we can allow the world to define us by human standards instead of Godly Standards.

Now, with Godly Standards, *As It Pleases Him*, here is what you must do: *"Therefore lay aside all filthiness and overflow of wickedness, and receive with meekness the implanted word, which is able to save your souls."* James 1:21. If you can save your own soul, then have at it! But, if you desire The Real Prophet to come forth, you cannot consume your own fruits or mangle the fruits of another. How do we make this make sense? According to Galatians 5:22-23, there is NO LAW against the Fruits of the Spirit or the use of them. Conversely, there are Spiritual Laws when we LACK the use of them, especially when PROPHESYING.

The moment we begin to consume our own fruits, jealousy, envy, pride, greed, arrogance, coveting, selfishness, and competitiveness will start forming plagues within the psyche with negativity and debauchery. All of which are hidden under something else. Now, what our something else is will vary depending upon what lies within. However, this does not render us unusable in the Eye of God; we just need Spiritual Training and Understanding, *As It Pleases Him*. What if we choose not to do so? We have free will to reject whatever, but the Prophet's Glitch will remain, making us unstable or wishy-washy.

The Prophet's Glitch

When lacking the use of Spiritual Fruits, *As It Pleases God*, we tend to become irresponsible, reckless, arrogant, judgmental, and disobedient as if no one else possesses the ability of prophecy. Just so we are crystal clear about this matter, the Holy Spirit is available to all in the same way that Spiritual Atonement is available to all as well. No one person has a Spiritual Lockdown on Spiritual Prophecies; however, with proper use, *As It Pleases God*, it gives one Divine Leverage and Trustability over the next person.

For example, the same things that I can do, you can do better. Really? Yes, really! You just need to become Spiritually Trained according to your Divine Blueprint while heeding the Spiritual Teacher or Lessons. In the Eye of God, the Spiritual Students must become better than the Appointed Teacher; if not, there is a Spiritual Glitch in the Matrix.

How do we get Spiritual Glitches or Malfunctions? If you omit your Predestined Blueprint, you will decrease your Spiritual Abilities by default. Then again, if you omit the Fruits of the Spirit, you will have a further decrease. If you refuse to behave Christlike, you are decreased a little more. Lastly, suppose you refuse the Holy Trinity (The Father, Son, and Holy Spirit). In this case, you will become Spiritually VEILED and sometimes turned over to a reprobate mind, even if you appear to have it going on or proclaim to be Heaven-Sent. Unfortunately, it is what you do behind closed doors that determines this!

For example, how you speak to yourself, your spouse, children, or anyone you think you do not need becomes the Writing on the Wall for reprobativeness or the exemption from it. Is this Biblical? Once again, I would have it no other way. *"And even as they did not like to retain God in their knowledge, God gave them over to a debased mind, to do those things which are not fitting."* Romans 1:28.

How do we get to a reprobate mind as Believers? Suppressing the truth, behaving waywardly, operating in outright disobedience, allowing dullness to penetrate the psyche, engaging in foolery, and willfully engaging in unrighteousness will do the trick. I could go on for days with this list, but we get the picture.

So, please allow me to Spiritually Align how reprobativeness can creep into our lives as Believers and unbelievers alike. Plus, how THE PROPHET from within knows what we refuse to acknowledge. *"For the wrath of God is revealed from heaven against all ungodliness and unrighteousness of men, who suppress the truth in unrighteousness, because what may be known of God is manifest in them, for God has shown it to them. For since the creation of the world His invisible attributes are clearly seen, being understood by the things that are made, even His eternal power and Godhead, so that they are without excuse, because, although they knew God, they did not glorify Him as God, nor were thankful, but became futile in their thoughts, and their foolish hearts were darkened. Professing to be wise, they became fools, and changed the glory of the incorruptible God into an image made like corruptible man—and birds and four-footed animals and creeping things. Therefore God also gave them up to uncleanness, in the lusts of their hearts, to dishonor their bodies among themselves, who exchanged the truth of God for the lie, and worshiped and served the creature rather than the Creator, who is blessed forever. Amen."* Romans 1:18-25.

As a result of being Spiritually Blind, Deaf, or Mute and having to endure the Wrath of God, some go to the dark side to tap into the Realm of the Spirit that the Blood of Jesus will not cover. Thus, another form of sacrifice must be rendered. Still, just because you do not understand what you are doing, it does not exempt you from the consequences of your actions, words, thoughts, intentions, or whatever. For this reason, you must account for what DISOBEDIENCE will cost you...and if you are not willing to account for the cost, it is better to leave the dark side alone. I was taught at a young age not to play with fire to avoid getting burned...and so it is when indulging in debauchery or violating the free will of another without repentance.

Understanding The Inner Child

Spiritual Discernment or Insight is wrapped in Spiritual Prophecy, even if we do not understand it as of yet. For example, there is a boy in every man, a girl in every woman, a puppy in every dog, a kitten in every cat, and so on. The moment we get too big for our britches, that boy, girl, puppy, or kitten will begin to act out, making itself known amid our proclaimed self-control or unresolved selfish efforts.

Why would the inner child act out? To let us know that we are becoming dull, stiff-necked, lukewarm, or uptight in some way, shape, or form. Then again, it is a possibility that it is being ignored. The bottom line is that it is a GIFT that we should ENJOY and never take for granted or abuse. Why? Our inner child has a direct link to the Fruits of the Spirit, as the first two fruits are LOVE and JOY. Why these two? They bring about laughter, which is MEDICINE for the soul.

For example, being that I am used to such a great capacity, most people think that I am so serious and unrelatable. But the truth is, I am from the country, I laugh a lot, and I enjoy doing so. I cannot hang around dry, dull, rude, and negative people for long. Why not? They drain my positive energy. More importantly, when you develop a *Spirit to Spirit* Relationship with God, you will find that He is very humorous. Realistically and relatably, when He makes me laugh, I know He is getting ready to give me PROFOUND Spiritual Insight or Divine Revelation about something or someone.

Where does the inner child hang out? Our inner child is within the psyche. Anything or anyone that has blood flowing through its veins has a smaller version of itself hidden within its DNA as a way of RELATING BACK to something. Unbeknown to most, this is where we get the word Religio from, and it is used as what we now call Religion. For the record, this is another reason why God has granted SCIENCE the ability to backtrack, analyze, and project to ensure we do not forget the roadmap of our Forefathers.

Plus, if we fail to speak life into that boy, girl, puppy, or kitten from within ourselves or others, it will decrease our Spiritual Language, Love Language, and People Skills by default. Why would this happen when we have perfected the Love Languages? Oh, my friend, this is how we are deceived! Everyone's Spiritual Language, Love Language, and People Skills are different, similar to having a different fingerprint, mindprint, footprint, and soulprint.

In the Eye of God, putting a soulprint of someone in a box is a recipe for disaster. Why? It creates limits that we will try to fit into or break out of in due time, seeking some form of freedom. Instead, the goal should always consist of creating stepping stones according to their Predestined Blueprint that would assist them in getting to a Cornerstone of Greatness. In all simplicity, when we can Spiritually Align others with their Divine Blueprint, *As It Pleases God*, it creates a triple-braided cord in our relationships, friendships, and work relations, making us the GO-TO person, regardless of whether we are overlooked, rejected, hidden, used, or talked about.

Why must we be overlooked, rejected, hidden, used, or talked about to be a GO-TO person? In the Eye of God, if one cannot handle being overlooked, rejected, hidden, used, or talked about, they are not ready for the Kingdom. Who am I to judge, right? No judgment is intended. The truth is that being overlooked, rejected, hidden, used, or talked about builds STRENGTH, teaching us what NOT to do to others. Without allowing them to teach us, *As It Pleases God*, we become WEAK in all things Spiritual. In addition, we will accumulate an entourage of rotten fruits while appearing strong and running our mouths too much, becoming the Go-Away or Stay-Away-From person!

According to the Heavenly of Heavens, we need the Fruits of the Spirit and the Holy Spirit to make that baby leap within any man, woman, child, animal, and most of all, God Almighty. And, once we have the Heart of God, *As It Pleases Him*, it is a WRAP! How so? We will become the Salt of the Earth with a flavor even our haters cannot deny. Our method of operation will become smooth as butter, flowing in the Spirit of Excellence amid our imperfections and sweet as honey, making people scratch their heads.

How is this humanly possible, especially when everyone is different? You see, this is where Spiritual Prophecy works best...the Holy Spirit will advise you on what to do, when to do, why to do, where to do, when to do, how to do, and with whom to penetrate the heart of man. If the penetration does not occur, you must step back into the Spiritual Classroom. Why? The Holy Spirit does not miss the mark; we do! All this means is that our Spiritual Compass is off and is in need of Spiritual Recalibration. Do not worry; it happens to us all...this is why we need to connect to the Holy Trinity, *Spirit to Spirit*.

Spiritually, in the Kingdom of God, there are no little U's or big I's when becoming a Vessel of God, *As It Pleases Him*. Although there are indeed Spiritual Levels, the Spirit does not discriminate against a genuinely willing and obedient soul who listens, learns, applies, grows, pursues, and gives back to the Kingdom of God when called upon, *As It Pleases Him*.

Now, on the other hand, we will run into problems when we add DISOBEDIENCE or POMPOUSNESS into our equational efforts. Why would we run into problems when we are prophesying in the Name of God? When operating in the Prophetic, we do not want to get it wrong, especially when all eyes are on us. However, when we are not operating with the Fruits of the Spirit or behaving Christlike, we will get a Spiritual Side-Eye from God Almighty.

As my ear has been to the ground for a minute, I have heard many prophesying that the Holy Spirit told them to get on social media to broadcast someone's business. Or, I have heard others put people on blast to destroy someone's life without advising them of their erring or gaining their agreement to do so, which is a lie from the Pits of Hell. All this is done for what? Views and clicks...Have we no shame! How can we become so comfortable saying the Holy Spirit said this or that when He did not say anything?

If broadcasting news or events is what we choose to do or our occupation, we have free will to do so because everyone is entitled to their own opinions and to do their jobs. But as a NEWS FLASH: We must leave the Holy Spirit out of it! The moment we bring the Holy Spirit into this matter, it changes the Spiritual Rules of the game.

According to scripture: *"Therefore I say to you, every sin and blasphemy will be forgiven men, but the blasphemy against the Spirit will not be forgiven men. Anyone who speaks a word against the Son of Man, it will be forgiven him; but whoever speaks against the Holy Spirit, it will not be forgiven him, either in this age or in the age to come."* Matthew 12:30-32.

Why is God so adamant about this? It impacts the psyche in ways that Science has yet to diagnose as of yet. Still, the side effects can indeed become evident to all through our thoughts, actions, reactions, words, biases, beliefs, and traumas.

Why is the diagnosis not available? Unfortunately, it is a Spiritual Matter; therefore, Science must operate in the Realm of the Spirit to UNVEIL a Spiritual Diagnosis. And being that everyone is different and on varying Spiritual Levels, we must be granted Divine Access for real, for real! If not, a Spiritual Violation may occur, possibly due to the violation of free will, but not limited to such. What is not limited to such consists of? Simply put, playing God with a Spiritual Diagnosis comes with a price or sacrifice that the Blood of Jesus may not cover. Now, to paint a picturesque view of this matter, this is similar to the Ark of the Covenant, where only certain people could touch it without perishing.

What if we are taught that the Blood of Jesus covers everything? Yes, everything except for blaspheming the Holy Spirit! What if we are not blaspheming? If we are attempting to force the hand of the Holy Spirit without agreement or violating Spiritual Laws out of selfishness, we are treading the line of blasphemy.

Overcoming Blasphemy

Blasphemy is the act of showing contempt or lack of reverence for God or anything SACRED. In addition, it can also refer to speaking about God in a disrespectful, immoral manner. Then again, it can also apply to the Divine Vessel He is using to carry out a certain MISSION or who is in Purpose on purpose according to their Predestined Blueprint. For this reason, we need to learn how to RESPECT each other, period! Without Spiritual Discernment, *As It Pleases God*, we DO NOT know who He is using to accomplish something or who is in training.

To better understand The Real Prophet from within, we must operate in Spiritual Authenticity to avoid getting the Divine Messages from God distorted or contaminated. If we cannot operate as such, *As It Pleases God*, we must remain a prophet in training for our protection from all things Spiritual. Why? God requires humility, respect, and the use of the Fruits of the Spirit. If we do not use them or we know nothing about them, our conveyance process can become easily manipulated and thwarted due to our conscious or unconscious desires, fears, traumas, or social influences.

Regarding our Q and A sessions, we must SPIRITUALLY POSITION ourselves to invoke the Hidden Prophet from within with the guidance of the Holy Spirit. Why do we need the Holy Spirit? Our Spirit, the Inner Genius or Prophet, must be adequately governed to ensure it is NOT selfishly misused or abused by worldly means to manipulate, abuse, misuse, insult, or destroy another.

Do we not have the power to cast down, reverse, or reject people, places, and things coming against our Internal Prophet? Yes, we do; however, there are Spiritual Rules and Protocols in doing so, *As It Pleases God*. *"The wisdom that is from above is first pure, then peaceable, gentle, willing to yield, full of mercy and good fruits, without partiality and without hypocrisy. Now the fruit of righteousness is sown in peace by those who make peace."* James 3:17-18.

God will not give us the answers to our Spiritual Lessons or Tests simply because we want them or to show off. He does it for the Greater Good of mankind or the Kingdom of God. Regardless of our intents, we cannot cheat the Spiritual System because we are designed to do the work, Spiritually Tilling our own ground, or better yet, DIG DEEP.

Where is the deep? Deep within our souls, as it relates to Spiritual Matters of the heart or the sifting of our worldly systems. So, we must QUERY and TEST the Spirit regarding all things. Why? With the Real Prophet from within, it is a requirement. Here is what we must know: *"Beloved, do not believe every spirit, but test the spirits, whether they are of God; because many false prophets have gone out into the world."* 1 John 4:1.

Testing The Spirit

In the same way, we expect someone to be accurate about a prophecy; we are required to TEST it as well. What are we testing? The goodness. 1 Thessalonians 5:21 says, *"Test all things; hold fast what is good."* If one does not know what is good from what is not, then it is time to get in the know, exercising discernment and wisdom, *As It Pleases God*.

How do we know what is good, especially when God will package our BLESSINGS in something or someone appearing bad, unkempt, or unpalatable? The key is to MASTER the Fruits of the Spirit. As a rule of thumb, God will allow the Fruits of the Spirit to supersede a dirty situation, circumstance, or event. What does this mean for Believers? It will contain a Win-Win with the appearance of a lose-lose, and it is our responsibility to exercise Spiritual Discernment to extract the Diamond or Gold from the dirt.

What if we do not like dirty things or what is beneath our class or standards? We are all entitled to our likes and dislikes, but if our hearts are unkempt or unhealed, what is the difference? Wait, wait, wait, do not answer this yet. Let me take another dig: When dealing with God Almighty, we must TEST the Spirit of whatever or whomever. If not, we may find ourselves walking around like boo boo the fool for judging what we did not take the time to

TEST, *As It Pleases God*. Remarkably, this process allows us to take the situations, circumstances, and events at hand, seeking God's Divine Perspective as well as the truth regarding our own. How? By our ability to ask the right fact-finding questions, we expect to receive Divine Answers. But more importantly, it helps us to put Biblical Scriptures into their proper context.

In the process of revamping our approach to all things, we must have a Christlike Perspective, period. By doing so, it helps to avoid partaking in ungodliness. Does this mean we must become perfect? No, it means we are quicker to repent, fast, and pray, going into our Secret Place to seek Divine Revelation or Healing. By far, this will help us gain Divine Wisdom, learn the necessary lessons, develop an understanding, and help others, *As It Pleases God*, without degrading ourselves or others in the process. Is this really possible? Absolutely. The moment we come to ourselves, understand who we are and why, purify ourselves, get into our Secret Place, and fast accordingly to become a Fruitful Vessel of God, we can truly step into the *Spiritual Know* or *Spiritual Classroom*.

Regardless of the pictures we paint for ourselves and others, the bumps and bruises of life are inevitable, exempting no one. Amid whatever or whomever, we must learn how to ask the right questions and seek the correct answers according to scripture as if we know nothing, seeking everything from God, *As It Pleases Him*.

What if we are the Real Prophet of God, and are not in need of questioning ourselves because we operate in wisdom? Let us take it to scripture, *"If anyone among you seems to be wise in this age, let him become a fool that he may become wise. For the wisdom of this world is foolishness with God. For it is written, "He catches the wise in their own craftiness"; and again, "The Lord knows the thoughts of the wise, that they are futile." Therefore let no one boast in men. For all things are Yours."* 1 Corinthians 3:18-22.

What is the difference between Spiritual Wisdom and worldly wisdom? One is from the Spirit via the Holy Spirit, and the other is worldly via any means. Why do we need to know the difference? Let us take it to scripture, *"Do you not know that you are the Temple of God and that the Spirit of God dwells in you? If anyone defiles the Temple of God, God will destroy him. For the Temple of God is holy, which temple you are."* 1 Corinthians 3:16-17.

Do we not have free will to do whatever we like? Absolutely. However, we must remember when it comes down to the wailing process, our *Spiritual Q and A*, or the notches we have under our belts, belong to God, period. How? Contrary to what we genuinely believe about who we are, our achievements, or our possessions, it is all vanity.

Spiritually, first and foremost, God deserves RESPECT in all things, regardless of whether we understand it or not. Secondly, we need to become GRATEFUL as well. Of course, we all like nice things and the comforts of life; however, we must change our perceptions to *As It Pleases Him*, not to please ourselves. According to scripture, *"Who then is Paul, and who is Apollos, but ministers through whom you believed, as the Lord gave to each one? I planted, Apollos watered, but God gave the increase. So then neither he who plants is anything, nor he who waters, but God who gives the increase. Now he who plants and he who waters are one, and each one will receive his own reward according to his own labor."* 1 Corinthians 3:5-8.

In the Eye of God, what we do, think, say, and how we behave matters because it is the WATER to our Spirituality or carnality. How is this possible? I can put it in my own words, but it will not do this chapter justice. Here is what we need to know: *"For we are God's fellow workers; you are God's field, you are God's building. According to the grace of God which was given to me, as a wise master builder I have laid the foundation, and another builds on it. But let each one take heed how he builds on it. For no other foundation can anyone lay than that which is laid, which is Jesus Christ. Now if anyone builds on this foundation with gold, silver, precious stones, wood, hay, straw each one's work will become clear; for the Day will declare it, because it will be revealed by fire; and the fire will test each one's work, of what sort it is. If anyone's work which he has built on it endures, he will receive a reward. If anyone's work is burned, he will suffer loss; but he himself will be saved, yet so as through the fire."* 1 Corinthians 3:9-14.

In being a Real Prophet of God, having *Spirit to Spirit* Sessions with Him about ourselves and others is wise and healthy, developing our people skills, *As It Pleases Him*. In addition, it aids in helping us balance and query ourselves. Even when pressure is applied, we are pushed to the limit, tested, or going through the fire.

Often enough, we have mistaken knowledge for being intelligent or being intelligently knowledgeable for wisdom. So, before we go any further, let us clear this matter from a Spiritual Perspective. Although they are all important, here is the breakdown:

- **Knowledge** is taught, bought, and sought after. In addition, it is ever-changing by God and man, wrapped in our hunger for learning or being in the know.

- **Intelligence** results from applied knowledge, know-how, how-to, understanding, wisdom, or perception.

- **Divine Wisdom** is pristine and unchanging, similar to the Law of Gravity. However, Divine Wisdom is inspired by God or other Spiritual means set forth by Him as a Spiritual Gift, benefiting the Kingdom of Heaven, or as a part of our Destiny-Enriched Provisions. It also incorporates using our conscience, instincts, senses, internal compass, and vibrational energy.

According to Divine Wisdom, we must weigh in on whether we exhibit secular or Spiritual Knowledge, Intellectualism, or Divine Wisdom. Does it make a difference? Absolutely.

We are in the most educated society in the history of mankind. Still, we are the most aloof from a Spiritual Perspective and in the Eye of God. How is this possible? Our morality is rapidly declining while becoming a bed of mortality from within. We are too blind to see it because we are clueless about what to look for and the reasons why. Yet, our inner man tells us something is definitely wrong or out of order, as we ignore or downplay it only to please ourselves.

What do we do? Where do we go from here? Let us take this chapter to the Spiritual Principles needed to provoke our rational state of questioning.

Character Building

According to the Heavenly of Heavens, the best way to begin to ask life the right questions is to understand Life's Instructions *As It Pleases God*. The Divine Instruction Manual of life and character building is hidden in the Book of Proverbs. Really? Yes, really! Even if we pretend we have it all together with pristine characteristics, there is always more to learn about God, ourselves, and others.

Regardless of where we are on the learning scale, if we cannot ask God, ourselves, others, and life the right questions or understand the answers, we are headed for destruction from the inside out. And, being that I do not wish ill will for anyone, allow me to open our eyes to a few things that will BLESS us if we take heed, helping in the wailing process, *As It Pleases God*.

Just so we are crystal clear, God is the ultimate SOURCE of Divine Wisdom. Any other way to lowercase wisdom is secondary, regardless of our thoughts, desires, conditioning, or beliefs. For the record, to get secondary wisdom comes with a known or unknown sacrifice.

Why is there a sacrifice involved? Once again, Divine Wisdom comes from God Almighty, and counterfeit wisdom or lower-level wisdom comes from a secondary source. Trying to beat the system without going through the Holy Trinity (The Father, Son, and Holy Spirit) or Spiritually Tilling our own ground will cost us something. What that something is, I do not know! Now, what I do know is that we must learn and understand the difference between Divine Wisdom, wisdom of another kind, and knowledge.

By NOT Spiritually Tilling our own ground, exempting God from our equational efforts, or NOT doing what we are called to do, *As It Pleases Him*, that something, the sacrifice, or the cost, may not be of our choosing! So, we must become cautious when bargaining for something or someone using borrowed wisdom as the gateway to please ourselves.

What is the big deal as long as we get what we want? All insight is not Divine Foresight, *As It Pleases God*. According to our Predestined Blueprint, everything we want may not be suitable for us. If we do not know by now, let me inform those with a willing ear to hear; it creates a Spiritual Taboo. Why is a Spiritual Taboo attached, especially when having free will? It is due to the elements of DISOBEDIENCE and the desire to alter Divine Order for selfish gain.

Think about this: How can we use the wisdom that God created to outsmart Him, especially when it takes the same amount of energy to add Him into our equational efforts to operate with Divine Wisdom, *As It Pleases Him*? Do we think for a minute God is going to look like boo boo the fool for us? That will not happen...not now...and not ever! *"Do not be deceived, God is not mocked; for whatever a man sows, that he will also reap."* Galatians 6:7.

God has set in motion how He desires for us to live. If we live contrary to what He has set forth without any form of repentance, without the covering of the sacrificial Blood of Jesus, and the ushering in of the Holy Spirit as our Guide, we permit the issues of life to pounce on us. How can this be our fault? No one is to blame here; we just need to step up our Spiritual Game, utilizing what is already available at our fingertips.

God has freely given us the Spiritual Tools and Weapons needed to contend with the enemy's wiles. However, we must follow proper Spiritual Protocol, *As It Pleases Him*, not ourselves.

What are the Spiritual Protocols for using our Spiritual Weapons properly? We must align ourselves and our lives with Biblical Scriptures without compromising ourselves, our Bloodline, or the Holy Ground of Scripture. In the simplicity of it all, we cannot use the Word of God to carry out evil practices or folly. If we do, the penalty of doing so is much higher for being lukewarm than not using anything at all, or going about our own way as a free agent, removing God from the equation totally.

In our *Spirit to Spirit* Relations with God, ourselves, and others can become our CORNERSTONE, ordained and guided stepping stones, a bridge, or an obstructed dam. We must decide if we are going to allow our wailing process to heal us for the Promises of God, or destroy us for the lack of knowledge and understanding. Of course, for the sake of the *Wailing Prayers to the Deep Reloaded*, we are going to choose to heal, so let us take this chapter up a notch.

Worldliness will not get us the Treasures of Heaven, as some would think; it can only get us an illusion in a bed of delusion. The

Treasures of Heaven are not of Earthen Vessel; they are intangibly from within, containing the Fruits of the Spirit. Contrary to what we have been deceived into believing about outer adornment to please ourselves or our insecurities, we must tap in from within, *As It Pleases God*.

Although this outer glitz or glamour looks fantastic to the masses, behind closed doors, the truth lurks to expose us, making us tremble in our boots. Why would this happen, especially as Believers? We have unrepentant flaws, unresolved trauma, or hidden imperfections we do not want to expose, which provoke internal fears, overzealous emotions, or negative thoughts.

The truth is, we all have our little quirks, no one is perfect, and we all have issues, even if we pretend we do not. In the Eye of God, it is okay to be who we are with a work-in-progress mentality while taking ourselves into the Spiritual Classroom to sort out our idiosyncrasies, *As It Pleases Him*.

According to the Heavenly of Heavens, the difference between our successes and failures is our PERSPECTIVES and PERCEPTIONS of selflessly PLEASING God or selfishly pleasing ourselves. Is there anything else? Yes, pleasing others!

People pleasers get a Spiritual Side-Eye from God, whereas a God-Pleaser, *As It Pleases Him*, becomes the Apple of His Eye. Can this really happen as Believers? Absolutely! And with Divine Protection and Care from the Heavenly of Heavens as well. For example, Deuteronomy 32:10 says, "*He found him in a desert land and in the wasteland, a howling wilderness; He encircled him, He instructed him, He kept him as the apple of His eye.*" From back then to now, this same Spiritual Principle exists for the sake of mankind.

As Believers, and on behalf of the Ancient of Days, to MASTER our perceptions and perspectives, we must pull out the Book of Proverbs. Why Proverbs? It is the Book of Wisdom, teaching us how to use Godly Principles in everyday life from a Spiritual Perspective with a Godly TONE we can understand. Also, it gives us the repercussions of not doing so as well.

Are our TONES Biblical? Of course. In the commission of our Spiritual Journey, *As It Pleases God*, we will need to master a few inflections:

- ☐ **A Stern Tone**: Displays sincerity without being rude, mean, or demeaning. "*And their eyes were opened. And Jesus sternly warned them, saying, "See that no one knows it."* Matthew 9:30. This is a 'Say what you mean, and mean what you say' tone of voice.

- ☐ **An Authoritative Tone**: Displays an influential inflection. "*Then they were all amazed, so that they questioned among themselves, saying, What is this? What new doctrine is this? For with authority He commands even the unclean spirits, and they obey Him.*" Mark 1:27. We cannot contend with the enemy with a wavering, insecure, or feeble decree.

- ☐ **A Humble Tone**: Displays a correctable, non-threatening, or understanding inflection. "*And a servant of the Lord must not quarrel but be gentle to all, able to teach, patient, in humility correcting those who are in opposition, if God perhaps will grant them repentance, so that they may know the truth, and that they may come to their senses and escape the snare of the devil, having been taken captive by him to do his will.*" 2 Timothy 2:24-26.

- ☐ **A Positive Tone**: Displays positive words of integrity, giving no ammunition for anyone to use against us. Doing so causes unjustifiable negativity to backfire or create a footstool. "*Likewise, exhort the young men to be sober-minded, in all things showing yourself to be a pattern of good works; in doctrine showing integrity, reverence, incorruptibility, sound speech that cannot be condemned, that one who is an opponent may be ashamed, having nothing evil to say of you.*" Titus 2:6-8.

- ☐ **A Soft, Gentle Tone**: Displays calmness and rationality. "*A soft answer turns away wrath, but a harsh word stirs up anger.*" Proverbs 15:1. More importantly, "*A wholesome tongue is a tree of life, but perverseness in it breaks the spirit.*" Proverbs 15:4.

- ☐ **A Patient Tone**: Displays a non-rushed demeanor. "*Through patience, a ruler can be persuaded, and a gentle tongue can* *break a bone."* Proverbs 25:15. When we are patient with God, ourselves, and others, we can break through barriers that a bad attitude or an unruly tongue will not penetrate.

- [ ] **A Happy Tone**: Displays a smile from the inside out, even if we have nothing to smile about; the Spiritual Implications of doing so are food for the soul. *"A merry heart makes a cheerful countenance, but by sorrow of the heart the spirit is broken."* Proverbs 15:13.

- [ ] **A Gracious Tone**: Displays a polished attitude of saying the magic words: please, thank you, excuse me, good morning, good evening, and you are welcome. *"Let your speech always be with grace, seasoned with salt, that you may know how you ought to answer each one."* Colossians 4:6.

- [ ] **A Honey Tone**: Displays sweet, savory, or luscious words; we often call this a sweet mouth, but it must be used correctly. But let us take it to scripture anyway: *"Pleasant words are like a honeycomb, sweetness to the soul and health to the bones."* Proverbs 16:24. If misused to manipulate, control, use someone, hurt, or cause any form of ill will, here is what happens: *"There is a way that seems right to a man, but its end is the way of death."* Proverbs 16:25. So, tread carefully with the honey.

- [ ] **A Righteous Tone**: Displays the ability to think before we speak. *"The heart of the righteous studies how to answer, but the mouth of the wicked pours forth evil."* Proverbs 15:28. Regardless of our conditioning, we cannot just ramble off, saying whatever we desire without reasoning or out of selfishness.

- [ ] **An Encouraging Tone**: Displays our mentorship abilities to share, motivate, strengthen, and teach others about the Good News. *"Strengthening the souls of the disciples, exhorting them to continue in the faith, and saying, We must through many tribulations enter the Kingdom of God."* Acts 14:22.

- ☐ **A Silent Tone**: Displays our ability to plead the 5th. We do not have to respond to any or everything. *"Even a fool is counted wise when he holds his peace; when he shuts his lips, he is considered perceptive."* Proverbs 17:28.

Regardless of our conditioning, background, or whatever, there is always more to learn, especially when dealing with a Spiritual Classroom of Divine Purpose, the process of bearing Good Fruit, or when we simply jump the tracks Mentally, Physically, Emotionally, or Spiritually.

As long as we have breath in our bodies, no one is exempt from the issues of life; therefore, we must increase our capacity to learn, understand, grow, and share. Doing so helps us to reel ourselves in positively, before going to the extreme or overboard in what we are doing, saying, or becoming. What is the purpose of being so careful? Disobedience, recklessness, unforgiveness, hatefulness, debauchery, and foolery can potentially spoil our Spiritual Fruits or place cracks in a stable foundation.

Once the heart and mind become open to the Spiritual Classroom, *As It Pleases God*, we give ourselves the upper hand in understanding a few things, such as:

- ☐ The Principles of God.
- ☐ The Mind of God.
- ☐ The Will of God.
- ☐ The Desires of God.
- ☐ The Personality of God.
- ☐ The Responses of God.
- ☐ The Move of God.
- ☐ The Expectations of God.
- ☐ The Methods of God.
- ☐ The Guidelines of God.
- ☐ The Truth of God.
- ☐ The Secret Wisdom of God.
- ☐ The Humor of God.
- ☐ The Divine Keys of God.

We are unique in our own individualized way, and God will open the Curtains of Holiness on our behalf if we dare to step outside of our comfort zones to receive what He has to offer. What is the catch? We must follow the Spiritual Rules, use the Fruits of the Spirit, exhibit Christlike Character, and be WILLING to move into our Divine Purpose, utilizing our Gifts, Creativity, or Talents according to our Predestined Blueprint.

Furthermore, we must also correctly discern between the DUALITY of right and wrong, positive and negative, just and unjust, as well as good and evil. Why must we understand duality as Believers? Without being able to Spiritually Discern or Divinely Contrast people, places, and things properly, or when we expose our hands prematurely, we can become an easy target of prey for predators. So, we cannot be ignorant of the devices used to sift us Mentally, Physically, Emotionally, and Spiritually.

What makes this so important in the Eye of God? If we are all over the place while proclaiming to be Holy-Ghost-Filled and Fire-Baptized and not know what is good or evil, right or wrong, just or unjust, and so on, we can subconsciously compromise a few things, but not limited to such:

- ☐ Our Spiritual Connection or Receivers.
- ☐ Our Spiritual Queries.
- ☐ Our Spiritual Answers.
- ☐ Our Spiritual Astuteness.
- ☐ Our Spiritual Integrity.
- ☐ Our Spiritual Understanding.
- ☐ Our Spiritual Respectfulness.
- ☐ Our Spiritual Boundaries or Depth.
- ☐ Our Spiritual Protocol.
- ☐ Our Spiritual Compatibilities.
- ☐ Our Spiritual Fruits.
- ☐ Our Spiritual Journey.

What is the purpose of knowing this information? Unfortunately, this is one of the reasons why Believers are fighting against their own about who is right or wrong. Not realizing that no one is 100%

right or 100% wrong! The goal is to KNOW and UNDERSTAND the DIFFERENCE in the Spiritual Duality we face in our Heaven on Earth Experiences to become the game changer in the Kingdom of God, feeding His sheep, *As It Pleases Him*. How do we begin this process? Begin with the FirstFruits of what we are setting in motion as fruits, seeds, and roots! And then, based on our findings, begin Spiritually Tilling (Cultivating) that ground.

Often enough, we take a lot of things for granted, but when it comes down to the Fruits of the Spirit, we should not play around. Why not? It is the Spiritual Tonic we need to satiate the inner thirst of the unnecessary, potentially debilitating issues of life. And if we do not perfect our wailing process to the point of having a direct connection to God in or out of our Secret Place, *Spirit to Spirit*, we cannot fault anyone.

We all have the same opportunity to receive all God offers; we simply need to get out of our own way. How do we get out of our own way, especially when we have to deal with ourselves and our shadows? We are all different, requiring something; however, listed below are a few items needed to unblock our internal progression, *As It Pleases God*, but not limited to such:

- ☐ If we need to repent, then repent.
- ☐ If we need to fast, then fast.
- ☐ If we need to roar out a '*Wailing Prayer To The Deep*,' then wail.
- ☐ If we need to ask questions, then ask.
- ☐ If we need to understand, then understand.
- ☐ If we need to seek, then seek.
- ☐ If we need to listen, then listen.
- ☐ If we need to step up to the plate, then step up.
- ☐ If we need to step down, then step down.
- ☐ If we need to do something, then do it.
- ☐ If we need to stop lying to ourselves, then stop.
- ☐ If we need inner healing, then allow the healing to take place.

When it comes down to the Kingdom of Heaven and what it has to offer, there will always be an underlying Spiritual Perspective.

Why is this so important in the Eye of God? A Kingdom must have ordinances to remain.

According to the Heavenly of Heavens, we have Spiritual Ordinances to keep a Temple from collapsing under pressure. Now, for the sake of the Kingdom, let us take it to scripture: *"But Jesus knew their thoughts, and said to them: Every kingdom divided against itself is brought to desolation, and every city or house divided against itself cannot stand."* Matthew 12:25.

How do we use the Book of Proverbs as a preventative method to keep from dividing ourselves, our lives, and our homes? In my opinion, it is best to read the scripture and then turn it into a question for ourselves, our spouse, our children, our environment, our associates, etc. For example, Proverbs 1:5 says, *"A wise man will hear and increase learning, and a man of understanding will attain wise counsel."* Listed below are questions I would ask myself based on this scripture:

- ☐ Am I exhibiting wise characteristics?
- ☐ Am I a good steward in my ability to listen effectively?
- ☐ Are my conversations understandable?
- ☐ Am I repeating back what I heard to confirm we are on one accord to gain agreement?
- ☐ Am I continuing to increase my learning capabilities?
- ☐ What am I learning?
- ☐ Why am I learning?
- ☐ Who am I learning from?
- ☐ Am I effective?
- ☐ Am I making a positive impact?
- ☐ Am I getting wise counsel?
- ☐ Am I receptive to those who know more?

Of course, I am a pro at asking and answering questions, so it may take a little practice to pull a lot of questions out of one sentence, but it is doable. How do I know? This is how I got started many years ago because I did not have any other choice if I wanted to understand something or someone properly. All in all, we do not all think alike or process information the same, so clarity is key.

In all due respect, I am compelled to share my journey with the Book of Proverbs. Many years ago, as I went to the restroom in the morning to do my due diligence, I read the Book of Proverbs daily. The more I read, the more I began to understand how to behave, and it also gave me a bird's eye view of how much I did not know.

As a result of yielding to the process, it revamped my character beyond what I could have ever imagined for myself. Why could I not imagine having excellent People Skills? I did not have anyone to teach me how to exhibit Christlike Character, even though I was already an adult in my early twenties. For this reason, I write to help those who may not have had the opportunity to have this information presented in such a manner.

Some laughed when I began to change positively for the Greater Good, *As It Pleased God*. But trust me, they are not laughing now. Why are they not laughing? First, they are still stuck on negative, declining in their character and People Skills. Secondly, my INTEGRITY is set, *As It Pleases God*. Plus, I will not curse my hand or mistreat anyone willfully.

What is the purpose of such Spiritual Devotion? I am held to a higher standard and accountability than most. Why? For the simple fact that I know better. Plus, I am Spiritually Trained by the Heavenly of Heavens to do better for the Kingdom's Sake. So, I must do better publicly and privately to PROTECT my Spiritual Anointing and ever so quick to REPENT when mistakes are made.

For this reason, there are some things that I am NOT going to do, period! Plus, to intentionally hurt others on purpose is not worth losing my Spiritual Gifts, Anointing, or Purpose. Nor do I want a negative seed to place a chokehold on me, my Divine Destiny, Predestined Blueprint, BLOODLINE, nor will I risk losing one of God's precious sheep due to my folly or negligence.

What is the big deal, especially when we all make mistakes? That one precious sheep is counting on me to Spiritually Download Divine and Relevant Information from the Heavenly of Heavens. Moreover, if I slip, not only do I have to account for that one lost sheep, but millions of them. Thus, I am NOT willing to take that risk; therefore, I am bringing it to the TABLE, doing my part. Whether it is accepted or rejected is not my job...I bring the MANNA and keep it moving in the Spirit of Excellence.

For the record, I do not have REAL Battle Scars for no reason. I went to WAR for this Divine Information, so I am not here to play patty cake with those posing distractions to get me off track. Nor am I here to sling mud pies or degrade anyone because I know that God has placed Divine Greatness in every Vessel sent here. Therefore, I am targeting the Diamonds in the Rough in Earthen Vessels, and I do not make it a secret.

Now, if one would like to perfect this process of questioning as well, here is how to begin to ask questions from the Book of Proverbs. Simply ask questions with these formations for problem-solving, planning, mapping, understanding, identifying, or targeted comprehension:

- ☐ What?
- ☐ When?
- ☐ Where?
- ☐ How?
- ☐ Why?
- ☐ With Whom? To Whom? By Whom?

Questionably, prefacing the Book of Proverbs in such a manner will create a viable platform for our *Q and A Sessions*. In addition, it will also aid in extracting and converting the relevant information needed, *As It Pleases God*, turning practical into Divine. What does this mean? Practical wisdom provides the Spiritual Gateway to Divine Wisdom.

We are all a work-in-progress, and properly querying ourselves, *As It Pleases God*, develops our Spiritual Eyes, Ears, and Mouth. So, when God sends us confirmation, we can recognize it. When God speaks, we will know His still, small VOICE. When the Holy Spirit guides our conversations, we will YIELD to the leading.

But if we do not use Spiritual Guidelines, we may not recognize the difference between Godliness and worldliness, causing us to become easily deceived, making evil or wickedness appear good. How is this possible? It is through a veil of darkness, covering those who do not know how to look for the LIGHT.

For example, if someone is saying God told them to do something negative, inflict harm to an innocent person, or do something evil, we already know this is not God. How do we know? According to scripture, *"These six things the Lord hates, Yes, seven are an abomination to Him:*

- ☐ *A proud look.*
- ☐ *A lying tongue.*
- ☐ *Hands that shed innocent blood.*
- ☐ *A heart that devises wicked plans.*
- ☐ *Feet that are swift in running to evil.*
- ☐ *A false witness who speaks lies.*
- ☐ *And one who sows discord among brethren."* Proverbs 6:16-19.

Once again, no one is perfect; this is why the repenting process needs to occur, preventing the unregulated growth of misbehaving. If we are satisfied with or do not recognize ill will, it is time to do something about it. To avoid asking the wrong questions, asking amiss, cursing our hands, violating the will of another, or contaminating our Bloodline, we must MASTER what God hates and what He loves.

Why do we need to know what God loves or hates? Somehow, amid living life, our culture has forgotten that our BLOODLINE is predicated on us, then the next generation, and so on. As Believers, being that our cycle of life is not over, we can do something about it. How? Our *Eternal Life* is NOW, allowing us to embrace life from God's Perspective and *As It Pleases Him*. Why? We can definitely see where our worldly views have gotten us! Where? Between a rock and a hard place, tossed to and fro by issues, primarily not of our own.

We have been GRANDFATHERED into a few things; however, we can break this Grandfather Clause if we take hold of our God-Given Birthright, Promise, or Blueprint. How do we break hindrances? By using our *Spirit to Spirit* Sessions of Q and A and the Book of Proverbs for things such as:

- ☐ For character development to become more Christlike in our approach to all things.
- ☐ To enhance our People Skills with Godly prudence to avoid being naive, unkind, rude, or repulsive.
- ☐ As a guide in our daily living to make good choices with proper discretion.
- ☐ For developing, maintaining, or severing relationships, as well as who or what to avoid.
- ☐ For principles in conducting good and wise business affairs.
- ☐ To avoid creating a pitfall for ourselves and others.
- ☐ For keeping our hands BLESSED and prosperous.
- ☐ Clues on how to remain diligent and effective.
- ☐ For polishing up our integrity with an understanding of Godly expectations.
- ☐ To develop self-control, correction, or chastisement.
- ☐ To better understand Spiritual Truths from God's point of view.
- ☐ To gain access to the Secrets of Wisdom or Divine Insight.

Why do we need to go through all of this? The best answer I can give is through scripture, *"Blessed are they that hear the Word of God, and keep it."* Luke 11:28. Listen, nothing is by chance, so if we desire answers beyond our human intellect, we must go to the Source, asking the right questions with a willingness and openness to receive while documenting our findings.

Our *Spirit to Spirit* Sessions with God are not required; they will always remain optional because we have free will. Still, if we desire to engage in such a manner, God does require us to focus while developing our righteousness. We do not want to get the ways of God wrong and then share the wrongness with the masses.

Spiritually, if we want to receive Divine Insight or Understanding, we must also use good judgment as well. Thus, we cannot become reckless, prideful, or gullible once we get what we want from God.

For example, I protect my Spiritual Gifts, Creativity, Talents, and Divine Blueprint, allowing no one to trample over them, regardless of how they feel, think, or believe. Why must I protect them if I truly place God first, *As It Pleases Him*? I still must do my part or duty of becoming and remaining a Good Steward, allowing their opinions to be theirs. And I DO NOT agree that it is my fault that they are clueless about their reason for being or Divine Blueprint, primarily when they have an opportunity to glean the information to become better, stronger, and wiser.

Listen, everyone is entitled to their opinion, and I know beyond a shadow of a doubt that we are ALL a work-in-progress. If they cannot go toe-to-toe with what I have been Spiritually Ordained to do, it is a distraction. But more importantly, I am the one who has put in the work, Spiritually Tilling my own ground, *As It Pleases God*, to get to where I am today while continuously upping the ante to become better, stronger, and wiser. Therefore, I do not play around with the Spiritual Maintenance needed for the upkeep, nor do I tolerate anyone spewing negativity over them.

How do I avoid negativity, scoffers, or dream killers? I remove myself, and if I cannot leave, I will Mentally, Emotionally, or Spiritually zone out, refusing to entertain folly or feed into it. If we can develop and maintain a *Secret Place, Meeting Place, or Prayer Closet* PHYSICALLY, with time, we also develop this zone Mentally, Emotionally, and Spiritually as a bonus package. Yet, it does take practice to zone into a peaceful state at the drop of a dime, but it is doable!

Spiritual Regrafting

Above all, as we are working on ourselves positively with God, *As It Pleases Him*, we have nothing to worry about. Why? Whatever He allows is a stepping stone for the building of our CORNERSTONE from the inside out, making us better, stronger, wiser, pristine, and astute. Conversely, the moment we stop working on becoming better, we have to contend with the frowardness of others to ruffle our feathers. Then again, we may find ourselves trying to fit in with worldly standards instead of Kingdom Expectations.

Who can benefit from the Divine Insight of having a *Q and A Session* with God, *Spirit to Spirit*? Anyone can reap the benefits if they are willing to put in the work to REGRAFT their Mind, Body, Soul, and Spirit, *As It Pleases Him*. However, listed below are a few examples of those who may be in dire need of Spiritual Regrafting, but not limited to such:

- ☐ A person who is unruly, who hates correction or cringes when being asked or told what to do, the Spiritual Regraft is crucial.

- ☐ A person who is negative, demeaning, or cruel, the Spiritual Regraft is crucial.

- ☐ A person who is always in the middle of drama or chaos, the Spiritual Regraft is crucial.

- ☐ A person who is battling with a history of having loose lips and sinking ships, the Spiritual Regraft is crucial.

- ☐ A person who cannot see the forest (the big picture) because of the trees (people) blocking it, the Spiritual Regraft is crucial.

- ☐ A person who is having a bout with self-defiant behaviors, attitude, or thoughts, who loves to wallow, the Spiritual Regraft is crucial.

- ☐ A person who is constantly consumed with a thwarted perception of thinking the worst about themselves and others, the Spiritual Regraft is crucial.

- ☐ A person who outright negatively judges, demeans, or criticizes those who appear less than them or without asking fact-finding questions, the Spiritual Regraft is crucial.

- ☐ A person who is self-righteous, having no regard for what others think, feel, or say, the Spiritual Regraft is crucial.

- ☐ A person who is abusive, Mentally, Physically, Emotionally, Spiritually, Financially, or Verbally, the Spiritual Regraft is crucial.

- ☐ A person who is okay with having temper tantrums as a full-grown adult, the Spiritual Regraft is crucial.

- ☐ A person who is having an identity crisis, trying to become someone or something they are not just to fit in, the Spiritual Regraft is crucial.

- ☐ A person who is only focused on what or who benefits them while manipulating or bullying others into unrighteousness, the Spiritual Regraft is crucial.

- ☐ A person who thrives on throwing people under the bus, the Spiritual Regraft is crucial.

- ☐ A person who is always on the take without giving back, the Spiritual Regraft is crucial.

- ☐ A person who outright pilfers from others with no remorse, the Spiritual Regraft is crucial.

- ☐ A person who thinks they are above God Almighty, the Spiritual Regraft is crucial.

- ☐ A person who has rotten fruits all over the place, the Spiritual Regraft is crucial.

This list is not designed to point the finger; it is designed to bring about an awareness of the things that could bring open rebuke from God or create generational curses. Of course, we all want to feel righteous or feel as if we are doing the right thing, but there must be some form of alignment as it relates to the Word of God, period. As a word of warning, we cannot manipulate scripture to cover our dirt or waywardness; we must own our truth, repent, forgive ourselves, and keep it moving **toward** righteousness, seeking the good, positive, productive, and fruitful.

With or without Spiritual Regrafting, can we just accept Jesus as our Lord and Savior, and be righteous without doing anything else? Unfortunately, the Kingdom of God does not work like this. First and foremost, to achieve a superficial state of total righteousness is called being self-righteous. Unbeknown to most, self-righteousness is considered foolery in the Kingdom of God, eventually leading to some form of public or private disgrace or shame.

Do not be alarmed; there is temptation lurking in everyone, regardless of whether we admit it or not. For the record, God looks at the heart posture, attitudes, motives, and behaviors of man.

Secondly, if we were completely righteous, we would have no reason to REPENT, right? From a Spiritual Perspective, self-righteousness is the root of our problems today, and if we do not learn how to tell the truth, we are only fooling ourselves, taking those we love into the abyss with us. How is this possible? The righteousness of the Kingdom comes through the Gateway of Humility, not pompousness.

Thirdly, from a Spiritual Perspective, thinking we do not have to do anything to become and remain righteous is one of the biggest forms of DECEPTION known to man. Why? Once again, we are known by our fruits, but if we pay attention, the last fruit is called SELF-CONTROL. If we do not have to do anything, or our righteousness would take care of itself, why would we need Self-Control? Or, more importantly, why would we need the Holy Spirit as our Comforter? Listen, *"Faith by itself, if it does not have works, is dead."* James 2:17. *"For as the body without the Spirit is dead, so faith without works is dead also."* James 2:26.

In the Kingdom of God, this self-defiant Spiritual hype is not necessary. We have innocent lives involved in our unrepentant debauchery, when all God is looking for is correctable humility, a repenting heart of transparency, and a willingness to exhibit good character and fruits, *As It Pleases Him*. But what do we do? We succumb to peer pressure, materialism, greed, loose lips, lust, jealousy, envy, coveting, idolatry, and the list goes on without any form of restraint or repentance due to our lack of understanding or willful folly.

Once again, *"For all have sinned and fall short of the glory of God."* Romans 3:23. However, it cannot become an excuse. Amid our vices, habits, quirks, traumas, or weaknesses, we must become aware of whatever it is, understand our WHY, and repentantly keep working on it without covering it up, as if there is no issue. This does not mean we must broadcast it to the world, but in the presence of God, we must come clean, period.

Now, if we have become a pompous Spiritual Bully, brainwashing God's sheep, telling them they are righteous when we know their behavior contradicts Christlike Character, then the bully is accountable for each one who has been misled. Why? God does not like us leading His innocent sheep to the slaughter, but let us take it to scripture, *"All we like sheep have gone astray; we have turned, everyone, to his own way; and the Lord has laid on Him the iniquity of us all. He was oppressed, and He was afflicted, yet He opened not His mouth; He was led as a lamb to the slaughter, and as a sheep before its shearers is silent, so He opened not His mouth. He was taken from prison and from judgment, And who will declare His generation? For He was cut off from the land of the living; for the transgressions of My people He was stricken."* Isaiah 53:6-8.

As a Spiritual Vessel, when leading God's sheep, we must know and understand the loving and kind characteristics and behaviors of righteousness. In doing so, we do not have to become weak, a people pleaser, a people chaser, holier than thou, or nail people to the cross, especially when we have our own cross to bear.

How do we develop in this area as Believers? We must engage in what puts a smile on God's face, *As It Pleases Him.* Listed below are a few examples, but not limited to such:

- ☐ We must place God first, developing a sovereign relationship with Him, ourselves, and others with no strings attached, full of genuine love.

- ☐ We must become unified in the Oneness of the Holy Trinity (The Father, Son, and Holy Spirit).

- ☐ We must develop our Spiritual Roots, yielding good fruits. Why? We are the *Tree of Life*, and we are known by our fruits. If we are not able to exhibit the Fruits of the Spirit, we must examine ourselves thoroughly. What is the purpose of doing so? We do not want the innocent to die or become sick Mentally, Physically, Emotionally, and Spiritually from our fruits. Instead, we want them to grow and live a better life because of them.

- ☐ We must anchor ourselves to the Word of God, aligning what we do, say, become, and how we behave with Biblical Scriptures to aid in our ability to think Godly and positive thoughts before taking action.

- ☐ We must pride ourselves on doing the right thing, being truthful, honest, and transparent, controlling our tongues from malice gossip, complaining, degrading, lying, or stirring up strife.

- ☐ We must diligently work on ourselves, correcting the correctable while creating a win-win to make the most of every God-Given opportunity.

- ☐ We must become trustworthy, exhibiting outright integrity, while quickly apologizing and self-correcting when we err.

- ☐ We must be willing to help, share, and encourage if it is within our power to do so; therefore, helping to break the Spirit of greed, selfishness, and coveting.

- ☐ We must exhibit respect to all, especially our Elders.

- ☐ We must give thanks, becoming grateful, peaceful, and content in all things.

- ☐ We must become peaceful, calm, merciful, forgiving, and reserved; therefore, enhancing our ability to listen, learn, and apply more effectively.

- ☐ We must become committed to the Mission of God, using our Gifts, Talents, and other Spiritual Tools to further the Kingdom of God.

In and out of our wailing process, developing our People Skills and sharing the Good News is our way out. Really? Yes, really. *"By this all will know that you are My disciples, if you have love for one another."* John 13:35. Now, on the other hand, for example, if we know someone is torn up from the floor up, Mentally, Physically, Emotionally, or Spiritually, being nasty, rude, or downright evil, we cannot tell them they are righteous, even if they believe they are. Why? Condoning this behavior leaves too many open doors for them to become sifted, soul-tied, or yoked by evil practices, then passing it along to their innocent Bloodline.

So, what do we do when faced with waywardness? We show them the *Spiritual Classroom* or how to have a *Q and A Session* with God, while sharing our Spiritual Fruits (Love, Joy, Peace, Patience, Kindness, Goodness, Faithfulness, Gentleness, and Self-Control), similar to what I am doing now. How is this possible without offending? This chapter is about learning how to ask questions, right? Therefore, if we learn how to ask the right questions, there is no need to offend anyone, especially when their answers are in their own words, provoking the elements of THOUGHT. Or, we can become an excellent story or parable teller, similar to how Jesus presented His messages.

Spiritually Speaking, we are here to help, encourage, mentor, teach, or nurture each other using the Fruits of the Spirit and Christlike Character along with our Spiritual Skills, Talents, Creativity, Passion, Knowledge, Wisdom, or Divine Blueprint. Still, it is NOT our job to fix people or condemn them to the PIT of Hell. Once again, we do not know what God is using to train, mold, or perfect them for their Predestined Blueprinted Purpose without Spiritual Discernment. Nevertheless, we must fix ourselves, *As It Pleases God*, allowing the Holy Spirit to fix the hole in us, and then become the Poster Child for the Kingdom of God, showing or sharing with others the RIGHT way, and then the Holy Spirit will do the rest.

CHAPTER 12

THE 4-FOLD

In or out of the folds, from the beginning until the end, there is always a need for existence. Now, to avoid nothingness, this innate desire is comprised of living in the true essence of the *Heaven on Earth* Experience, *As It Pleases God.* From Genesis 1:1 to Revelation 1:1, we can tiptoe around our Spirituality, but with this chapter, we will bridge the gap from our back then to our right now. As there are many levels to *Heaven and Earth*, there are also various levels with layers of variations in us as well. But more importantly, in a time such as this, the surface level (worldliness) is not going to get us what we need. Why? God requires us to dig deep for the sake of the Kingdom of Heaven, which is the Spiritual Level of fulfillment we long for, secretly.

    For the *Wailing Prayers To The Deep Reloaded*, the previous chapters should have already prepared us in a few ways. If not, it is best to revisit them. Why must we revisit them for the Greater Good? They are designed to prepare us for the '*Marriage Supper.*' What is this? Before we go any further, let us take this to scripture: "*Let us be glad and rejoice and give Him glory, for the marriage of the Lamb has come, and His wife has made herself ready. And to her, it was granted to be arrayed in fine linen, clean and bright, for the fine linen is the righteous acts of the saints. Then he said to me, "Write: Blessed are those who are called to the marriage supper of the Lamb!" And he said to me, "These are the true sayings of God." And I fell at his feet to worship him. But he said to me, See that you do not do that! I am your fellow servant, and of your brethren who have the testimony of*

Jesus. Worship God! For the testimony of Jesus is the Spirit of Prophecy." Revelation 19:7-10.

Regardless of where we are or who we are, preparation is a must. Why do we need to prepare as Believers? Let me answer this with another question: 'Would we show up to a dinner party undressed?' Of course not! We would not do so in the natural; therefore, we should not want to do so in the Supernatural. For the record, do not allow anyone to say that we do not have to do anything but accept Jesus as our Lord and Savior and then sit on our hands doing nothing. We must PREPARE!

In a commitment to becoming Christlike, *As It Pleases God*, self-control is a must. Chosen or not, we cannot run around cutting someone's ear off as Simon Peter did in John 8:10 without correction. Listen, there is no Purpose coming forth through the Holy Trinity (The Father, Son, and Holy Spirit) without corrective training, preparing, testing, and presenting.

The superhero facade must stop. We cannot paint the picture of being zapped into the Christlike vintage overnight. God's sheep or new Believers are getting hurt by this. How do I know? I was one of them. I was deceived into believing we would be instantly transformed into a state of perfection. So, in my newfound journey in my early days, I began to try to live perfectly, crucifying myself when I made a mistake, not knowing what to do to self-correct or how to heal.

In my cluelessness, I began to use a Christian couple I admired as a role model. Then, one day, I witnessed them getting into an argument, saying and doing things I could not fathom doing or saying to another human being. I was literally devastated and traumatized to the core of my being. Although this happened when I was in my early twenties, it confused me beyond what I could have ever imagined.

My WHY

As odd as it seems, no one ever told me that our Spiritual Journey with God comes with working on ourselves on a moment-by-moment basis. No one ever told me to use the Fruits of the Spirit. No one ever took me by the hand to give me a step-by-step analysis of consequences and repercussions, and why I needed to avoid certain behaviors. No one ever taught me how to ask the right questions and seek the truth from within. No one ever taught me how to use my Spiritual Armor to contend with the enemy. How will I ever know if I am not taught, right? In my opinion, I was left to fend for myself in Spiritual Training Wheels.

Well, the life of Hard Knocks had a plan for me, serving no mercy. Actually, knowing what I know now, it was the best thing that could have ever happened to get my Spiritual Wheels turning in the right direction, *As It Pleased God*. After being hung out to dry by the wiles of the enemy while laughing in my face, dragging me through the dirt, and throwing me under the bus, I decided to leave a LEGACY of Divine Information for the next man, helping them understand their Spiritual Training Wheels.

The blood, sweat, and tears I shed could not be rendered in vain, nor could I allow another person to remain oppressed without having the information available to them. Therefore, I had to DIG DEEP and Spiritually Fight with my God-Given Tools, Skills, Creativity, and Blueprint, helping others to do likewise by answering the hard questions we do not know how to ask.

Why is answering the tough Spiritual Questions so important? I am very analytical by Divine Design, so the surface answers were not getting it. Nor could people serve me fluff to digest when it comes to my Heavenly Father. I knew too much about Spirituality but failed to understand it entirely, as my conscience and instinct alerted me to misinformation or contradictions.

As the confusion progressed, I could not blame anyone. Why? I knew deep down from my Spiritual Encounters it was my God-Given responsibility to provide answers from the Heavenly of Heavens. I had been answering adult questions in a child's body my whole life as my formal training ground. As an adult, I knew it was time to take it up a notch to answer the Spiritual Questions in a grown-up human body. Therefore, I had to take my focus off man and get into the Spiritual Classroom of knowing and understanding the Word of God for myself, *As It Pleased God*.

Why was the Spiritual Classroom necessary? If I wanted to be Spiritually Equipped, *As It Pleased God*, I had to Spiritually Prepare to work for the Kingdom of God with the Divine Authority to place His sheep in the Fold and remove them from the Fold. Is this

Spiritual Training Biblical? *"All Scripture is given by inspiration of God, and is profitable for doctrine, for reproof, for correction, for instruction in righteousness, that the man of God may be complete, thoroughly equipped for every good work."* 2 Timothy 3:16-17.

Testimonial Marriage

In my commitment to this Spiritual Journey, God gave me a scripture, helping me in ways beyond human comprehension. Now, I am compelled to share it with the world: *"I will instruct you and teach you in the way you should go; I will guide you with My eye."* Psalm 32:8. With this Spiritual Guidance, coming back to share my findings and teachings of Spiritual Truths, *Spirit to Spirit*, this is my 'WHY.' Had it not been for the oppression and evident Battle Scars, I would not be adequately equipped to bring this information to the Spiritual Table, holding nothing back for the *Testimonial Marriage* of the Holy Trinity. Before we move on, here is what we need going forward:

- ☐ Faithfulness.
- ☐ Truthfulness.

If we are not authentic, or if we are a liar, it taints our Spiritual Linen. Here is the secret: Before telling a lie or incriminating ourselves publicly, simply plead the 5th, taking it to God, as discussed in Chapter 10. By far, this is our Spiritual Right! Why? There are certain things we can set in motion with man that have irrevocable consequences, contaminating our Bloodline. Therefore, we must tread with caution when battling with loose lips or sinking ships with a careless tongue.

We must adorn ourselves with the Fine Linen FREELY given to us through the Holy Spirit by Jesus. What does this mean for us? We must make an EFFORT to have clean hands and a pure heart as we cover ourselves with the Blood of Jesus as Spiritual Atonement and use the Holy Spirit to guide, correct, and protect. Just so we are crystal clear, in this Divine Union, this is a *'Take me as I am to become better*' Relational Union. Not a '*Take me as I am, and do no more*' deal-breaker. We have to try to put on the Fine Linen, *As It Pleases God*, instead of stubbornly leaving it as-is, pleasing ourselves.

As we get back to our Levels of Spirituality, let us peel back a few layers to avail ourselves to receive an invitation. Listed below are the layers for ROBING ourselves in anticipation of our ONENESS at the Spiritual Table:

- ☐ Layers of our Divine Purpose.
- ☐ Layers comprised of Divine Strategies.
- ☐ Layers of selecting our Pride.
- ☐ Layers of our 24-Hour Anointing.
- ☐ Layers of the Expelling of Toxins.
- ☐ Layers of the Wailing Process.
- ☐ Layers of our Eternal Life Now.
- ☐ Layers of our Fasting Gaps.
- ☐ Layers of our Fasting Chambers.
- ☐ Layers of our Secret Place.
- ☐ Layers of our Q and A Sessions
- ☐ Layers of our 4-Fold Effect.

Please make no mistake about it: We are not speaking of outer linen; we are speaking about INNER LINEN to determine our FOLDS. How? Let us take it to scripture, "*As the Father knows Me, even so I know the Father; and I lay down My life for the sheep. And other sheep I have which are not of this fold; them also I must bring, and they will hear My voice; and there will be one flock and one shepherd.*" John 10:15-16.

The Fold Breakdown

As it relates to the *Wailing Prayers To The Deep Reloaded*, our Folds are extremely important. What is the 4-Fold effect? It is the Folds to prevent worldly division among ourselves to obtain our *Eternal Life* now. What are they?

- ☐ The Fold of the Mind.

- ☐ The Fold of the Body.
- ☐ The Fold of the Soul.
- ☐ The Fold of the Spirit.

Is this Biblical? According to scripture, let me deliver this message in 4 parts as well to establish importance.

- ☐ "Now Enoch, the seventh from Adam, prophesied about these men also, saying, "Behold, the Lord comes with ten thousands of His saints, o execute judgment on all, to convict all who are ungodly among them of all their ungodly deeds which they have committed in an ungodly way, and of all the harsh things which ungodly sinners have spoken against Him." Jude 1:14-15.

- ☐ "These are grumblers, complainers, walking according to their own lusts; and they mouth great swelling words, flattering people to gain advantage. But you, beloved, remember the words which were spoken before by the apostles of our Lord Jesus Christ: how they told you that there would be mockers in the last time who would walk according to their own ungodly lusts. These are sensual persons, who cause divisions, not having the Spirit." Jude 1:16-19.

- ☐ "Maintain Your Life with God - But you, beloved, building yourselves up on your most holy faith, praying in the Holy Spirit, keep yourselves in the love of God, looking for the mercy of our Lord Jesus Christ unto Eternal Life. And on some have compassion, making a distinction; but others save with fear, pulling them out of the fire, hating even the garment defiled by the flesh." Jude 1:20-23.

- ☐ "Now to Him who is able to keep you from stumbling, And to present you faultless Before the presence of His glory with exceeding joy, To God our Savior, Who alone is wise, Be glory and majesty, dominion and power, Both now and forever. Amen." Jude 1:24-25.

In the building of our Mind, Body, Soul, and Spirit for the edification of the Kingdom of God, they are the distinctive measures associated with having DOMINION. If we leave out any one of them, it creates an imbalance or a form of division among ourselves and others.

The **Mind** brings us into becoming conscious of our thoughts, forming our perceptions, and feeding the Body, Soul, and Spirit, positively or negatively. *"For to be carnally minded is death, but to be spiritually minded is life and peace."* Romans 8:6.

The **Body** is the vessel that makes us world-conscious, forming the connection to what we see, hear, touch, taste, and smell. Our bodily senses bring forth action, putting our words, thoughts, and soulish desires in motion, positively or negatively. *"But solid food belongs to those who are of full age, that is, those who by reason of use have their senses exercised to discern both good and evil."* Hebrews 5:14.

The **Soul** brings us into the consciousness of our likes, dislikes, Purpose, instincts, traumas, and Genius capabilities. Not to mention, it is also our giant file cabinet of life, storing the perception of our experiences. *"For what profit is it to a man if he gains the whole world, and loses his own soul? Or what will a man give in exchange for his soul?"* Matthew 16:26.

The **Spirit** is our direct connection to God, making us God or Spirit-Conscious; yet, it is dormant or active based upon free will. *"Do you not know that you are the Temple of God and that the Spirit of God dwells in you?"* 1 Corinthians 3:16.

Here is the deal: We have a choice to use the 2-Fold, Mind and Body; the 3-Fold, Mind, Body, and Soul; or the 4-Fold, Mind, Body, Soul, and Spirit. Does it make a difference? Absolutely. If we want to live an empty life, the 2-Fold works well. If we want to live a chaotic, emotional life, the 3-Fold works better. However, if we have a desire to live a fulfilled, balanced lifestyle, *As It Pleases God*, we must use the 4-Fold Effect.

God dwells in the Spiritual Realm, and if we desire to connect to Him, *Spirit to Spirit*, we must ACTIVATE or AWAKEN our Spirit. By choosing to do so, we also need to do a few other things as well:

- ☐ We must develop a positive mindset.

- ☐ We must bring our emotions under control.
- ☐ We must not allow the lusts of life to control the body.
- ☐ We must use the Fruits of the Spirit and behave Christlike.

If we omit the 4-Folds, the enemy will have us for lunch, toasting and roasting us with the issues of life, thwarting our perception of God into a bed of doubt, emotional debauchery, and mental instability. Better yet, if we desire to have the Spiritual Guidance of the Holy Spirit, He can only connect through our AWAKENED Spirit to become ONE with us.

Just in case we do not know: Our Spirit lays dormant if we allow our psyche to rule and reign; therefore, the Holy Spirit will NOT violate our free will, making us serve God. However, the moment we decide to awaken our Spirit, allowing the Holy Spirit to take over, He will chastise our soulish ways, taking us into the Spiritual Classroom and teaching us the things and ways of the Kingdom.

Our Spiritual Life is full of meaning, but it must be sought after with the proper conduct. We cannot run around thinking we rule the world without understanding Kingdom Truths or without being in Purpose on purpose, knowing nothing about our Predestined Blueprint. The Kingdom Truth about what? It is more like the Divine Truth about WHOM (The Father, Son, and Holy Spirit).

Listen, just so we are clear before we move on, God is in everything. If He created us, them, and it, He is a part of the seen and unseen. Yet, He is not formed out of any of it. We cannot put God in a box, carve Him into stone, etch Him into a piece of wood, or create whatever to limit Him. He designed and created it all, with us all, and through us all. Without Him, *As It Pleases Him*, or what He inspired us and others to do, according to our Predestined Blueprint, we will miss the true BLESSINGS set before us.

The Real Reality

As this is the last chapter in this book, as it relates to our wailing process, what are we missing here? We are missing an understanding of who we are. How is this possible when we do not have an identity crisis? We are the only creation of God that lives the way we do. We live comfortably, but we are ungrateful, and we fail to share with others as we should. We have more than enough to eat, but we will not feed our brothers or sisters who have missed a meal, not to mention several. Yet, the birds of the air and the beasts of the field have to totally depend on God for their next meal, and they never complain.

Let us take this up a notch: The animals we love to watch sleep in trees, caves, burrows, or on the ground, and they never complain. They live in the heat, cold, rain, snow, storms, and wind without turning up their noses or degrading other animals for where they live. But more importantly, each animal has a level of instinctual respect for us, and what do we do? We disrespect them, violating their habitats and wrecking their homes to provide comfort for ourselves without even giving thanks to God for migrating them to another area, not including the vegetation lost.

What is the purpose of knowing information about animals? The entire ecosystem serves a purpose; the moment we misalign ourselves with it, discontentment, imbalance, or disorder secretly sets in. Why? It is all connected. We are connected. Regardless of whether we realize or acknowledge it, it is so in the Eye of God.

Please allow me to reel this in to create Divine Relevancy. Here we are, we live our lives the way we desire without giving thanks to God for keeping us safe, giving us a bed to sleep in, a roof over our heads, food on the table, shoes on our feet, a car to drive, schools for education, extracurricular activities to keep us busy, and the list of BLESSINGS go on.

Yet, on the other side, in the Animal Kingdom, they must stay on constant alert, not knowing if they will become the next meal for the predator that is protecting their Bloodline. And we, as a people who have DOMINION, do not have time for our own.

Let me dig in a little deeper: As an animal, can one imagine running for our lives every single day, outrunning the unknown, and not complaining? Although we are not them, they stay in their lane, living out their purpose of being fruitful and multiplying, period.

In all reality, as we are in the constant pursuit of whatever or whomever, due to our lack of understanding, we do not give a rat's tail about the BLESSINGS or curses we are leaving behind for our lineage as long as we get what we want right now. How can we not see what is before our very eyes? Or is it that we choose not to see?

In or out of the wailing process, please do not make this mistake. What mistake? The mistake of developing the nerves to become ungrateful or complain about our BLESSINGS, even if they do not appear as such. Why should we not complain as Believers, especially when having free will to express ourselves? God will shut us down from the inside out because we are truly BLESSED among all of His creation!

God loves us all, but we must know this: *"Happy is he who has the God of Jacob for his help, whose hope is in the Lord his God. Who made heaven and earth, the seas, and all that is in them; who keeps truth forever, Who executes justice for the oppressed, who gives food to the hungry. The Lord gives freedom to the prisoners. The Lord opens the eyes of the blind; the Lord raises those who are bowed down; the Lord loves the righteous. The Lord watches over the strangers; He relieves the fatherless and widow; but the way of the wicked He turns upside down."* Psalm 146:5-9.

What would be the purpose of getting turned upside down? This is done to shake us up a little. Why? When we become settled in the ways of the world, He politely lets us know who is in charge. God is predicated on systems, strategies, designs, concepts, and order to cater to His creation. If we do not understand our place as a Child of God, and if we do not own up to the reason He created us in the first place, then we are out of order.

Listen, regardless of what we are going through, how we feel, or what we do or do not have, God BLESSES us to be a BLESSING. But more importantly, believe it or not, someone is wailing for the same people, places, and things we take for granted; therefore, we must step up our gratefulness, squashing the desire to complain.

If we engage in the wailing process without establishing the point of origin (Our Father, which art in Heaven), we avail ourselves to entertaining other sources outside of Heaven.

For example, suppose we are behaving like a hellion on wheels all day long with an uncontrollable tongue, exhibiting defiant behaviors and negative habits, casting doom and gloom all over the place, and then stepping into the presence of God without repenting or any form of correction. In this case, the evil or negativity is still at full alert from within. If one does not believe me, then can one tell me where it went? In all due respect, if it is still operating after being in the presence of God, then it is still there...what manner of Spirit is this?

Remember, it was DISOBEDIENCE in the Garden of Eden that separated us from God in the first place, getting us into this mess. So, do we think for a minute that He would advocate this sort of behavior? The answer is NO.

In the life of Jesus, He spent more time casting out evil Spirits and healing blindness; therefore, it is imperative to invoke the Holy Spirit to do likewise with us. How is this possible? Once again, we must repent of all ungodly behaviors, and in the wailing process, we must:

- ☐ Truthfully, direct our wailing prayer to a specific place. For example, *Our Father, which art in Heaven.*

- ☐ Respectfully cast down (cancel) and replace the negative behavior with a positive result, including the applicable Biblical Scripture or affirmation. For example, I cast down fear, and I replace it with courage, in the Name of Jesus. *"For God has not given me a spirit of fear, but of power and of love and of a sound mind."* 2 Timothy 1:7.

- ☐ Forgive and let go, making all attempts to do the right thing. If a mistake is made, we must keep trying. So, repeat the process, not suffering from any form of defeat or thoughts of giving up. Why? We must become patient with God, ourselves, and others because some things are indeed a process or a Spiritual Classroom.

- ☐ Claim the victory, ruling over our heart posture, and keep it moving, exhibiting the Fruits of the Spirit, even if we have to start with one fruit at a time. God will honor our diligence; I am living proof! But more importantly, let us take it to scripture, *"I have chosen you, and ordained you, that you should go and bring forth fruit."* John 15:16.

The wailing process is not something we should joke about, nor should it be taken for granted. *'Wailing To The Deep'* has a profound impact on our Destiny Enriched Provisions, regardless of whether we understand them or not. For this reason, we must MASTER relating to God, *Spirit to Spirit*. To ourselves, *Self to Spirit*. And to others, Brother to Brother, Sister to Sister, or Brother to Sister, to open the Floodgates of Heaven and our Spiritual Negev of Divine Provisions.

What is the Spiritual Negev? It is Spiritual Provisions (An Underground Cistern) hidden amid something else that people, places, things, and money (man-made currency) cannot buy! In my opinion, it is like an intellectual battle vs. a Spiritual Battle of objectives with Workable Provisions based on pleasing ourselves or PLEASING God. Simply put, our blueprint with limits vs. God's Divine Blueprint with the unlimited potential of Divine Greatness.

Without having the Holy Spirit to facilitate our character, attitude, mindset, and lovability, our vision can become thwarted, causing God to set limits on how, what, and whom He provides, zapping our Supernatural Favor.

What can the Holy Spirit do for us that money cannot buy? Although we cannot limit the Holy Spirit, listed below are a few things money cannot buy:

- ☐ Money cannot buy: Inner serenity of peace and comfort with God, ourselves, and others for edification, self-control, and a direct connection to the Realm of the Spirit. This invokes supernatural faith, uncommon favor, and our unique, fashionable style from a Spiritual Perspective.

- ☐ Money cannot buy: Inner charactorial conviction or correction with justifiable truths without sugar-coating the hidden power of *Repenting, Fasting, and Praying* in the REGRAFTING process.

- ☐ Money cannot buy: Inner guidance with a grid-worthy distinction, making the Word of God applicable to our daily living in or out of our *24-Hour Anointing*.

- ☐ Money cannot buy: The empowerment of our Inner Genius overriding *Toxic Influences*.

- ☐ Money cannot buy: The anointing of our Gifts, Talents, Calling, Creativity, or Fruits to unveil our Spiritual Eyes, Ears, and Mouth for the Kingdom of God.

- ☐ Money cannot buy: The Spiritual Guidance with the Pen of a Ready Writer as we *Strategize* our Plan of Action or our next move.

- ☐ Money cannot buy: Inner Revelation of the Great Unknown, unveiling our *Spiritual Folds*.

- ☐ Money cannot buy: Inner unspeakable joy, quenching our thirsts or pangs of hunger in or out of our *Secret Place*.

- ☐ Money cannot buy: The infallible Teacher in or out of our *Q and A Sessions* or Spiritual Classroom.

- ☐ Money cannot buy: The inner or outer voice of utterance, reason, prophecy, or intercession, in and out of the process of 'Wailing To The Deep.'

- ☐ Money cannot buy: The gifted spark of genuine creativity, wisdom, and knowledge from God's Divine Perspective.

- ☐ Money cannot buy: Spiritual Illumination, unveiling the elements of our *Eternal Life* now.

If we downplay or omit what money cannot buy, neglecting the role that the Holy Spirit plays in our daily lives, it may cause us to doubt ourselves, creating a vicious cycle of déjà vu, self-sabotage, or self-righteousness. As a result, we will find ourselves buying love, counterfeits, and getting mad at God when we make a mess.

So, let it be known that from this day forward, we were created to learn from anything and everyone, deciphering through the information, choosing the positive, and discarding the negative to create a win-win.

Understanding Doubt

Suppose we are Spiritually Blind, Deaf, or Mute. In this case, we will begin to miss out on the simple things in life, as doubt becomes our motivating factor, creating all types of known and unknown Spiritual Disasters or causing us to become accident-prone.

How does doubt come into the picture when we have everything we want? Doubtfulness creeps through the crevices of our lives when we think we do not need anyone. Then again, it could come from thinking we have it all together, as if we are perfect, or when we become bound to the negative. As a result, our super-inflated egos create potholes of hidden insecurities, causing us to become seemingly difficult, pompous, or ungrateful. Unfortunately, our People Skills suffer, creating a cycle of people flowing in and out of our lives with unfruitfulness or rotten fruit.

The goal of this final chapter is to help us grasp the 4-Fold Effect, releasing life's chokehold and bringing us to the Revelatory Marriage Supper. How is this possible? Through our ability to effectively wail, repent, and fast to awaken ourselves from our sleep to the Word of God and the Testimony of Jesus.

Developing Our People Skills

The Spiritual Laws pertaining to relationships are just as important as the Law of Gravity. How do we make this make sense, comparing our People Skills to gravity? First, the force of attraction between any two masses makes our People Skills relevant in the matter of INTERPERSONAL CONNECTION. Secondly, gravity is designed to pull everything toward the earth's core, and being that we are comprised of the elements of the earth, we are drawn to the core of our design as well. Simply put, we are connected. How are we connected? Relationships are the core factor of how God designed us from the BEGINNING in Genesis, and it is how He will close it out as well in Revelation.

The heart of man (the soul) is designed to relate to God, self, and others, *As It Pleases Him*. When the bonds are broken or violated, it pulls us back to the earth from the inside out. But the most graphic thing about this process is that it consumes us in a slow metamorphic way, especially if left uncorrected or unrepentant. Unfortunately, the breakdown becomes noticed in our words, thoughts, actions, reactions, biases, traumas, and conditioning. All of these play a vital role in our People Skills, positively or negatively.

What do we need to do to enhance our People Skills? Although everyone has a story to tell, here are a few pointers on how to do so, but not limited to such:

- ☐ Accept ourselves for who we are, and likewise with others. We do not need to be like someone else because our Destiny is tied to our authenticity. Remember, God did not make a mistake when He created us.

- ☐ We must respect God, ourselves, and others with our actions, words, thoughts, attitudes, body language, etc. Without respect, we become repulsive or putrid by default.

- ☐ We must quickly forgive ourselves and others with no strings attached. Remember, forgiveness is not for them; it is for us.

- ☐ We must give thanks in all things to God, ourselves, and others. Keep in mind that ungratefulness and disobedience are sore spots for humanity, so tread carefully.

- ☐ We must be willing to share, selflessly activating the Law of Reciprocity. In the Eye of God, selfishness is not what He had in mind for us because it will ruin relational bonds beyond repair.

- ☐ We must exhibit compassion and mercy. These two character traits are the bedrock of keeping the psyche from crucifying people. Unbeknown to most, without same way we have the right to accept or reject chaos and confusion.

Even if we cannot see our way in or out of relationships, we still must see ourselves clearly, *As It Pleases God*. Therefore, we must thoroughly examine ourselves.

According to the Heavenly of Heavens, when we are able to see ourselves, we are then ready to see God face-to-face. Blasphemy, right? Wrong again. We are able to see God through ourselves, and if we cannot see Him through our People Skills, our Spiritual Fruits, and our Christlike Character, then we have work to do.

Please allow me to Spiritually Align: *"When I was a child, I spoke as a child, I understood as a child, I thought as a child; but when I became a man, I put away childish things. For now we see in a mirror, dimly, but then face to face. Now I know in part, but then I shall know just as I also am known. And now abide faith, hope, love, these three; but the greatest of these is love."* 1 Corinthians 13:11-13. So, when we look at ourselves in the mirror, if we do not see faith, hope, or love, we can begin with love to open our Spiritual Eyes. Once accomplished, faith and hope will come automatically.

Spiritually Speaking, we are all a work-in-progress, and our love of people will be tested first before the unveiling of the full portion of our Spiritual Gifts, Talents, Creativity, Calling, or Divine Blueprint. Is this Biblical? I would not have it any other way. *"Pursue love, and desire Spiritual Gifts, but especially that you may prophesy. For he who speaks in a tongue does not speak to men but to God, for no one understands him; however, in the Spirit he speaks mysteries. But he who prophesies speaks edification and exhortation and comfort to men."* 1 Corinthians 14:1-3.

What about the other Spiritual Gifts? To perfect the other Spiritual Gifts, we must start with our relationships. We must MASTER the ability to speak to the heart of man, and not just our hearts. Without the communicative efforts of love, we cannot fully penetrate the heart of man positively or effectively. The bottom line is that we must know how to talk to people. But more importantly, this is a form of our selfless contribution to receive more of what the Holy Spirit has to offer, *As It Pleases God*.

What if we fail at our People Skills? We become limited with our Spiritual Gifts as it relates to our *Eternal Life* and Kingdom Purposes. Unfortunately, with all due respect, this is how we get self-appointed members proclaiming to be apostles, prophets, evangelists, teachers, miracle workers, healers, helpers, and administrators, speaking in a variety of tongues and imitating the Heavenly Spiritual Gifts with a trail of rotten fruits.

How do we recognize the self-appointed? We must pay attention to their PEOPLE SKILLS while kindly asking the right questions. Why? They operate with a basket of rotten fruits, full of hatefulness, envy, jealousy, strife, coveting, competitiveness, pride, and waywardness. Unfortunately, a self-assumed mask can only last for a short amount of time. Once again, they are limited; they cannot remember their lines because it is unnatural. Therefore, the mask must come off to be who they really are when provoked, tired, offended, caught off guard, or vexed.

Now, on the other hand, if our basket has any spoiled fruits, we must take a step back and fix it! What do we do if we are doing the right thing, and our People Skills are up to par, yet the wolves in sheep's clothing are on our trail? When someone attempts to bring shame to our names out of selfishness, do not worry about it. Keep moving forward in the Will of God because slander is a hidden sign or smokescreen of jealousy, envy, or covetousness. All we need to do is read it, understand it, learn from it, and keep it moving in the Spirit of Excellence, not allowing anyone or anything to kill our dreams.

On the other hand, if we refuse to own our rotten fruits or fix our mess while under a true Spiritual Anointing, it creates a whole new ballgame. The game of pretense without God, or when pleasing ourselves, leads to unmet desires or expectations. When we are not living up to the expectations of God, we will tend to unconsciously fault others for our lack, placing our expectations on others, leading to another unmet need. Over time, we will continue to go around the mulberry bush of compounded unmet expectations in a cycle of déjà vu.

What do we need to do to make changes? We must recognize we are going in circles and then make a conscious decision to stop it. How? Repent, Fast, Pray, Forgive, Cover ourselves with the Blood of Jesus, Invoke the presence of the Holy Spirit, apply

Scripture, use the Fruits of the Spirit, and behave Christlike! Is this the answer to everything? It is for anything that has us in bondage, yoked, or soul-tied. However, it is up to us to break it!

What if we do not have what it takes? If you are reading this book, you have what it takes, period. All you need to do is take one step at a time, placing one foot in front of the next, using the Divine Information God has placed in your hands.

According to the Heavenly of Heavens, I have given the What-To-Do and Why-To, and the Holy Spirit will guide you into the How-To. Regardless of whether you are walking on eggshells or not, the wailing process works; there is no need to recreate the wheel. God's System is not broken; it is simply underutilized, *As It Pleases Him.*

At this point, you are *In The Spiritual* Know, and you are now equipped for the Spiritual Journey. You have what it takes! Believe it, drop your nets, *As It Pleases God,* and *GO FISHING.*

Many BLESSINGS to you and yours, and do not forget to share this book to lock in the Divine Wisdom that the Law of Reciprocity has shared with you. GROW GREAT!

Dr. Y. Bur

www.ingramcontent.com/pod-product-compliance
Lightning Source LLC
Chambersburg PA
CBHW071708160426
43195CB00012B/1621